INTO THE
KILLING
ZONE

INTO THE KILLING ZONE

The Real Story from the Frontline in Afghanistan

SEAN RAYMENT

CONSTABLE • LONDON

Constable & Robinson Ltd
3 The Lanchesters
162 Fulham Palace Road
London W6 9ER
www.constablerobinson.com

First published in the UK by Constable,
an imprint of Constable & Robinson Ltd

ISBN: 978-1-84529-693-3

Printed and bound in the EU

PEFC
PEFC/16-33-111
CATG-PEFC-052
www.pefc.org

CONTENTS

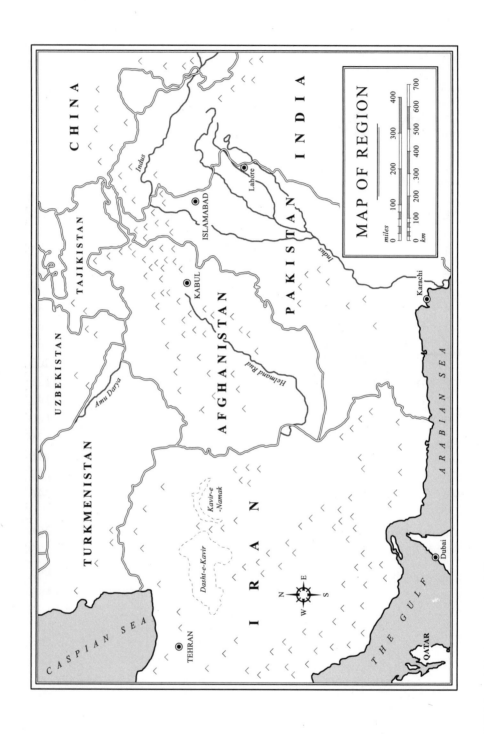

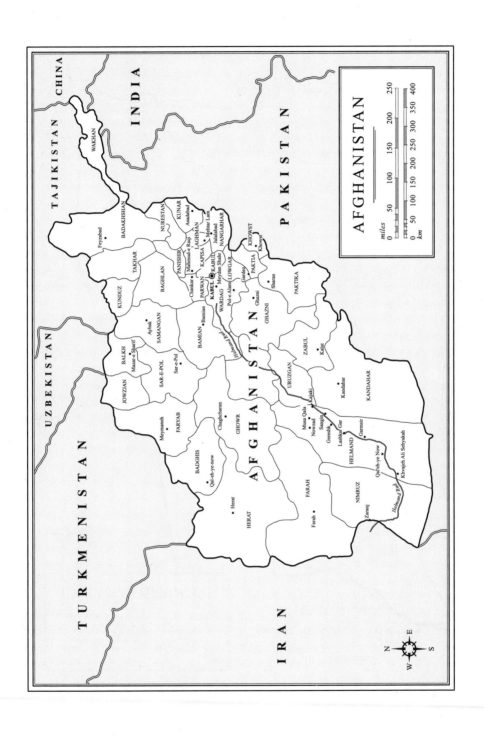

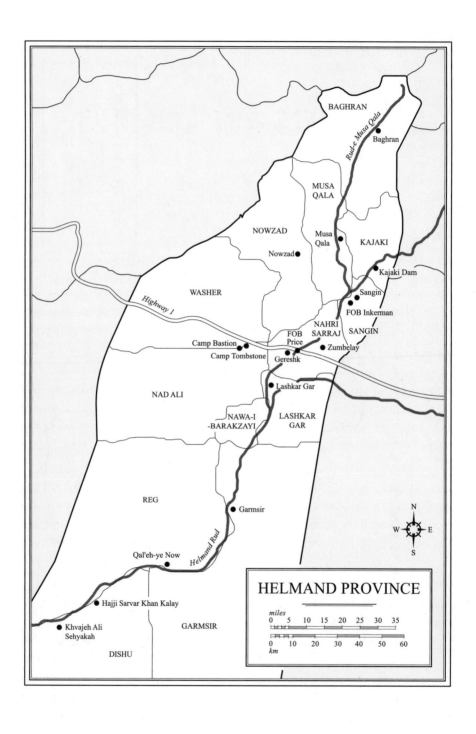

BAGHRAN

Rud-e Musa Qala

Baghran

MUSA
QALA

NOWZAD

Musa
Qala

KAJAKI

Nowzad

Kajaki Dam

WASHER

Highway 1

Sangin

FOB Inkerman

NAHRI
SARRAJ

SANGIN

FOB
Price

Camp Bastion

Zumbelay

Camp Tombstone

Gereshk

NAD ALI

Lashkar Gar

NAWA-I
-BARAKZAYI

LASHKAR
GAR

REG

Garmsir

N

W   E

S

Qal'eh-ye Now

Helmand Rud

Hajji Sarvar Khan Kalay

HELMAND PROVINCE

Khvajeh Ali
Sehyakah

GARMSIR

miles
0   5   10   15   20   25   30   35

DISHU

0   10   20   30   40   50   60
km

1

THE INFIDELS ARE COMING

Inkerman Patrol Base, Upper Sangin Valley, 30 August 2007

The whispered words 'Moving in five minutes' ripple along the column of soldiers standing in the dust of the Helmand desert. Tense faces are illuminated beneath a clear moonlit sky. After hours of waiting and preparation, we are finally setting off to hunt down the Taliban in the Green Zone, a lush green strip of land which borders the Helmand river and which, incidentally, is also the most dangerous part of Afghanistan.

The soldiers call it bandit country and for good reason. This is where the Taliban hold sway, this is their turf and this is the place where the majority of British soldiers have been killed and injured – the last just ten days ago when he was shot through the head by a Taliban sniper.

It's one in the morning and, despite a cool breeze that is blowing across the brown-baked desert, I'm sweating beneath my helmet and body armour. Five minutes comes and goes. There's a delay but we are not told why. The soldiers check and recheck their weapons and equipment for a final time. Rifle, bayonet, ammunition, hand grenades, tourniquet, morphine, field dressing, water, rations, spare socks – almost everything the modern British soldier needs for fighting in Helmand. The other thing is luck.

I sit on a small wall and think about my family back in the UK and wonder what the hell I'm doing here. Images of my wife, Clodagh, and my two small children, Rafe and Luca, flicker through my mind. I hum a tune to myself which Luca sang on almost every day of our summer holiday in Scotland just a few weeks ago and tears well up in my eyes. I'm filled with the sense that I might never see them again, and it makes me angry.

The Company Sergeant Major, Terry Taylor, walks down the line and says to me, 'Everything okay, Sean?' 'Yes, fine. Can't wait,' I reply a little too earnestly, but what I really want to say is 'No, Sergeant Major, everything is not okay. Actually, I'm scared stiff and, rather than go out there and face being killed or blown-up by the Taliban, I would like to stay here and get a good night's sleep and fly home on the next plane, thanks very much.'

But of course I don't. The fear of being called a coward is sometimes a greater motivator than the fear of being killed and, besides, I know I am not alone in feeling scared and that's a curiously comforting feeling.

The 120 soldiers who are about to march out on the operation are coming to the end of their six-month tour in Afghanistan. Each one of them has now fought in so many battles that they have forgotten things which, just a year ago, they thought they would never experience. Each man has seen colleagues fall and die in battle and now they are ready to go home – no one wants to be the last man killed or injured in Helmand.

Seventeen years ago, when I was an officer in the Parachute Regiment, I would have given anything to lead men in battle. Standing here now as a Fleet Street journalist sent to cover the conflict in Helmand by the *Sunday Telegraph*, war – or the prospect of being in the thick of it – does not exactly have the same appeal.

When the British Army arrived here in March 2006, John Reid, the then Defence Secretary, said that he hoped that it could leave in three years' time without having fired a shot. By the time I find myself standing here at Patrol Base Inkerman 18 months later, awaiting the order to move, over 1.5 million bullets have been fired and 63 British soldiers and Marines have been killed fighting the Taliban. Hundreds more have been injured.

Helmand is now one of the most dangerous places on earth and we are in the most dangerous part of the province. In the next few minutes we will leave the relative safety of the patrol base – I say relative safety because the British officer who died ten days ago was killed right here.

Another message floats along the column of soldiers who, like me, have now become impatient and want to get on with the mission: 'Prepare to move.' This is it. I look along the line of soldiers and can see young faces illuminated by the glow of cigarettes being sucked for the final time. Others are hauling their impossibly heavy packs on to their backs. There is a flurry of activity and then, without ceremony, we move silently beyond the walls of Patrol Base Inkerman.

The long-awaited Operation Palk Ghar has started. In an hour or so we will be in the Green Zone.

Walking through the patrol base gate, I am struck by the enormity of the moonlit desert. In the distance a dog, no doubt woken by soldiers, is barking – so much for catching the Taliban by surprise.

The soldier in front of me turns around and says in a loud whisper, 'Keep your spacing.' The further we are apart, the less chance he has of being injured if I step on a landmine. As we move along a pitted track, which in this part of the country serves as the main road, I'm suddenly aware that my survival over the next 24 hours is at the mercy of chance. The very fact that I am a journalist, and not a soldier, is not going to protect me from a carefully laid landmine or a sniper's bullet – as far as the Taliban are concerned I am fair game, just like the 120 soldiers from C (Essex) Company 1st Battalion The Royal Anglian Regiment.

As we move past a series of dwellings, I search out the ground ahead of me for anti-personnel mines. My eyes are on stalks as I try to walk in the footprints of the man in front of me. It is the prospect of stepping on a landmine which worries everyone most of all. The Taliban will often wait to see the direction in which troops are approaching before laying a few mines along a track – it is a tactic that has proved successful in the past, which the men of the Royal Anglians know to their cost.

Anti-personnel mines are designed to maim, not kill. A military doctor friend of mine told me many years ago that as well as blowing off a foot or a leg, a landmine can also remove a soldier's testicles. The thought of such a gruesome injury is almost too much to bear. I am annoyed with myself that I have managed to drag this distant memory up from my past – but, try as I might, it is a thought that I know I will not be able to eradicate from my mind for the next 24 hours.

The sense of acute vulnerability is something I had felt before but that was when I was a Captain in the Parachute Regiment in Northern Ireland, a different war against a different enemy, but with the same fears. Back then, in 1990, I commanded the 3rd Battalion of the Parachute Regiment's Close Observation Platoon on covert counter-terrorist operations in Belfast. I was younger, fitter and virtually devoid of any responsibilities outside of my military life. If I was unfortunate enough to be shot dead by an IRA terrorist or blown up by a carefully placed booby trap, I would only be missed by my family and friends.

Every time I went out on patrol, I had the same feeling of being vulnerable and exposed, which of course I was. Fortunately for me and the soldiers I commanded, however, most of the missions in which I took part were covert operations at the behest of the UK's Special Forces network in Ulster. For the IRA to be able to plan an ambush or to know that we were about to arrive on their patch would have meant that they would either have been fantastically lucky – or that there was a serious intelligence leak somewhere much further up the chain. Luckily, neither happened and, after two years of continuous operational activity, my platoon returned to England in 1991 without a single casualty.

The Inkerman Patrol Base was created in July 2007. At that stage it was the most isolated, vulnerable and northerly outpost in the Sangin Valley. The idea behind its creation was that it would act as a buffer to the strategically important town of Sangin, 12km further down the valley, from where the Taliban had been routed a few months earlier. Inkerman was effectively acting as a 'tethered goat'. It was a 'come on' to the Taliban. If the Taliban were attacking Inkerman, they wouldn't be attacking the strategically important town of Sangin, or at least that was the theory, and it was a tactic which, more or less, was working.

For those soldiers based in Inkerman, however, the threat of death and injury was ever-present. A few days before I arrived, Private Tony Rawson was killed when he was shot through the head by a Taliban sniper whilst on patrol in the area. The following day, Captain David Hicks, the second-in-command of C (Essex) Company 1st Battalion The Royal Anglian Regiment, was killed and five other soldiers were injured during an attack on the base. And, just a few hours before I departed on Operation Palk Ghar with the majority of C Company, the base was mortared by the Taliban.

An officer from the Royal Anglians, who was a friend of David Hicks and who had been involved in action in every British base in the province, later told me that he thought Inkerman was by far the most dangerous place in Helmand.

After 20 minutes we stop in a small hamlet and a soldier crawls towards me and whispers, 'If we get ambushed and you find yourself in the killing zone, stick with me.' I ask him what he means by 'the killing zone'. 'It's the area of ground in an ambush where you have the greatest chance of being killed. If you're in it, you're in the shit.' He then smiles and says, 'And if I'm dead, you're probably fucked.'

Just before we move, another message is sent down the line. The interpreters have intercepted a Taliban communication: 'The infidels are coming. We are ready for them.'

The Taliban's message emphasized to me that we were facing an intelligent, wily and dangerous enemy, with hard-won experience of guerrilla warfare earned over decades of conflict. History should have warned us not to underestimate them.

2

THE RISE OF THE TALIBAN

On a particularly chilly Christmas Eve in 1979, Leonid Brezhnev, the ailing leader of the Soviet Union, ordered an elite force of Soviet airborne troops to seize the airport on the outskirts of Kabul, the capital of what was then called the Democratic Republic of Afghanistan.

Despite widespread international condemnation at the time, the decision by the Soviet leadership to 'invade' Afghanistan was a reluctant one and was only taken after repeated requests for military assistance by Afghanistan's communist government. Only when the Soviets believed that the Afghans might look to the US for assistance did the Kremlin finally agree.

The actual decision to invade was made in secret by a very small group of Soviet leaders against the expressed and forceful opinion of the military who, having studied military history, were aware that Afghanistan was the graveyard of many military campaigners who had been convinced that Afghan tribesmen, with their obsolete weapons and sandalled feet, were no match for a modern and professional army.

The invasion stunned the world and sent relations between the East and West to a new low. Jimmy Carter, the then US President, described the invasion as 'the most serious threat to world peace since the Second World War'. Despite the international condemnation, however, the most memorable joint international response was nothing more than the boycott of the Moscow Olympics the following summer.

Declassified Soviet documents reveal that as early as 1980 – less than a year after the first deployment of troops – the military leadership realized that there was no military solution to the situation in Afghanistan and a political solution was sought.

The crack Soviet troops who landed in Kabul on that cold winter morning in 1979 were the vanguard of the Soviet Union's 40th Army.

On paper, the 40th Army, which was commanded by Marshall Sergi Sokolov, was a powerful force. It was composed of three motor rifle divisions, an airborne division, an assault brigade, two independent motorized rifle brigades and five separate motor rifle regiments. In numerical terms, this comprised around 1,800 T62 tanks, 80,000 men and 2,000 armoured fighting vehicles as well as hundreds of pieces of artillery – a force somewhere close to the size of the modern British Army but with more tanks. Despite its size, however, the army possessed two fatal flaws. Firstly, it was mostly composed of poorly trained reservists who had absolutely no experience of anti-guerrilla warfare. Secondly – and this returned to haunt the Soviet leadership – there was a complete failure to anticipate either the influential role of Islam or the importance of tribalism within Afghan society.

The Soviet troops' initial mission – to guard cities and installations – was soon expanded into combat and kept growing over time. Although the Soviet troops were supposedly in Afghanistan to protect civilians from anti-government forces, they soon found themselves fighting the people they had been sent to protect.

Military operations to pursue and capture the mujahideen leaders often failed through a lack of intelligence and had to be repeated, leading to greater casualties amongst the Soviet troops.

In the next ten years, as the Soviet military became sucked into a bitter insurgency, more than 13,000 young men would die, the majority killed in carefully planned ambushes as their heavy, armoured vehicles slowly trundled along twisting mountain roads. Others would die a more harrowing death at the hands of their mujahideen captors, who became infamous for beheading Soviet prisoners during the war.

The Soviet leaders and the generals had never planned for a lengthy occupation. Initially, the aim of the invasion was to prevent their communist neighbour from descending into chaos and turning Westwards for help. The history of the occupation can be traced back to a coup in April 1978, which saw a select band of Soviet-trained officers seize power and install Nur Muhammad Taraki, a revolutionary leader of the communist People's Democratic Party of Afghanistan, as President.

During the first 18 months of rule, the new government applied a series of Marxist-style reforms, which proved unpopular with the majority of Afghans who were deeply immersed in tradition and Islam.

Decrees were issued setting out changes in marriage customs and land reforms. Thousands of members of the social elite, the religious establishment and the intelligentsia were persecuted and imprisoned. Many were also tortured and summarily executed for crimes against the state.

Afghanistan's religious leaders declared a jihad, or holy war, against the communist regime. In effect, this amounted to a crusade in defence of Islam. The impact was immediate. After months of purges of the Army of the Democratic Republic of Afghanistan, entire regiments defected to the resistance. By the end of 1979, the actual strength of the Army had plummeted to less than half of its original 90,000. In March 1979, the city of Herat revolted and virtually all of the Afghan Army's 17th Infantry Division mutinied and joined the rebellion. The city was eventually reoccupied after it was bombed by the Soviet Air Force.

History had already demonstrated on numerous occasions that Afghanistan was a land inhabited by natural fighters who were rarely conquered. Instead, the Soviet plan in 1979 was very simple. The generals planned to stabilize the situation, strengthen the Afghan Army and withdraw all of their forces within three years.

The Soviets had trained to fight in large formations using tanks, artillery air power and shock troops over a front of hundreds of miles. They were not equipped to fight low-level counter-insurgency operations against a religiously motivated resistance force in hostile and mountainous terrain.

In the early days of the jihad, the mujahideen were an uncoordinated and ill-equipped force bound only by their collective desire to rid Afghanistan of a communist government. The Russian invasion changed all of that. The UK, the US and China, as well as a host of other countries, began sending aid in the form of cash and weapons to the mujahideen via the Pakistan Inter-Services Intelligence Agency (ISI), the foreign intelligence service of Afghanistan's nearest neighbour.

As the months passed the war began to develop into a classic insurgency versus counter-insurgency struggle with each side targeting the other's means of supply. The *modus operandi* of the mujahideen was to attack Russian convoys whenever and wherever possible. There was no real attempt to hold ground or overrun bases because they knew that they could never compete against the Russians in a conventional battle.

In return, the Soviets bombed rural villages, destroyed crops and landmined vast swathes of the country in an attempt to decimate popular support for the mujahideen and to limit their freedom of movement. In a bid to escape the violence, more than 7 million refugees fled the country for sanctuary in neighbouring Pakistan, where they remained for almost a decade.

The Soviet tactics also forced the mujahideen to carry most of their food and supplies into Afghanistan from Pakistan and create secret bases inside Pakistan so that they could continue the fight against the Soviets. On paper the mujahideen were no match for the might of the Soviet Army. The communist troops were better trained and equipped. They had massive air power in the form of fast jets, strategic bombers and the lethal and much-feared Hind helicopter gunships. However, there was little appetite amongst the Soviet military for the war in Afghanistan and even less amongst the young Russian conscripts who were sent to fight and die.

Bristling with weaponry, the Hind was equipped with a 12.7mm multi-barrelled heavy machine-gun and could carry 1,500kg of bombs. It was also loaded with anti-tank rockets and smaller, 57mm fire-and-forget rockets. Working in pairs and providing air cover for Soviet convoys, the Hinds would fly up and down Afghan mountain valleys searching out the mujahideen and destroying anything that appeared remotely suspicious. It is little wonder that the mujahideen dubbed them the 'devil's chariots'. One Afghan commander once famously said, 'We do not fear the Soviets. We fear their helicopters.'

In one of the most successful covert operations ever undertaken, which lasted from 1982 to 1985, an estimated 12,500 foreigners were trained in bomb-making, sabotage and urban guerrilla warfare in camps set up inside Afghanistan with the help of a $500m CIA slush fund provided by the US government. At the time these men, some of whom later went on to become active members of the Taliban were heralded by President Ronald Reagan as 'freedom fighters'.

The covert programme was known as Operation Cyclone. For the US, the funding of the insurgency became an integral part of the Cold War. Of all the aid supplied by the CIA to the mujahideen, it was probably the donation of the FIM–92 Stinger anti-aircraft missile systems which made the greatest impact, although many field commanders, among them Ahmad Shah Masoud, stated that the Stinger's impact was exaggerated. While the mujahideen were able to destroy Hinds as they were about to take off or come into land, the helicopters' anti-missile flares limited the Stinger's effectiveness. Under the stewardship of the CIA, the mujahideen became expert saboteurs. Virtually any state-owned organization became a viable target.

Despite the hundreds of body bags filled with teenage Russian males which were flown back to Moscow and other cities every week, there seemed to be little interest in the Afghan War from the political elite until Mikail Gorbachev came to power in 1985. He ordered his generals to secure victory within a year. However, he soon realized that the war was unwinnable and thus ordered them to begin drafting an exit strategy.

In 1988, following months of negotiations at the United Nations (UN), half of the Soviet military force withdrew from Afghanistan. On 15 February 1989, the remainder of the force left the country.

After ten years of bitter and bloody fighting in which the Soviet Union lost 13,833 men, Russia's leaders finally accepted that they were trapped in a war that could never be won. Although they had killed more than 1.3 million Afghans, the Soviet–Afghan War was a disaster from which the Soviet Union never really recovered. Within seven months of the withdrawal of troops, the Berlin Wall had been pulled down and the Soviet Empire began to implode.

Civil war raged in Afghanistan after the Soviet withdrawal. By 1992, Muhammad Najibullah, who had been President since 1987, agreed to step down in favour of a transitional government. The President was influenced by a promise from the United Nations that a stabilization force would be sent to the country following his resignation. However, the peacekeepers never arrived and the mujahideen filled the power vacuum. An uneasy truce existed for a short period between the rival factions, but a mixture of greed, an obsession with power and a desire to settle old scores led to fighting which would last until the emergence of the Taliban in 1994. By then, vast swathes of the country – some estimates suggest up to a third – had been turned to rubble.

During this desperate period, Afghanistan was carved up along various factional lines, with many of the mujahideen commanders establishing themselves as local warlords. It was against this background that the Taliban became powerful. Former mujahideen who had become disillusioned after their victory over the Soviets had formed the nucleus of a movement that followed the teachings of

Mullah Mohammad Omar, a former mujahid fighter who was based in Kandahar Province in the south of the country. The group, many of whom were madrassa (Islamic school) students, called themselves Taliban, which means 'students'. Their aims were to restore stability and to introduce a highly conservative form of Islamic law. They successfully attacked local warlords, many of whom had become hated figures amongst the rural Afghans who often suffered under their rule, and the Taliban soon gained a reputation for military prowess. By this time, the movement had already attracted the support of Pakistan, which saw the Taliban as a way to secure trade routes to Central Asia and to establish a Kabul government that would be friendly to its own interests. Pakistani traders quickly became some of the Taliban's strongest financial backers.

In September 1995, the Taliban achieved one of their greatest victories when they captured the city of Herat and succeeded in cutting off the land route connecting Afghanistan to Iran. The Taliban's mastery of mobile warfare also enabled them to take control of Kabul after Masoud, one of the most charismatic mujahideen warlords, was forced to retreat north to the Panjshir Valley.

Within months of the Taliban's victory, Osama bin Laden, who was born into a wealthy family in Saudi Arabia but turned his back on a life of luxury and excess to join the fight against the Soviets, returned to Afghanistan. A year later, he moved to Kandahar where he began to develop a close relationship with Mullah Omar, who was now the head of the Taliban. Although bin Laden had developed a reputation as a fearless mujahideen fighter during the Soviet occupation of Afghanistan, it is his creation of the international terrorist network known as al-Qaeda that has gained him worldwide notoriety. Created in 1988, al-Qaeda, which literally means 'the base', has drawn its members from across the Muslim world. In simple terms, it is an international alliance of militant Islamist terrorists. Although it has no formal structure, it has managed to attract thousands of recruits.

By 1996, bin Laden had issued the first of his two fatwas (declarations of war) against the West – the other was in 1998. He said that Muslims should kill civilians and military personnel from the US and other allied countries until they withdrew support for Israel and removed their military forces from Islamic countries.

Such was the closeness between al-Qaeda and the Taliban that by

1997 a unit of al-Qaeda-trained fighters known as the 055 Brigade were integrated into the Taliban militia and remained with them until 2001.

By 1997, the full impact of the Taliban's rule was beginning to be felt across the country, which was renamed the Islamic Emirate of Afghanistan. Mullah Omar assumed the title Amir-ul Momineen (commander of the faithful). In areas under their control, the Taliban enforced their version of Islamic law. Women were no longer allowed to work outside the home in activities other than healthcare. The general view of women was that they should be seen but not heard because they drove men away from the true Islamic path and into temptation. They were also prohibited from attending university, and girls' schools in Kabul were closed, although primary schools did continue to operate in many other areas across the country. Women were not allowed to be treated by male doctors unless accompanied by a male chaperone. A strict dress code was enforced for women, while men were required to wear beards and refrain from western haircuts and dress. Virtually every conceivable type of entertainment, including music, television, videos, playing cards, kite-flying and most sports and games, was banned. Violation of the Taliban laws could result in a public flogging or even execution for crimes such as adultery.

Throughout 1997 and 1998, the Taliban made repeated attempts to extend their control to the north of Afghanistan where one warlord, General Abdul Rashid Dostrum, the head of a powerful Uzbek militia, had effectively carved out a separate state within Afghanistan.

Fighting continued to wage throughout Afghanistan, most of which went unnoticed in the outside world. Afghanistan was viewed as a country which was in total turmoil and presided over by a band of religious zealots. The world's view of Afghanistan began to change in August 1998, when the US launched a series of air strikes on suspected training camps where followers of Osama bin Laden were being turned into international terrorists. The strikes came in the wake of the bombings of US embassies in Nairobi and Dar es Salaam. In 1999, the UN imposed sanctions on the Taliban for their role in international terrorism and called on Mullah Omar to hand over bin Laden. Taliban aircraft were prevented from taking off and landing and the country's assets abroad were frozen. The Taliban's failure to hand over bin Laden led to an expansion of international sanctions, which included an arms embargo and travel restrictions on some government officials.

After the 1998 bombings, bin Laden and several other members of al-Qaeda were indicted in the US Criminal Court. The Taliban consistently protected bin Laden from extradition requests by claiming that he had 'gone missing' in Afghanistan, that 'Washington cannot provide any evidence or any proof' that he was involved in terrorist activities and that therefore he was a 'man without sin'.

It could be argued that the world really began to take notice of the Taliban in March 2001, when Mullah Omar ordered the destruction of the Bamiyan Buddhas. The statues, one of which was 36m tall and the other 53m, had been carved into the caves at Bamiyan 1,800 years ago. The act shocked the world and was condemned by the United Nations Educational, Scientific and Cultural Organization (UNESCO). Although Mullah Omar had initially supported the preservation of Afghanistan heritage, and Japan had offered to pay the preservation costs of keeping the statues in good and safe order, his view had changed radically by 2001. Under a decree issued by the Taliban leadership, all representations of humans, including those in museums, had to be destroyed in accordance with Islamic law, which prohibits any form of idol worship. The government of Pakistan implored the Taliban to reconsider, but to no avail. Saudi Arabia and the United Arab Emirates later denounced the act as savage. For many in the western world, the destruction of the Buddhas put the Taliban on the international map and demonstrated that Afghanistan was a country prepared to act in total defiance of worldwide pressure. It was a foretaste of events that in just a few months would change the world forever. On 9 September 2001, Ahmad Shah Masoud, known as the 'Lion of the Panjshir' and a sworn enemy of the Taliban, was assassinated in a suicide attack by two members of al-Qaeda posing as a camera crew.

With the dramatic success of the Taliban in the late 1990s, the various warlords who had been at war with each other following the Soviet withdrawal had little choice but to align themselves against the Taliban. The United Front for Afghanistan Liberation was formed. The organization became known as the Northern Alliance in the western media because most of the factions supporting it came from the north of Afghanistan. The Alliance received outside support from Russia, India and Iran, primarily because of a united fear of the now visible growth on or within their borders of militant Islamists.

Masoud's assassins were two Arabs claiming to be Belgians who were originally from Morocco, but their passports later turned out to be stolen. One of the two men set off a bomb in either a video camera or a belt. Masoud died within 30 minutes, although his death was officially denied until 13 September. One of the attackers died in the attack and the other was shot while trying to escape.

On 11 September (9/11), two days after Masoud's death, 19 terrorists hijacked 4 commercial airliners en route to California from Logan International, Dulles International and Newark airports on the eastern seaboard of the US. Each airliner had a fuel capacity of nearly 24,000 gallons. Two of the airliners were flown in to the World Trade Center, one each into the North and South Towers, one was flown into the Pentagon and the fourth crashed near Shanksville, Pennsylvania. The attacks killed almost 3,000 people, including the 19 hijackers. The term 'asymmetric warfare' also entered the public lexicon for the first time.

After the 9/11 attacks, investigators in the US, the UK and a host of other friendly countries rapidly began accumulating evidence which implicated Osama bin Laden, who refused to admit any involvement in the attacks. In fact, it was not until 2004, prior to the US presidential election, that bin Laden publicly acknowledged al-Qaeda's involvement.

As the evidence mounted against bin Laden, the US issued a series of demands to the Taliban, including delivering up al-Qaeda leaders located in Afghanistan, closing all terrorist training camps and giving the US full access to the training camps to verify their closure. The Taliban refused to speak directly to President Bush, claiming that talking with a non-Muslim political leader would be an insult to Islam, but they did make statements through their embassy in Pakistan. On 21 September, the Taliban rejected all of the US demands, maintaining that there was no evidence in their possession linking bin Laden to the attacks of 9/11.

By this stage the international community was beginning to mobilize against the Taliban. Just 24 hours after the Taliban rejected the US demands, the United Arab Emirates and later Saudi Arabia withdrew their recognition of the Taliban as the legal government of Afghanistan, leaving Pakistan as the only remaining country with diplomatic ties. It has been suggested that on 4 October 2001 the Taliban covertly offered to hand bin Laden over to the Pakistani ISI for trial in an international tribunal that operated according to Islamic Sharia Law, but the Pakistan government, perhaps knowing that such a move would enrage the US government, is understood to have rejected the offer.

Although it was never reported at the time, it has since emerged that moderates within the Taliban met with US embassy officials in Pakistan to work out a way to convince Mullah Omar to turn bin Laden over to the US and thus avoid its impending wrath. On 7 October, just hours before the aerial bombardment of Afghanistan was about to begin, the Taliban also made an open offer to try him in an Islamic court in Afghanistan. The offer was rejected by the US as 'insincere' and hours later British and US air forces began to attack targets inside Afghanistan. The cities of Kabul, Jalalabad and Kandahar, the so-called spiritual home of the Taliban and where Mullah Omar had his headquarters, were all targeted.

Fifty Cruise missiles launched from US and British ships and submarines in the Gulf attacked key installations and suspected terrorist training camps. Dozens of strike aircraft from carriers were also involved in the first wave of devastating attacks. To demonstrate to the people of Afghanistan that this was not a war against them but against the terrorist forces inside their country, two C–17 Globemaster transport jets delivered 37,000 military ration packs by airdrop to Afghan civilians.

Essentially, the air campaign set out to paralyse the Taliban. Its command over its forces dispersed across the country effectively ceased to exist within hours of the start of the war. Within a few days of unrelenting bombing, many of the terrorist training camps had been destroyed, as had most of the virtually obsolete anti-aircraft defences in the Taliban's possession.

Despite these successes, the Taliban positions facing the Northern Alliance held. Within the first two weeks of the campaign, the Alliance began to demand that US strike aircraft should be used to carpet-bomb the Taliban in the north. The campaign rolled into November and the US began to use weapons that had originally been developed for the Vietnam War. Fifteen thousand Daisy Cutter bombs were used against Taliban positions and AC–130 gunships were deployed. Both the US and British Special Forces also began to link up with the Northern Alliance.

The Taliban's poor understanding of the tactics of conventional warfare played into the hands of the US and British Special Forces who were able to call in devastating air strikes against Taliban troop concentrations at will. But it wasn't all one-way traffic. Although Taliban fighters were being killed in horrifically large numbers, support from Pashtun tribesmen was flooding into the region from the Pakistan border.

On 9 November 2001, the battle for Mazar-i-Sharif began when US jets began carpet-bombing the Taliban defenders. By the early afternoon, the Northern Alliance had seized the city's main military base and airport. By the early evening, what remained of the Taliban forces was in full retreat south. On the following day the Northern Alliance began combing the city looking for anyone suspected of being a Taliban sympathizer. Many people, some undoubtedly innocent, were shot in summary on-the-spot executions. An estimated 520 Taliban fighters who were found hiding in a school were also massacred.

The fall of Mazar-i-Sharif initiated the total collapse of Taliban opposition throughout the north. In the time-honoured Afghan way, many local commanders simply switched sides rather than fight an enemy they had absolutely no hope of defeating.

Kabul, the capital that had already been ravaged by years of war, fell on 12 November. The Taliban fled under the cover of darkness. By the time the Northern Alliance arrived the following afternoon, the only remaining opposition was a small group of foreign Arab fighters hiding in the city's park. All were killed in a gun battle that lasted just 15 minutes. By 16 November, the Taliban's last stronghold in northern Afghanistan was besieged by the Alliance.

The Taliban leadership was in chaos and even the most optimistic of the organization's commanders must have known that the game was up. It was only a matter of time before they were crushed by the US and the Northern Alliance. What was left of the Taliban's fighting arm headed to a cave complex known as Tora Bora, 45km southwest of Jalalabad, close to the border with Pakistan. By the middle of November, an estimated 2,000 al-Qaeda and Taliban fighters had dug themselves into highly fortified positions within the mountains for what was expected to be a fight to the death. It was also within the many caves of the mountain complex that the CIA believed Osama bin Laden was hiding.

At first the US attempted to force the Taliban and al-Qaeda fighters out of their hiding places by using B52 aircraft to blanket-bomb the mountain ranges. However, it was obvious to the US military that at some stage troops would have to be sent in to 'clear' the caves of the Islamic fighters. This was an unenviable task and both the British and US Special Forces commanders, who were effectively controlling events on the ground, were acutely aware that the body count amongst friendly forces could be high. It was at this point that the CIA, equipped with suitcases full of US dollars, began raising a local militia who, they hoped, would do the bulk of the fighting.

Slowly, the militia, supported by US and British Special Forces, began to clear the caves. It was a dangerous and painstaking process. US bombers would hit an area believed to be housing al-Qaeda or Taliban forces. Once the bombers had pulled away the ground troops would move in to either capture or kill any survivors. The fighting lasted for almost a month before a rather shady deal was done between the Taliban and the local militia leaders. At first, it was assumed that the Taliban were merely being given a period of time in which to hand over their weapons. It is now believed that this was a ruse to allow senior members of the Taliban and al-Qaeda to escape. For months afterwards, US Special Forces scoured the countryside searching for al-Qaeda while paying vast sums of money for information on Osama bin Laden's whereabouts. No trace of bin Laden was ever found. It is now assumed that the al-Qaeda high command slipped away into the Pakistan tribal areas to the south and east. Many of them are believed to be still living there today.

One of the campaign's most extraordinary battles, partly because much of it appeared on television, took place in the city of Kunduz, where hundreds of Taliban fighters had surrendered following days of air attacks by US bombers flying in from the Gulf. The prisoners were taken to the Qala-i-Jangi fortress, where they were questioned by CIA interrogators. The prisoners should have been searched for weapons by members of the Northern Alliance, but some of the Taliban had secreted small arms and weapons within their clothes. The Taliban waited for the right moment to strike. It came when John Michael Spann, a CIA interrogator, was questioning groups of prisoners. They pounced on the unsuspecting agent and he was beaten to death in seconds while other prisoners attacked guards and seized their weapons. In a few short minutes, a fully blown revolt was underway involving an estimated 600 fighters. Within an hour-and-a-half, the jail was in the prisoners' hands and they had armed themselves with rifles, machine-guns and grenades. It was immediately clear that the Northern Alliance had neither the capability nor the intent to deal with the situation so members of the UK's Special Forces – the Special Air Service (SAS) and the Special Boat Service (SBS) – were ordered to move into the area to provide assistance.

Television crews witnessed much of the fighting and, for the first time in their history, British Special Forces were filmed in battle. Westerners speaking with British accents, but not in uniform, were seen firing machine-guns into the fort from vantage points outside. One SAS soldier was seen taking aim with a sniper rifle after a Northern Alliance fighter pointed to a target. The battle lasted for 7 days. Fewer than 100 Taliban prisoners survived and around 50 Northern Alliance soldiers were killed.

By the end of November 2001, Kandahar was the last remaining Taliban stronghold and was facing a force of nearly 3,000 tribal fighters led by Hamid Karzai, who would later become the country's first post-Taliban President. Meanwhile, the first significant US combat troops had arrived. The prize target in Kandahar was the capture of Mullah Omar, the leader of the Taliban, who was believed to be hiding in the ancient city. A task force of around 1,000 US troops, supported by helicopter gunships, was established in a base south of the city. Meanwhile, US bombers using laser-guided weapons began to destroy targets within Kandahar. By December, Mullah Omar was ready to strike a deal which would allow him and his top generals to escape but the US government rejected the compromise. Instead, US Rangers assaulted the city's airport in a dramatic parachute drop. The Taliban's control of Kandahar – its so-called spiritual home – came to an end on 7 December 2001, but Mullah Omar and his cohorts had already escaped in a convoy of motorcycles. He remains on the run to this day.

Following the fall of Kandahar a *Loya jirga*, or grand council, of Afghan factions, leaders and former exiles met to decide on the next step in the future of their new country. It was decided that an interim Afghan government would be established in Kabul under the leadership of Hamid Karzai.

The US established it main base at the former Soviet air base in Bagram, where the British SAS and SBS were also based. Bagram housed the CIA holding centre where all al-Qaeda suspects were taken for interrogation prior to being flown to Guantanamo Bay.

Despite these rapid successes it soon became clear that neither the Taliban nor al-Qaeda had given up. Elements of the Taliban began to regroup in a range of mountains known as the Shahi-i-Kot, in Patika Province. Meanwhile, the Americans and the British began to build up their forces. Up until now this had largely been a war conducted by British and US Special Forces, but it was clear that the need for conventional troops to conduct large-scale clearance operations had become urgent. Intelligence estimates suggested that by March 2002, a growing force of Taliban and al-Qaeda fighters was based in the mountain range. The US and British Special Forces believed that the intention of the fighters was to turn the area into a base from which they would launch hit-and-run guerrilla operations similar in style to that of the mujahideen who a decade earlier were fighting the Russians. To counter the threat, the US devised Operation Anaconda. US airborne troops and Special Forces, together with Afghan militia units, were transported into the mountains via helicopter to conduct a series of search-and-destroy operations against the rebels. Armed with AK47s and rocket-propelled grenades (RPGs), the insurgents used classic guerrilla tactics against the US troops. There was no attempt to force the US troops back or to take land. The insurgents simply attacked the Americans, then withdrew to their caves and waited for the inevitable US air strike to pass. The US troops found the fighting exhausting, mainly because most of it occurred above 3,000m where the air is very thin. US commanders also initially drastically underestimated the size of the insurgent force. Original US estimates, based on intelligence from local militia groups, suggested that somewhere between 100 and 200 fighters were hiding in the mountains. It later emerged that the guerrillas numbered somewhere between 1,000 and 5,000 men and they were being reinforced, although these figures may be highly exaggerated. By the end of the Operation Anaconda around 400 insurgents had been killed in the fighting. Eight US troops were killed and seven Afghan soldiers also died, while there were scores of wounded on both sides.

However, just as in the battle of Tora Bora, it is now known that hundreds of Taliban and al-Qaeda fighters escaped into the Pakistan tribal area of Warizstan. The insurgents once again regrouped and by the summer of 2002 they were launching cross-border raids against the US.

The UK's contribution to the war in Afghanistan was not solely limited to the use of its Special Forces. In November 2001, 2nd

Battalion The Parachute Regiment, which was part of 16 Air Assault Brigade, was put on 48-hours' notice to prepare for a deployment to Afghanistan. In fact, the first elements did not depart until New Year's Eve. The mission was called Operation Fingal, and 2 Para were to form part of the British contribution to the UN-authorized International Security and Assistance Force (ISAF) and to provide a secure environment for the recently formed interim government. ISAF came into being in December 2001 and Lieutenant General John McColl, then a major general, led the first mission with contributions from 16 nations.

Essentially, the troops were sent to bring security to Kabul and to improve the effectiveness of the Kabul police. Although the Taliban influence in the capital was now weak, criminality was surging with violent gangs robbing at will. It soon became clear to the ISAF commanders that if the confidence of law-abiding Afghans was to be won then the capital had to be a safe and secure place where local people could begin to lead their lives with some semblance of normality. If this failed then, it was feared, support for the Taliban would return.

Conditions for the troops were harsh. They were housed in freezing buildings at the height of the Afghan winter, which proved to be a tremendous challenge. Food was mainly based on British Army 'compo', which despite being nutritious is no substitute for fresh rations where morale is concerned. Under the command of Lieutenant Colonel James 'Bash' Bashall, a friend and former colleague from my days in 3 Para, the battle group immediately began a series of high-profile joint patrols with the Afghan police. The Paras were involved in several contacts with criminal gangs but, despite some minor injuries, there were no fatalities. As well as conducting joint patrols, the Paras embarked on a series of 'hearts and minds' projects and helped to renovate 18 schools and 14 police stations. As conditions improved and the locals began to accept and trust the Paras, it was decided that by way of celebration a football match should be organized in a local stadium. Just a few months earlier, football had been banned under the Taliban and the stadium had been used for public executions. The match, which saw a team from ISAF play an Afghan United, attracted a crowd of more than 30,000.

Although the Paras tour proved to be highly successful, questions began to arise as to the nature of the UK's role in Afghanistan. It appeared that there was concern at the very highest levels within the military as well as in the UK Parliament.

Admiral Sir Michael Boyce, who in 2002 was the Chief of the Defence Staff, publicly warned of the UK getting 'our hand caught in the mangle' of Afghanistan. Peter Kilfoyle, a former Labour Defence Minister, raised the spectre of Vietnam and said that the UK ran the risk of being sucked into an unwinnable war.

Despite these concerns, the UK agreed to a US request to send a force of 1,700 troops to assist in the hunt for the Taliban and al-Qaeda fighters who had fled to the mountains close to the Pakistan after the fall of the old regime. The mission was known as Operation Jacana and the officer in charge of the British force was Brigadier Roger Lane of the Royal Marines.

The battle group was composed around 45 Commando and it was ready to take part in operations from mid-April 2002 onwards. Geoff Hoon, the then Defence Secretary, warned the British public that it should be under 'no illusions' of the risks involved. Military analysts constantly appeared in the daily newspapers warning of the dangers facing British troops and suggested that a 'bloody' campaign lay ahead.

The Commandos were located at the sprawling former Soviet air base at Bagram, a 45-minute drive north from the capital Kabul. Although the Russians had vacated it 13 years earlier, the signs of the Soviet occupation were still very visible. Russian ground attack aircraft were still in the same position as they were when the base was abandoned in 1989. The threat from mines, both anti-personnel and anti-tank, was a great concern. Shortly before I arrived at Bagram to report on the role of the Commandos in April 2002, a sergeant in the Royal Engineers had his foot blown off after stepping on an anti-personnel mine in an area which had supposedly been cleared of explosives.

From the moment I arrived at Bagram, it was repeatedly sold to me and other journalists that the Commandos were about to embark upon an operation the dangers of which could not be underestimated. We waited with bated breath.

Despite the warnings of casualties, bloodshed and bitter fighting, the operation began slowly. The first mission into 'enemy territory', called Operation Ptarmigan, later turned out to be effectively just a dress rehearsal for future operations. At the time, however, the press pack at Bagram was told that the operation's aim was to flush out any cave complexes and to search and destroy them.

The next mission, the 11-day Operation Snipe, took place about ten days later at the end of April. Once again, the operation was launched with much fanfare amid warnings that the fighting would be tough and casualties were to be expected.

Soon after the Marines arrived on the ground, Downing Street announced that Operation Snipe was a 'substantial offensive operation' aimed at a 'key terrorist base'. However, the enemy remained as elusive as ever and the only material success of the operation, a hidden weapons cache which was destroyed by the Marines, was later found to belong to an Afghan ally of the coalition.

It was clear that the Marine officers who had been briefing the press in Bagram were starting to feel the pressure of the apparent lack of fierce fighting. The more we were told of the dangers facing British troops, the less they failed to materialize. In fact, the only casualties the Commandos had suffered was a vomiting bug which had been imported from the UK and left 39 Marines bedridden. By this stage, I and other correspondents had been withdrawn from Bagram. News editors can be tough and demanding individuals and the *Sunday Telegraph* had already written off Operation Jacana as a non-event.

The final debacle came on 17 May 2002 when the Ministry of Defence (MoD) in London directly contradicted Brigadier Lane over suggestions that his men were involved in a major battle against the Taliban. Earlier in the day, speaking from a podium close to the press tent in Bagram, Brig Lane announced that an 800-strong force composed of Royal Marines and coalition forces had deployed to southeastern Afghanistan to assist an Australian patrol which had been ambushed by al-Qaeda and Taliban forces.

Perhaps relieved that his troops were finally in action, the Brigadier announced to the world's press: 'Clearly there is a substantial force there. The mission is to destroy them. We can confirm that the coalition has made contact with the enemy and some have been killed.' The MoD clarified the situation, stating that while coalition forces had been in contact with the enemy, the Marines had not. To the casual observer, such confusion could be put down to the fog of war but, for many journalists who had been following the Marines in Afghanistan, this was just another mission which had been oversold to the press.

Shortly after I returned to the UK, I had a meeting with a very senior military official. It had been a long-standing appointment and most of the conversation centred on Afghanistan, the war on terror and the possibility of military action against Iraq. The officer, who spoke to me on the condition of anonymity, then asked me about the Marines in Afghanistan. I said that from what I saw 45 Commando were a first-class, highly professional and well-led unit whose role had been undermined by an over-zealous public relations campaign. I then asked him what he thought of the operation. The officer immediately rounded on Brigadier Lane and told me that, from what he had seen on television and learnt through reports via the MoD, Lane was incompetent and should be sacked.

The following morning I reported my conversation to my news editor. There was a great deal of discussion over whether or not we should run the story. It was apparent that to do so would be highly controversial, for the *Sunday Telegraph* would be effectively criticizing an officer in the field while in the middle of a military operation. It was obvious that such a story would be popular with many of our readers but for us the question was whether it would be the right decision. In the end, the stature of the source swung the decision in favour of running the story. If he had been a middle-ranking officer who was simply airing his petty, inter-services prejudices, I would not have taken his comments seriously. But this was different. The source was a three star officer – equivalent in rank to a general – who was happy for me to use his comments providing that he was not named. The story provoked a storm of criticism from Geoff Hoon, the Defence Secretary, who described it as nonsense and said that Brig Lane had his total support. However, the story refused to disappear and by the following Monday, Admiral Sir Michael Boyce, the Chief of the Defence Staff, stated in a briefing to journalists at the MoD in London that 'Expectations had been ramped up, with the result that the Marines felt flat and disappointed.'

With hindsight, it was no surprise that the Taliban or al-Qaeda failed to show themselves. The Royal Marines are excellent combat troops; they were supported by British artillery and they had US Apache helicopter gunships and A–10 Warthog tankbusters on call. By comparison, the Taliban were a lightly armed militia, which moved either on foot or in pick-up trucks. The Commandos' role was worthwhile. They were part of a larger force that prevented the Taliban from operating with impunity in that part of Afghanistan at that particular time.

Unfortunately for the troops of 45 Commando, some officers serving with them 'oversold' their mission to the media and, when reality failed to live up to the hype, the military came under fire.

Briefing journalists in operational theatres is always a tricky business. If the threat is under-played and casualties are sustained, commanders will be castigated for underestimating the enemy. Operation Jacana ended in July 2002 and contact with the enemy was never made. The reason why the Marines could not find the Taliban or al-Qaeda forces was because they were long gone before the Marines arrived, even if they were there in the first place. It seems likely that the intelligence behind the mission was fatally flawed. Eight months later, in March 2003, the UK's military forces would be deployed on another operation for which the intelligence would also later prove to be fatally flawed. Operation Telic, otherwise known as the invasion of Iraq, was based on the presumption that Saddam Hussein had arsenals full of chemical and biological weapons.

I'm still unsure whether or not it was correct for the *Sunday Telegraph* to run a story criticizing Brig Lane. As a newspaper journalist, my job is to write articles which set the agenda and that is something the Brig Lane story clearly achieved. Would I write a similar story again given similar circumstances? Yes, because that is my job. Ultimately, it is up to the editors to decide whether or not such stories should be run. Just like a soldier, it is sometimes necessary for a journalist to put their personal qualms aside and have faith in their superiors.

While the Commandos may have struggled to locate al-Qaeda, the UK's Special Forces units, which were composed primarily of the SBS and the SAS, including its territorial battalion, had been extremely active. In fact, the troops had been so busy that mid-ranking officers and senior non-commissioned officers privately began to question whether or not they, as 'special forces', were being used correctly.

Through various contacts I had developed during my years as a journalist and through my time in the Parachute Regiment, I learnt that two of the SAS's brightest officers and future Commanding Officers of the regiment – whose names I will not disclose for reasons of personal security – both believed that the regiment had been largely misused on many operations in Afghanistan. Basically, the SAS is a unit of hand-picked, highly trained and resourceful troops who conduct unconventional operations, often but not always behind enemy lines. In

Afghanistan, however, they were increasingly ordered to conduct operations which should have been the preserve of a well-trained infantry unit.

One of those operations took place in northern Afghanistan in November 2001. The plan was relatively straightforward: US war planes would provide air cover while 80 men from A and G Squadrons of the SAS assaulted a series of al-Qaeda-held bunkers with the aim of capturing or killing senior members of the terrorist organization.

The operation went well until the troops were forced to take on a bunker system further away from the point they had originally attacked. As they moved forward in a classic infantry formation, they were ambushed from the side and began taking casualties.

The most seriously injured was a young SAS trooper whose ankle was shattered by a bullet from an AK47. Later, the lower half of his leg had to be amputated. Three other soldiers suffered arm, chest and leg wounds caused by grenade fragments and bullets. One of the squadron commanders, a major who was later awarded the Military Cross for his part in the attack, escaped serious injury by a hair's breadth: a bullet tore into his webbing and ripped off his water bottle while two others struck the ceramic breast-plate of his body armour.

The fighting was described as a 'close quarter battle at its most intense'. One SAS soldier who took part in it later recalled: 'Targets were being engaged at a distance of 10 feet. It was a case of who had the steadiest hand won.' More than a dozen of the enemy died in the attack and their strongholds were destroyed; there were no SAS fatalities.

It had been another hard-fought but clear victory for the troops of the SAS. As the smoke cleared, however, a realization quickly descended on the hot and exhausted sabre squadron that this mission had not been the 'special' type of mission for which the SAS had been created. During the post-operation debrief the following day, one of the elite unit's squadron commanders turned to a colleague and made a surprising admission. 'This was not one for us – 1 Para could have done it better,' he confessed.

It is now accepted that during the overthrow of the Taliban in Afghanistan in 2001 the SAS took part in a number of operations that could – and should – have been carried out by infantry units, such as the Paras or the Royal Marines. A new commanding officer was appointed to the regiment and a new brigadier took over as the Director of Special Forces. Both men subscribed to the notion that the SAS should be allowed to return to its roots and concentrate on conducting 'special' rather than 'conventional' operations. And that is exactly what happened following the invasion of Iraq and the return to Afghanistan in 2006, which was called Operation Herrick.

After the fall of the Saddam regime in Iraq in 2003, the SAS were co-located in Baghdad with the US Special Forces in a single unit known as Task Force Black. Working as a coalition entity, Task Force Black was originally responsible for hunting down members of the old regime but that mission later morphed into fighting insurgents and the organization which came to be called Al-Qaeda in Iraq or AQI.

Back in Afghanistan the Taliban were beginning to regain their confidence and began to plan for the insurgency that Mullah Omar had promised. However, at home the main focus began to switch to Iraq. By September 2002, it was more or less clear that the UK and the US planned to invade Iraq amid claims that Saddam Hussein had developed weapons of mass destruction and was prepared to use them against the West. The relatively short and sharp military operation to oust the Taliban from power, and turn a failed state into one with potential, appeared to have given the Bush administration the false impression that the same could be achieved in Iraq.

By September 2002, the Taliban had begun recruiting from the madrassas from which they had originally risen in the Pashtun areas of Afghanistan and Pakistan. Taliban leaders combed the towns and villages in search of easily influenced young men and teenagers and urged them to join a new jihad against the coalition and the US. The Taliban printed pamphlets which likened the coalition to the Russians a decade earlier and secretly distributed them in the towns and villages of the notoriously lawless border region.

Small, mobile training camps in Helmand, Uruzgan and Kandahar provinces were reportedly established. Volunteers were taught how to make improvised explosive devices, usually from mines or artillery shells from the many secret ammunition dumps which were created by the mujahideen during the Soviet occupation.

The Taliban, with the help of al-Qaeda, began to devise new tactics. Groups of up to 50 Taliban fighters grouped together to attack isolated military outposts, convoys of Afghan Police or Army soldiers and US bases with rockets and mortars. After the attack the groups would split up into smaller teams of five or ten men and melt away into the local countryside before regrouping for another attack a few days later. It was worrying for the coalition that the tactics were reminiscent of those used with such great success by the mujahideen against the Soviet forces ten years earlier.

To coordinate the strategy, Mullah Omar named a ten-man leadership council for the resistance, with himself at the head. Five operational zones were created and assigned to various Taliban commanders, such as the key leader Mullah Dadullah, who was placed in charge of Zabul Province operations.

One of the first signs that the Taliban were resurgent came with the launch of Operation Mongoose in January 2003, when troops from the US 82nd Airborne Division launched an attack against around 100 insurgents allied to the Taliban in the Adi Ghar cave complex, which is close to the town of Spin Boldak in Kandahar Province by the border with Pakistan. Newspaper reports at the time said that 18 fighters had been killed and that the site had become a base for supplies and a staging post for Taliban recruits arriving in Afghanistan to take up arms against the US. Although the operation was a success for the coalition, it clearly demonstrated that the Taliban had not been destroyed and were capable of reorganizing and recruiting.

As the summer of 2003 approached, the frequency and ferocity of the attacks against Afghan Army posts intensified in what became known as the Taliban heartland, an area called Dai Chopan which is mainly in Zabul Province but also extends into Kandahar and Uruzgan provinces. Dozens of Afghan military and police officers were killed and several US soldiers also died.

Attacks against the new regime in Afghanistan continued throughout 2003 and 2004. Although the Taliban had been ejected from power in Afghanistan, it was now clear to the US government, and possibly the British, that they were far from beaten. It was also clear that if Afghanistan was to have a future, ISAF would have to move beyond the boundaries of Kabul and towns like Mazar-i-Sharif in the north, down into the south of Afghanistan where the Taliban influence was strong and growing. Such a mission would require more troops and more money. The cost would also be paid in the blood of those chosen for the task.

3

THE ROAD TO WAR

By early 2005, the planning for the deployment of 16 Air Assault Brigade as part of the ISAF expansion into southern Afghanistan was already in full swing. The process was being driven in part by the US military, who had been hunting al-Qaeda fighters who had managed to melt away after the fall of the Taliban regime. That mission was called Operation Enduring Freedom (OEF) and the quarry the US Special Forces were after were the mastermind behind 9/11, Osama bin Laden, and the leader of the Taliban, Mullah Omar.

For months the US generals had been keen to reduce their commitment in the south of the country and replace it with a large multinational force which would be responsible for bringing security to the whole of southern Afghanistan.

The plan was for the UK to form part of a multinational Brigade, along with the Dutch and the Canadians. Each nation would be responsible for one of the country's southern provinces and British troops were allocated the task of pacifying and reconstructing Helmand – a province which was effectively one large opium factory and where the Taliban had spent the last three years regrouping.

The task of deciding what size of force should be sent to Afghanistan fell to a planning team of senior officers based at the Permanent Joint Planning Headquarters (PJHQ) inside a vast underground complex on the outskirts of London in Northwood, Middlesex. The 'bunker', as those who work there affectionately know PJHQ, is the place from where all operations are run; consequently, it is largely staffed by the best officers in the armed forces.

The plan would be critical to the success of the forthcoming operation in Helmand. Staff officers had the challenging task of trying to predict what the troops on the ground would need to sustain them for the duration of their tour. The first challenge was to decide how many men to send and where they should be based. In 2005, Helmand had virtually zero infrastructure so any force would have to be self-sustaining. This meant that the main base would have to be accessible by both air and land. It would also need to accommodate up to 5,000 troops, generate enough water for them and deal with their sewage. The planners also needed to estimate the necessary amounts of food, ammunition and medical supplies, as well as the numbers of helicopters and armoured vehicles. In short, it was a monumental undertaking.

In an ideal world, the planners should have been able to draw on the entire resources of the British military. However, that was not the case in 2005. The UK, along with the US and a few other coalition partners, was bogged down in an increasingly nasty counter-insurgency war in Iraq. The lack of post-war planning had come back to haunt the coalition in spectacular fashion, especially in Baghdad, where dozens of US troops and hundreds of civilians were being killed every week. In the south, where the British were based, the insurgents had just perfected an improvised explosive device (IED) which was capable of destroying the Army's infamous 'Snatch' Land Rovers. These were vehicles that had been primarily designed for operations in Northern Ireland and offered no protection from IEDs for those inside. For many soldiers, any operation which involved travelling in these vehicles filled them with dread.

The drain on resources caused by the UK's continuing involvement in Iraq was a major headache for the planners at PJHQ. The general assumption amongst the UK's top brass in 2004–5 was that by the time the Afghanistan mission started to build up steam, the Iraq operation would effectively be over. Like almost all other assumptions made before and during the invasion of Iraq, this proved to be hopelessly wrong.

Rather than deploying a full brigade with four battle groups comprising some 7,000 men, the size of the force was capped by the MoD at just 3,150. It was a decision that Ed Butler, the Commander of 16 Air Assault Brigade, would later describe as 'barking'.

One of the officers on the PJHQ planning team was John Lorimer, who was then a full colonel and a deputy assistant chief of staff. A high flyer, he had already learnt that he was due to take command of 12 Mechanized Brigade, one of the Army's deployable units, and would take them to Iraq as well as Afghanistan. Patrick Mercer, who at the time was a Tory MP but had previously been the Commanding Officer of 1st Battalion The Worcestershire and Sherwood Foresters Regiment, and who had also taught Lorimer at the Army's Staff College, thought that the British plan was 'a nonsense'. Much to Lorimer's increasing annoyance, on more than one occasion Mercer publicly said that if the plan for Afghanistan which the British were about to put into operation had been presented to him by a student at Staff College, he would have had no hesitation in failing them.

Under the ISAF expansion plan, the UK, Canada, the Netherlands – the three main nations, as well as Denmark and Australia – would form a multinational force which would create a series of provincial reconstruction teams (PRT) responsible for different areas of southern Afghanistan. While the UK would lead a PRT in Helmand, the Netherlands and Canada would lead similar deployments in Uruzgan Province and Kandahar Province respectively.

In the early part of 2005, it was also generally assumed that the British PRT would become involved, at least to some extent, in counter-narcotic operations. This was a position which was reinforced by John Reid, the Defence Secretary, when he told the House of Commons in January 2006 that 'We cannot go on accepting Afghan opium being the source of 90 per cent of the heroin which is applied to the veins of young people of our country.'

Just days after his inauguration as Afghanistan's new president, Hamid Karzai made an impassioned plea for international help in which he described opium production as Afghanistan's 'cancer'. It seemed, therefore, that, as well as assisting in the reconstruction of southern Afghanistan, British troops would also be involved in the eradication of the poppy and therefore of the production of opium.

PRTs had already achieved a certain amount of success in the north of Afghanistan in the town of Mazar-i-Sharif. A second, smaller, UK-led PRT was later established in Meymaneh. The PRT in Mazar included personnel from the Foreign and Commonwealth Office and the Department for International Development, and was aided by around 100 troops to support development programmes alongside the Afghan authorities. By creating a secure environment, the PRTs allowed reconstruction to take place, which meant jobs offering decent wages could be created and thus improve the lifestyles of hundreds of Afghans who had known nothing but poverty, hardship and war for almost two decades.

The move into the north was known as Phase One of the ISAF expansion. Phase Two was the expansion into the west of the country. Phase Three was to be the ISAF expansion into the south, a far more dangerous and challenging operation than that which had been successfully achieved elsewhere in Afghanistan, where the threat from the Taliban and al-Qaeda was much less.

Helmand is the largest province in Afghanistan and remains the main poppy growing area in the country. It was also known to be a hotbed of Taliban activity. It lies within the Pashtu-belt, the traditional home of the Taliban. The only foreign language presence in the area was a small US force of around 100 soldiers. Covering 54,584km^2, Helmand Province is long and thin, running from the Pakistan border up towards the centre of Afghanistan. While the north and central regions of the province are mainly mountainous, the centre to the south is composed mainly of undulating and dusty land. The provincial capital is Lashkar Gar, a city that had previously come under the influence of both the Russians and the US. In the 1960s, Helmand was the centre of a US development programme and was nicknamed 'little America'. Tree-lined streets were created in Lashkar Gar, and a network of canals and a hydro-electric dam were also built, but the project was abandoned when the communists seized power in 1978.

Although wheat production takes place on the fertile land either side of the Helmand river, the cultivation of the poppy and the production of opium is by far the biggest industry in Helmand. It is estimated that 50 per cent of the opium that finds its way on to British streets comes from Afghanistan and 80–90 per cent of that comes from Helmand.

The Taliban banned the cultivation of the poppy for opium in 1997, a year after seizing power. Despite attempts to enforce the ban, some of which were quite brutal and often involved the very real threat of death, production continued. By 2000, Afghanistan's opium production still accounted for 75 per cent of the world's heroin supply. On 17 July, the Taliban reissued a decree that all opium production would cease and by February 2001 production had tailed off hugely. In July 2001, just eight weeks before the attacks of 9/11, the US government gave the Taliban $48 million for reducing opium production by 99.86 per cent. After the regime fell, opium production soared and by 2005 Afghanistan was supplying 87 per cent of the world's opium.

As well as deploying 3,000 troops into Helmand, the British Army would also be dispatching its newly acquired Apache helicopter gunship. The Apache was a long time in coming to the British Army. The need for a new attack helicopter was first identified in the early 1990s, with the initial suggestion that 125 would be needed. The contract for the Apaches was finally issued in 1995 but the number ordered had been reduced to 67.

The Apache is a formidable helicopter. It has a 30mm cannon slung underneath the nose of the aircraft and it is also fitted with Hellfire missiles and CRV7 rockets. The helicopter can also be fitted with 76 Felchettes, each filled with 80 12cm tungsten darts, which are supposed to be used against soft-skinned or lightly armoured vehicles but are equally as lethal against troops in the open. When they are all fired together in a single volley, the rockets burst open to create a cloud of darts which have the effect of stripping flesh from the bone. However, it is the doughnut-shaped Longbow radar system, which sits on top of the helicopter's rotor blades, that really sets the British version of the Apache apart from its rivals. The elevated position of the radar dome allows the pilot to detect, attack and destroy targets while the rest of the helicopter can be hidden behind a hill, trees or a building. The helicopter can also share targeting information with other Apaches that might not have a line-of-sight to the target. This allows a group of Apaches to engage a series of targets with only one radar dome being revealed. The Longbow radar can put an attack into effect in 30 seconds. The processors inside determine the location, speed and direction of travel of up to 256 targets. It is also fitted with a bewildering array of night-vision and target-acquisition devices, which means that it can function in virtually all weather conditions, day or night. Attached to the pilot's helmet is a display unit which projects data images on to the pupil of the right eye, allowing him or her to read the computer screens while looking directly ahead.

The Apaches were due to come from 9 Regiment Army Air Corps, which was based at Dishforth Airfield in North Yorkshire. When I visited the unit in June 2005, it was clear that everyone from the commander downwards was aware that at least six of the helicopters would accompany the Paras the following May – even though no one I spoke to was prepared to be quoted on the record.

While the Apache is obviously a very effective weapon system, it has one vital flaw – it has no capacity to carry troops, so Chinooks would also form a vital part of the operation in Afghanistan.

As well as Apaches, the task force would be able to call upon the support of six GR7 Harrier ground attack aircraft, which had been based at Kandahar in support of the US-led OEF mission since September 2004. The task force would also have access to a wide variety of other air assets such as the lethal US Army A–10 Warthog tankbuster.

In marked contrast to Operation Telic – the war in Iraq – troops who deployed to Afghanistan on Operation Herrick would be properly equipped with the correct weapons, body armour and equipment. There were concerns, however, as to the wisdom of embarking on two foreign campaigns at the same time.

Under the 1998 Strategic Defence Review, the British Army was configured to undertake only a limited number of operations at any one time. The review stated that the size and shape of the British force should be able to undertake either two concurrent medium-scale operations – one a relatively short, war-fighting deployment and the other an enduring non-war-fighting operation – or a single full-scale operation. For many in the Army, however, embarking on a dangerous and demanding mission in Afghanistan while British troops were still involved in a highly volatile and long-term operation in Iraq was asking too much of the armed forces. No one I spoke to at the time doubted the need to ensure that the Taliban had to be removed if Afghanistan was not to become a breeding ground for international terrorism. However, there were concerns over whether the UK, with its military commitments in Iraq, could take on another – and in many ways more demanding – military challenge.

The UK's armed forces have a combined strength of around 182,000 personnel of which about 101,000 are in the Army, 36,000 are in the Royal Navy and Royal Marines and 45,000 are in the Royal Air Force. Most of the troops currently taking part in land operations come from the Army, the Royal Marines and elements of the RAF. Troops available for operations tend to be posted to one of the Army's seven deployable brigades, namely: 16 Air Assault Brigade, 1 Mechanized Brigade, 4 Mechanized Brigade, 12 Mechanized Brigade, 19 Light Brigade, 7 Armoured Brigade and 20 Armoured Brigade. 3 Commando Brigade, which is part of the Royal Navy, is also available for deployment on operations and is composed of 3,500 men.

With one 'enduring' operation already taking place in Iraq, which consumes the best part of a brigade, the result is that three brigades are immediately taken out of the system: one brigade is preparing for operations, another is actually on operations and a third is recovering from operations and needs to undergo a period of rest and retraining. So, if the UK's armed forces are committed to two operations requiring two brigades, a total of six are taken out of the system, leaving just two and these brigades are often used to reinforce those units already on operations. It was against this backdrop that the first concerns began to arise as to whether there were enough troops in the system to send a large enough force Afghanistan. The prime concern on many military minds was the question: 'What would happen if both operations needed to be reinforced at the same time?' The apparent answer was that they would come from the Middle East reserve force based in Cyprus. This acknowledged that there was only one battalion trained, acclimatized and ready to deploy at short notice on operations in either Afghanistan or Iraq.

Concern over the lack of a mobile reserve force was a factor which would emerge time and again at the highest levels in London and at NATO headquarters in Brussels over the next few months.

As the preparations progressed, it became clear that the task force would be based around a 3 Para battle group with a platoon of volunteers from the Royal Irish Rangers, who had recently returned from a tour of duty in Iraq, as well as a platoon of Gurkhas and reservists from the Paras' territorial 4th Battalion, known as 4 Para.

The battle group would be supported by D Squadron of the Household Cavalry Regiment Reconnaissance, who are equipped with the aged but very effective Scimitar armoured vehicles. 16 Air Assault's integral reconnaissance forces, the Pathfinders, were also due to take part in the operation, as were elements of the brigade's teams of gunners, engineers, mechanics, signallers, logisticians, Royal Military Police and medics.

Although the Paras are just one of a large number of regiments which make up the 36 battalions of the UK's infantry, they remain a unique organization in the British Army. Apart from the SAS, they are the only infantry regiment that has its own selection procedure – P Company – which all officers, non-commissioned officers and private soldiers must pass before they can serve in the regiment.

In P Company, which takes place at the Infantry Training Centre at Catterick in North Yorkshire, Parachute Regiment recruits and those personnel volunteering to serve with the airborne forces must conduct a series of gruelling physical and mental tests designed to push them to the very limits of their endurance. Of those who volunteer to take up the challenge of joining the 28-week Para recruitment training course, only 48 per cent pass.

However, perhaps the best gauge of the regiment's character is that its soldiers make up more than 50 per cent of the entire strength of the Special Air Service, which selects individuals from across the whole of the Army.

To earn their wings, like all of the airborne forces, Paras must also complete the basic military parachuting course at RAF Brize Norton in Oxfordshire. The Royal Marines also have an intense physical selection course – the Commando course – but they are part of the Royal Navy.

Life in the Parachute Regiment can be tough and uncompromising. Professionalism is expected and demanded from all ranks at all times and those officers or soldiers who do not measure up either leave the Army or are persuaded to join other regiments. Such demands lead to a breed of soldier who is courageous, loyal and a world-class fighter.

After the Falklands War in 1982, the Parachute Regiment went through a dauntingly quiet period in the Army. While large parts of the armed forces departed to the Gulf in the latter part of 1990 to take part in the first invasion of Iraq the following January, the Paras remained firmly rooted in the UK. My battalion, 3 Para, was coming to the end of a two-year residential tour in Ulster and, even though I had already decided to leave the Army the following year, I and many of my fellow officers looked on jealously as what seemed to be the entire rest of the Army readied itself for war.

Apart from routine operational deployments in Ulster, it was not until the Kosovo emergency in 1999 that the Paras were to enter operational service again. Following Kosovo they saw action in Sierra Leone (2000), Macedonia (2001), Afghanistan (2001) and Iraq (2003, 2005) – in short the Parachute Regiment has never been busier than in recent years.

The Brigade finally received its marching orders for Afghanistan in the autumn of 2005 and the long-awaited preparations and training packages swung into action.

Details of the plan to send a British task force into Afghanistan were to be made public in late November 2005, but this was delayed until the following January because of a series of disagreements with other NATO parties over rules of engagement, the size and make-up of forces and basic command and control functions. The lack of NATO cooperation and the refusal by some countries to allow their troops to be deployed on combat missions in dangerous parts of the country were factors that would dog the entire campaign.

The delay was also having an impact on the commanders who were attempting to ready their troops for the operations which lay ahead. It is worth remembering that even by late November 2005 the intelligence coming out of Helmand was limited. It was known that the Taliban had seized control of some areas, but details of their strength, locations and means of supply were very limited.

The first reconnaissance of Helmand involving British forces took place in February 2005. Lorimer did not take part in the recce.

Brig Ed Butler, the Commander of 16 Air Assault Brigade, was one of the few senior officers in the British Army who had any recent experience of fighting in Helmand – he served on operations in the province when he was commander of 22 SAS. He fully expected to be asked to take part in the PJHQ recce. Somewhat astonishingly, the call never came. His staff officers in the brigade thought that their 'lofty' counterparts at PJHQ had missed a trick.

From the moment the PJHQ plan appeared – even in draft form – Brig Butler and his staff officers were concerned. Frustrated at being left out of the planning process, something which one officer described as 'unfortunately not being unique in the history of the British army', Brig Butler explained to his staff at his headquarters in Colchester, Essex, that the plan was calculated 'not on the basis of what is needed to achieve success but on the basis of what was available for the operation'.

One brigade staff officer said: 'If those who were to execute the plan had been allowed to plan the plan, in terms of force generation and troop numbers, we would have probably come up with different figures. Right from the very beginning the plan lacked flexibility and was unrealistic.'

The officer, who was one of Ed Butler's advisers, told me:

I knew, with the troop numbers we had and the helicopter that we had, we were pushing our luck. The feeling in the brigade was that, if everything went swimmingly and the enemy didn't have a vote, then it might just be achievable.

But looking back I think PJHQ underestimated the ground and the enemy. There was an underestimation of the number of troops needed to achieve the task and of the problems with mobility, in getting around that piece of real estate.

With his experience, Butler was one of the few people in the Army to be aware of the scale of the problem. He was familiar with the terrain and he knew that we would be totally reliant on helicopters. However, as one of his staff officers said, 'You live with what you're given.'

Another officer said that Butler privately thought the plan was 'barking'. The brigade commander made it clear in a series of memos over several months to senior officers at PJHQ that he was not being given the proper resources for the type of mission he was being asked to undertake.

The general consensus within 16 Air Assault Brigade was that the force needed to be composed of at least two battle groups of around 1,500 to 1,800 men, plus a theatre reserve and all the other units, such as medics, signallers, engineers, mechanics, which allow a brigade to function. Commenting on what was believed to be needed in Helmand, a brigade staff officer said:

> You needed two manoeuvre battle groups plus a theatre reserve and with all the added bits and pieces you were talking about a force of 5,000 to 6,000. Would we have got 5,000 to 6,000 troops if the brigade commander had been involved in the planning? The answer is no but I think I would have some pretty strong objections from the word go before we got into a situation that we couldn't actually get out of.

Thus, the tone was set for the Helmand task force. Like much of the Army they were being asked to do too much with too little. Before anyone in government seemed to appreciate the size of the undertaking, it was too late. The MoD, not PJHQ, capped the size of the force at 3,150. It was decided that the force would consist of a battle group and a PRT and would be commanded by full colonels, a decision which would later be reversed.

The announcement that the Paras had been waiting for finally happened in the House of Commons on 26 January 2006. The Defence Secretary told MPs that the UK was sending a military task force into Helmand, which would face 'risks and difficulties'. In his speech Mr

Reid said that the British force would not be in Helmand to 'wage war' or to carry out the kind of 'seek-and-destroy' operations which the Americans had been mounting under OEF. Instead, he said, the British mission would be defined as denying terrorists an 'ungoverned space in which they can foment and export terrorism'.

Despite Mr Reid's assertion that British troops would not be hunting down the Taliban, the military had other ideas. 'If we get a sniff of the Taliban we will go after them and kill them. We won't wait for them to attack us – that's why we are bringing Apache', a senior officer told me in the months leading up to the deployment.

It was also made clear to journalists through government briefings in the early part of 2006 that the PRT's highest priority would be tackling Helmand's opium trade. It was suggested that by a combination of education programmes and cash incentives, Afghanistan's impoverished farmers would turn away from planting the lucrative poppy. Shortly after such aspirations appeared in the media, another contact who was directly involved in the planning of the operation told me that the 'counter-narcotics' element was a complete red herring. 'That's for other people to worry about – it's not the job of soldiers. Despite what the government might want people to believe, we are not going in to Helmand to take on the drug lords, we are going there to kick out the Taliban.' And his words, even at that early stage, proved to be absolutely correct.

Mr Reid's claims that British troops would not be taking part in seek-and-destroy operations seemed to be at odds with briefings being given to the senior officers from 3 Commando who, even at this early stage, were beginning the planning process for their deployment to take over from 16 Air Assault Brigade in October 2006. Documents from what was clearly an internal PowerPoint presentation were leaked to me in April 2006. They clearly showed that there were plans to launch operations to root out the Taliban.

One of the documents, entitled 'Execution – Tac CONOPS', showed a map of Helmand with areas identified as locations of suspected Taliban activity. In these areas, the document clearly said, 'insurgents/criminals' would be found and tracked. Their sanctuaries and locations would be disrupted and they would be 'defeated (eventually)'. Again, when I asked another soldier, whom I had known for many years, to explain exactly to what type of operations these documents were referring, he said, 'It would be wrong to say that British troops would be taking part in search-and-destroy operations because that is not a phrase used by the Army – but we will be taking part in operations which amount to the same sort of thing. We call it cordon-and-search.'

A few days after my resultant article was published in the *Sunday Telegraph* in April 2006, John Reid appeared to be reconsidering the role of British forces in Helmand when he told BBC Radio 4 that soldiers may launch offensive missions that involve hunting down and killing insurgents. During the interview on Sunday, 23 April, he said:

Although our mission is primarily reconstruction, it is complex and dangerous because the terrorists will want to destroy the economy and the legitimate trade and the government that we are hoping to build up. Of course, our mission is not counter-terrorism but one of the tasks will be to defend our own troops and the people we are here to defend and to pre-empt, on occasion, terrorist attacks on us. If this didn't involve the necessity to use force we wouldn't send soldiers.

Mr Reid's spin doctors were keen to make the point that this was not a policy U-turn, but a clarification of the message the Secretary of State wanted to get out to the public. An explanatory note was sent to journalists via Mr Reid's office, saying that British troops would be involved in counter-insurgency operations, but not anti-terrorist operations. There is a difference, of course, but it is a fine one. As far as the soldiers were concerned, they were being sent to Afghanistan to kill the Taliban.

Around the same time, various reports began appearing in the national press stating that the force deploying to Afghanistan required more troops. I had been told by a number of contacts that Lieutenant General David Richards, who was the commander of the British-led Allied Rapid Reaction Corps, which was due to take command of the NATO mission in the summer of 2006, wanted the UK to supply an extra battle group of around 1,000 men. The General wanted a mobile reserve force that could be flown across the whole of southern Afghanistan to reinforce units which were under Taliban attack. This request, I and other journalists were told, had been denied because the UK was still too committed to operations in Iraq to send any more troops into Afghanistan. This was always strongly denied by the government, which claimed, even during 2007, that the number of troops in Afghanistan was not dependent on the number serving in Iraq.

At every conceivable opportunity, the government was making the case that the size of the force being sent to Afghanistan was large enough for the job in hand. And yet, despite media reports stating that General Richards was said to have asked for more troops, this was denied by Mr Reid. Nevertheless, as the months progressed more troops were sent out and within a year the number of troops serving in Helmand had more than doubled.

The Defence Secretary went on to say that the role of the British forces in Helmand was fundamentally different to that of the US forces elsewhere in Afghanistan: 'We are in the south to help and protect the Afghan people to construct their own democracy.'

Mr Reid then made a statement which would haunt him for the rest of his time as Defence Secretary. He declared to the world's media, 'We would be perfectly happy to leave in three years and without firing one shot because our job is to protect reconstruction.'

It was also around this time that the UK received a reminder, in the form of an RAF Harrier being destroyed at Kandahar airport, that the fight against the Taliban had not gone away. The Taliban had been routinely firing rockets at the airport for months; most failed to hit their targets but this time they got lucky and hit a GR7, one of six which had been based at the airfield in support of OEF since the previous September.

As 2005 drew to a close, concerns began to emerge within the head-quarters of 16 Air Assault Brigade over the lack of helicopters and the number of fighting troops that would be available for operations. The entire task force would have just six Chinook transport helicopters and four Lynx helicopters. Although the Chinook can carry heavy loads and up to 40 men in full kit, the Lynx can carry just four passengers. In the height of the summer, the heat effectively grounded the Lynx. It was virtually unable to fly during daylight hours. Given the arduous conditions in Helmand, high altitude, dust and heat, British commanders knew it would take a great deal of effort to keep all the aircraft airworthy at all times. Also, the use of helicopters would be limited by the number of air-hours they can fly before they need a major service. Furthermore, it would be necessary to keep at least one Chinook free from operational duties so that it could deal with the evacuation of casualties.

Brig Butler returned to Helmand in the autumn of 2005 to conduct a detailed reconnaissance with key officers from his headquarters. The recce merely confirmed his worst fears about the PJHQ plan.

Even before he departed for Afghanistan, Brig Butler knew that helicopters were going to be the key to the success of the mission. One of his staff officers at the time said:

> When we did a detailed tactical 16 AA recce in the autumn of 2005, we started looking at helicopter hours, time and distance estimates and the number of contacts, which to be fair we underestimated, and things like the rates of ammunition expenditure. We always recognized that we would be truly stretched.

Brig Butler was aware that the failure to withdraw troops from Iraq in 2006 would have an impact on his mission. He ensured that his PJHQ bosses – Air Marshal Glen Torpy and, later, Lt Gen Nick Houghton – were made aware of his concerns in a series of 'loose minute' memos he wrote in late 2005 and early 2006.

The issue of helicopter shortages was even raised by members of the House of Commons Defence Select Committee in April 2006, who said that they were deeply concerned that British troops would not have enough air cover or helicopters to launch operations against the Taliban. However, there were no more helicopters available – 16 Air Assault Brigade would just have to make do.

The first task of the Afghanistan operation was to build the camp where the British troops would be based. This monumental task fell to 850 men from 39 Regiment Royal Engineers. A vast, flat and dusty plain close to Route 1, the main road through Helmand, was chosen for the location of Camp Bastion, which it would grow to become the largest base ever built by the British overseas. By the time it was completed, Camp Bastion would occupy an area of 20km^2.

Using heavy machinery, brute force and a lot of sweat, the engineers set about the task in February 2006, just as the short Afghan winter was coming to an end. In haste, the relatively small force began building roads, pitching tents and erecting a perimeter fence over 22km long.

As well as building a secure camp which could accommodate several thousand troops, the engineers had to build an airstrip which could handle the vast number of Hercules sorties that would be required to turn the compound into a functioning military base.

Camp Bastion sits in a flat, featureless area of the desert in central Helmand. It is ringed by watchtowers housing soldiers who spend hours every day, sweltering in the heat, trying to spot any Taliban fighters foolish enough to try and launch an attack against them. In the distance, mountains – when they can be seen, for the heat often distorts the horizon – denote the varied terrain of Helmand.

The creation of the camp was vital for it would be the main logistics base and an air bridge to Kandahar and on to the UK. The makeshift airstrip at Bastion took an enormous pounding from the heavily laden Hercules as they arrived hourly from Kandahar, carrying everything from men to mortar shells, as well as food and water.

The airstrip also took its toll on the aircraft. Tyres were routinely ripped to pieces on landing. Break and hydraulic pipes were slashed by razor sharp stones being kicked up from the desert floor as the wheels touched down. Even the undercarriage doors took a serious beating. Despite all of these potentially hazardous circumstances, not a single aircraft was lost. The Hercules has been a great servant to the British military since it first came into service over 40 years ago, but it is not invulnerable to attack from the ground. Ten British personnel were killed when a Hercules was shot down in Iraq by a suspected insurgent anti-aircraft missile in January 2005. At that stage, it was the largest loss of life sustained by British forces in a single incident since the start of the war in Iraq.

It is estimated that Camp Bastion cost around £1billion to build. Troops live in air-conditioned tents – the temperature in the summer regularly reaches 50°C – with showers and toilets. A gym and a NAAFI, where troops can watch satellite television while drinking coffee, tea and other non-alcoholic drinks, were also built.

Everything in Bastion has to be imported, from the food in the canteen to the Hesco ramparts which protect every walkway from mortar, rocket attack or small arms fire. Hesco blocks are large steel rectangular-shaped baskets, about 1.5m high by 1m wide, which are filled with earth and stacked to form walls and ramparts. Rather than run for cover, troops are simply advised to hit the deck.

Deploying on operations is always something of a surreal experience for soldiers. Within a matter of hours you are transported from the security of your own home, surrounded by your family, into a hostile combat zone where people are trying to kill you.

When I was serving in the Paras, my combat zone was West Belfast and the enemy were the IRA and, to a lesser extent, the Protestant para-militaries. The door-to-door trip from my home in southwest London to Palace Barracks, just outside Belfast, took around four hours. From the moment you stepped off the plane at Belfast International Airport you had to be on your guard.

I always found the trip from the airport, through the city centre and into Palace Barracks quite stressful. I was often picked up by two soldiers from the Close Observation Platoon which I commanded, and as a matter of standing procedure both would be armed with semi-automatic pistols and one with a powerful Heckler Koch assault rifle. However, I always believed that it would be relatively easy for the IRA to spot Army personnel arriving at the airport and then ambush them en route. Luckily, during my two years in the province no such attacks occurred. Most of the routes to the airport went through Protestant areas and the basic theory was that the IRA never felt comfortable operating outside the districts where, at the very least, there was sympathetic support for their cause.

I am sure that those troops who left the UK or Germany for Helmand in early 2006 had exactly the same sense of trepidation that I always had on those airport runs.

Troops heading for operations overseas usually depart from RAF Brize Norton, flying out in aging white Tristars. For those flying into Iraq and Afghanistan, a helmet and body armour are mandatory pieces of equipment for both civilian and service personnel alike. The trip to Kabul – the first staging post en route to Helmand – takes around eight hours. To reach Camp Bastion, troops transfer to a Hercules transport aircraft fitted with a fully equipped defensive aids suite, which should protect it from any surface-to-air missiles threat.

By the beginning of May 2006, a large portion of the 3,150 troops who made up the task force had arrived in Helmand via a two-week acclimatization programme in Oman, which the MoD never wanted to admit to because of so-called host-nation sensitivities. Decoded, this means that, as a Muslim country, Oman did not want it publicized that it was giving aid to a non-Muslim nation which was about to conduct military operations in a fellow Muslim country.

The troops quickly settled into their new quarters in Camp Bastion. The camp was a massive culture shock for many in the Brigade. In the early days of their arrival, water was only available for a couple of hours a day, power cuts were constant and the food was produced from the Army's 'compo rations'. It was the energy-sapping heat and the ultra-fine dust, however, which initially proved to be the soldiers' greatest enemy, for the Taliban were yet to show their faces. It was virtually impossible to stay clean in such conditions and there were fears that the dust might begin to affect some weapon systems but this problem rarely, if ever, materialized.

As the troops began to settle into their new home, Brig Butler set about putting his plan into operation. In essence, he wanted to secure a 'Helmand triangle' linking Camp Bastion, Lashkar Gar and Gereshk, which would be cleared of the Taliban and thereby create the security conditions which would allow reconstruction to begin. At the same time, elements from his force would also begin training or 'mentoring' members of the Afghan National Army (ANA) and the Afghan National Police (ANP). These troops were known as Operational Mentoring and Liaison Teams (OMLTs, pronounced 'omelettes'), and this task largely fell to the men of the 7 (Parachute) Royal Horse Artillery.

In those early days of the so-called 'break in battle', it was hoped that over time the size of the triangle would grow as the Taliban were pushed further back and the ANA and the ANP would begin to take over responsibility for security.

The first Brigade troops to arrive in Helmand were the Pathfinders. Their historical role was to recce ahead of the main Brigade force, establishing parachute dropping zones and helicopter landing zones. The Pathfinders select troops from across the Army, including the Parachute Regiment, and many of its number later go on to serve with the SAS.

The Pathfinders arrived in March 2006, while Camp Bastion was still being built. They conducted their pre-deployment training in the Kandahar area before moving into Helmand. The Pathfinders' main piece of equipment was the Land Rover WMIK, which was generally referred to as the Wmik, pronounced 'wimik'. The acronym stands for Weapons Mounted Installation Kit. This essentially involves connecting a metal frame to a stripped-down Land Rover, which then allows a .50 calibre machine-gun to be fitted to the vehicle. The 50, as it is known to the troops, is a fairly formidable piece of equipment. Although many of those deployed to Helmand were originally made in the 1950s, they will take out anyone foolish or inexperienced enough to think that a brick wall, tree or building might provide them with cover from fire. It has been said that such is the power of the weapon that just the shockwave created when a bullet zips through the air can kill a man. In addition to the 50, the Wmik was also fitted with a general purpose machine-gun (GPMG).

The Pathfinders' first task was to move by road to Forward Operating Base (FOB) Price. FOB Price sits just outside the strategically important town of Gereshk, close to the Helmand river, in an area known to have been heavily infiltrated by the Taliban. The Pathfinders' mission was to develop a detailed tactical picture of the terrain and enemy presence, which could then be passed on to the main force of Paras who were due to arrive in the next few weeks. Such information would be vital if the Paras were to hit the ground running. They would need to know where the old Soviet minefields had been laid, which villages were friendly to the coalition, and therefore could be regarded as safe, and which were likely to be supportive of the Taliban.

With the arrival of the 3 Para battle group, the Pathfinders left FOB Price and set off for the north, looking for the Taliban.

One of the many patrols in the area became locked in a firefight with the Afghan National Police, who later claimed that they thought the Pathfinders were the Taliban. The Pathfinders always found this excuse hard to believe and their worst fears were later confirmed when intelligence was obtained which suggested that the ANP had actually been infiltrated by the Taliban.

The threat posed by Soviet mines, which had been laid two decades earlier, was demonstrated in dramatic fashion just a few days after the Pathfinders' 'battle' with the ANP, when a vehicle hit a mine and one of the recce team's engineers lost a leg.

The Pathfinders' presence in the north proved fortuitous. Just a few days into the programme the brigade headquarters in Camp Bastion received word that the security situation in and around the town of Musa Qala, north of Helmand, was deteriorating. First reports suggested around 400 Afghans had been killed in a series of protracted firefights between the Afghan security forces and the Taliban.

Tension had been growing in the town, where a sizeable Taliban presence had been intimidating the locals and carrying out sporadic attacks against the ANP. By late May, the attacks were becoming more frequent and ferocious, so Brig Butler ordered a force to be sent to the region to support the ANP and the ANA.

The operation began on 17 May 2006, when the Pathfinders were told that a poorly trained police force of around 100 Afghans were surrounded by a 500-strong Taliban force in Musa Qala. The police needed help and they needed it quickly. It was hoped that just like the 7th Cavalry, the Pathfinders would arrive in the nick of time and save the surrounded and isolated police from certain death.

Privately, however, the Pathfinders suspected that the enemy strength had been highly exaggerated to ensure that the British would act, but it was clear that the policemen holed up in their station were in trouble. Casualty figures revealed that the police had already lost 13 men. British commanders were only too well aware that losing the town to the Taliban would present the enemy with a strategic as well as a propaganda victory over the British.

Time was clearly of the essence for the Pathfinders, but it was vital that, in their eagerness to get to Musa Qala, they did not allow themselves to be ambushed by using the most obvious routes into and out of the town. Instead, they used mountain roads and dried-up river beds, called *wadis*, which offered the best compromise between speed and stealth.

The Pathfinders arrived on the outskirts of Musa Qala on the 19 May. Fears of a massacre immediately disappeared.

From their mountain vantage point, which overlooked the town, they could see the Taliban in full retreat with the police in hot pursuit. The Pathfinders attached themselves to the end of the column and joined in the hunt. Within a few hours the Pathfinders were deep in enemy territory, in an area where Mullah Omar is believed to have fled after the fall of his regime in 2001. By the following day, as the temperature edged towards 50°C, the convoy arrived at the town of Baghran, where the fighting restarted. The police were unwilling to push on into the town so the British called in air support. It may have been coincidental but, following the arrival of a US B1 long-range bomber, the Taliban resistance melted away. If any of the Taliban had been at Tora Bora a few years earlier, or had heard stories from those who survived, they would have only been too well aware of the destructive firepower that such aircraft can deliver on to a target.

With the fighting over, the Pathfinders began making their way back to Musa Qala, fully aware that they were in enemy territory and that the risk of ambush remained ever present.

As the troops arrived at Paysang, where a large gorge offered a perfect ambush site, the British troops began to get very suspicious. As they moved steadily along the road, they were met with small arms fire from the Taliban. Rounds from AK47s zipped past their heads and RPGs smashed into the ground close to the Pathfinders' column.

Immediately, the Pathfinders' 50 swung into action and the valley was filled with the deafening rattle of machine-gun fire. John Reid's desire for British troops not to fire a shot in anger disappeared in an instant.

Those amongst the Taliban who chose to raise their head above a rock or from behind a tree or building were risking life and limb. Once a target was identified, the gunner would carry on firing even if the enemy was hiding behind a wall. For the Taliban on the receiving end of the fire, the effect must have been terrifying.

With the arrival of the Afghan National Police, an assault against the Taliban was launched. The British struck from one direction and the Afghans from another. The Taliban were caught in a deadly pincer movement. The fighting raged on for most of the day until the Taliban were finally suppressed by an A–10 Warthog, with its fearsome 30mm cannon from which there is no protection.

The five days of fighting had left 60 people dead. By the time the exhausted Pathfinders arrived at Musa Qala, locals were once again leaving following threats by the Taliban. However, when the ANP told them of how they had beaten and killed large numbers of Taliban, the locals decided to stay in the town. It was exactly the result that Brig Butler wanted. The British knew that word of the battle would quickly pass through the towns and villages of the area.

However, the British commanders were also aware that the Taliban would strike back, and in force: it was just a question of time. A US company from the 2/87th Infantry Regiment eventually relieved the Pathfinders, but they would be back in Musa Qala in a matter of weeks. On that operation, victory over the Taliban would not be so easily won.

4

TETHERED GOATS

Helmand's '120-day wind' started to blow as the first soldiers began to arrive at Camp Bastion in late March 2006. Swirls of ultra-fine, talcum powder-like dust descended on the Paras, exhausted by the 15-hour journey from Brize Norton via Kabul, as they marched in unison down the ramp of the Hercules. It was not the friendliest of welcomes.

For many of the soldiers, whose average age was just 19, this was the first time they had been abroad in their relatively short lives and they were in a land where a large number of the inhabitants intended to spend the next six months trying to kill them.

The nature of the mission had been drilled into every man for the last six months. Their job was to provide security so that reconstruction could begin. It was a simple mantra but the task, every man knew, was immense and fraught with danger. Success was by no means guaranteed. While the UK government held on to the belief that the Army might be able to leave Afghanistan in three years' time 'without having fired a shot', the Paras knew that they were in for a tough fight. It was not lost on some of those teenage soldiers that they were about to embark on an adventure from which some of them might not return.

Within hours of arriving at Camp Bastion, which then resembled a tented refugee-type encampment, the briefings began. They were warned of the dangers posed by a particularly venomous scorpion whose sting can kill in 15 seconds – no anti-venom has yet been found. Also, they were told how the dreaded diarrhoea and vomiting, known as 'D and V', could lay waste to a fit platoon of 30 men. Home could not have been further away.

A few weeks earlier, during the seemingly endless pre-deployment briefings at their headquarters in Colchester, the troops had been promised that they would be living in large, comfortable, air-conditioned, state-of-the-art tents and would be fed on fresh rations. 'Don't worry about the dust,' they were told, 'you will be able to wash in hot showers with an unlimited water supply.'

Defence Secretary John Reid's delay in announcing the Helmand mission to the House of Commons meant that the engineers started building the camp two months later than had been originally planned. Instead of sleeping in air-conditioned tents, the troops spent the first ten days of the deployment housed in 5.5m × 7m tents which had been last used on Salisbury Plain. Fresh rations were non-existent and the soldiers survived on ten-man ration packs. Water was still limited to a few hours a day and power cuts were irritatingly common. Any of the younger Toms, the Paras' word for young private soldiers, who were foolish or inexperienced enough to complain about the living conditions were chided with the reprimand: 'If you can't take a joke, you shouldn't have joined.' The Paras were experienced enough to know that it could be worse, much worse, as they were soon to discover.

Within a couple of days the Paras got back down to training and honing their platoon-level tactics. The soldiers practised section and platoon attacks, anti-ambush drills and first aid. Weapons were zeroed, so that the soldiers would hit what they aimed at. Commanders began to get a feel for the ground and started to become familiar with those people they had come to Helmand to help, as well as those they had come to kill.

What struck all of those new to Helmand, and that was 99 per cent of the men, was the hostile nature of the terrain, the vastness of the country and the poor quality of the roads. Helmand had changed little in the past 500 years. Many homes had no access to the outside world. Only the more prosperous villages had electricity; the majority of homes were lit with kerosene lamps. Helmand was, in effect, a pre-industrial society where levels of ignorance were high and the vast majority of the people unquestioningly obeyed the words of the local mullah. The Paras were soon to learn that many of these leaders were in league with the local drug lords and the Taliban.

By the middle of May 2006, the whole of 3 Para had arrived but it would be another six to eight weeks until the brigade achieved Full Operational Capability – the point at which, in theory, it is ready to conduct war-fighting operations.

As the month of May turned into June and the temperatures hit their high point, the troops started to become increasingly busy. Although the Paras had spent months training on Salisbury Plain in Wiltshire and at the Sennybridge Training Camp in South Wales, the training continued apace in Helmand.

The brigade had established a permanent presence in the towns of Nowzad and Musa Qala, which had prevented the areas from falling into the hands of the Taliban. However, this had also meant that the platoon houses or District Centres were starting to attract significant amounts of enemy fire. The preferred weapon of the Taliban was the ubiquitous AK47, closely followed by the RPG, but they were also equally adept with the 107mm Chinese rocket and the Russian Dshk 12.7mm heavy machine-gun – a powerful weapon capable of obliterating a substantial brick building. One soldier described the experience of being attacked in one of the towns where the British were based: 'You just had to keep cool and make sure every shot counted, the more they came the more we dropped. It was intense and nothing prepares you for it, you simply go into training mode and deliver everything you have been trained to do.'

Both Brig Butler and Lt Colonel Stuart Tootal, the Commanding Officer of 3 Para, had decided that the time was now right to launch a major full-scale operation against the Taliban, who were becoming an increasingly menacing force in Nowzad.

Lt Col Tootal was a highly driven, intense and intelligent officer who was an expert in counter-insurgency and had previously served on Operation Telic during the Iraq War. Tootal was aware that the task before him was enormous. One of the greatest problems he faced was the lack of intelligence available. No military unit had previously operated in Helmand and the Taliban held sway in vast parts of the country. They were not about to give up their position lightly.

Initially, the environment was relatively benign. For the first six to eight weeks the Paras and the Taliban watched each other carefully. The Paras soon learnt that they could enter a hamlet or village and be welcomed by smiling locals only too keen to offer them cups of sweetened tea. The Paras were initially encouraged by the reception but on the third or subsequent visits to the same area they would be attacked. Thus the British troops struggled to get an accurate intelligence picture. It was not that their initial intelligence was wrong: the problem was that none existed in the first place.

Nowzad, it was decided, was the place where the Paras would make their mark. The town had changed little since medieval times. High mud walls, several feet thick, which decades and probably centuries of Afghan sun had baked to a rock-like hardness, separated areas from one another.

Lt Col Tootal and his staff planned to confront the Taliban and ideally kill or capture their leaders in a 'cordon-and-search' mission called Operation Mutay. The operation, which took place on 4 June 2006, was centred on a large high-walled compound situated in a 'bocage' – an area consisting of dense orchards, irrigation ditches and many inter-connected walled compounds.

Put simply, it was the perfect place in which the Taliban could hide and easily ambush anyone trying to enter. Visibility within the bocage was, at best, around 70m and movement by foot was extremely restricted, funnelling anyone entering into obvious killing zones.

Once again, intelligence was sketchy. The basic intelligence picture suggested that Taliban were in the area – 'No shit, Sherlock!' was the view of most soldiers when told this – but there were no details on numbers, locations or weaponry.

The task of searching and clearing the compound fell to the men of A Company, which was commanded by Major Will Pike whose father had commanded 3 Para some 24 years earlier during the Falklands War. Maj Pike was a tough and uncompromising officer who, up until the Afghanistan operation, was not yet sure whether, like his father, he wanted to make the Army his life.

The men of A Company were supported by Patrols Platoon, the equivalent of the recce platoon in other infantry regiments, and the Gurkhas were tasked with providing a cordon to the east and west of the search area with the aim of preventing movement in and out of it. The term 'cordon-and-search' is not really a suitable description for the operation. In essence, the Paras were effectively sealing off an area into which dozens of heavily armed troops would be deployed with the aim of killing or capturing any Taliban inside. The operation would more than likely take place in full contact with the enemy. The risk of casualties was high.

One junior officer made the following observation in the hours before the battle:

There was a great sense of anticipation in the hours before the operation began. For many of us, this was going to be our first real taste of combat. There were a lot of nerves. We knew that the

Taliban would put up a fight and we knew that we might take casualties. Most of the men just spent the time packing and repacking their kit and checking their weapons. You could see that some of the guys were apprehensive but the NCOs got amongst them and made sure they were kept busy.

A small unit of the Afghan National Police, together with the District Police Chief, also took part in the operation to give the locals the impression that this was an Afghan-led mission. In simple terms, the plan was for the Gurkhas and the Patrols Platoon, both of whom were already based in the town, to leave their base ten minutes prior to the arrival of A Company and establish the outer cordon. The Gurkhas were also responsible for escorting the District Police Chief and a number of the ANP, who would join up with A Company to demonstrate the Afghan involvement in the operation. A Company were to land in four Chinooks to the north and southwest of the target area, immediately sealing it off, and the search would then begin.

In the sky above, the Paras would be supported by Apache attack helicopters, US A–10 Warthogs and B1 Bombers throughout the entire operation. H-Hour, the time at which all operations begin, was 1200hrs on 4 June 2006 and L-Hour, the time at which the heliborne force was due to land, was 1210hrs.

Prior to the start of the operation, orders were delivered by the Commanding Officer to commanders of all the main units due to take part. In turn, these commanders worked out their plan and delivered their orders to their subordinates and so on until everyone taking part knew exactly what they were meant to do and when to do it.

As well as the main plan, commanders also had to prepare for a number of unscripted contingencies, such as what to do if one of the helicopters was shot down en route or had to turn back to base because of a mechanical problem. Will the mission be aborted? What is the plan if troops are ambushed and cut off in the search area? What is the plan if troops are found to be missing in action? However, it was also vital that everyone remained flexible and were not laden down with information because, as any soldier will tell you, 'No plan survives contact with the enemy.'

Once the orders process was complete, the rehearsals began. The commanders and soldiers alike knew that they would be at their most vulnerable when the helicopters were coming into land. The Chinook is a pretty big target and one lucky hit from an RPG could be catastrophic.

The soldiers practised exiting from the helicopters and what they would do if they came under fire. They also concentrated on house-clearing skills and the casualty evacuation (casevac) procedure. House-to-house fighting is both dangerous and exhausting. Soldiers can be attacked from multiple firing points, the soldiers also had to assume that every room in every dwelling could be booby-trapped.

The operation was planned to take place at the hottest point of the day and every man knew that the heat could be as deadly as the Taliban. As well as carrying enough water to sustain them through the duration of the mission, the soldiers would also be carrying helmets, body armour, full ammunition scales, morphine, field dressings, radios, a 24-hour ration pack and additional ammunition for weapons like the GPMG. Each platoon would also carry its requirement of electronic counter measure (ECM) equipment. ECM is designed to block radio signals at specific frequencies in order to prevent the Taliban from ambushing soldiers with IEDs triggered by remote control. In total, modern infantry combat requires every soldier to be an athlete who can carry up to 90lbs in battle and have the mental discipline and training to counter the effects of both extreme heat and extreme cold.

For those taking part in the operation, 4 June began with an early breakfast. Those of a more robust disposition chose the cooked option while many others simply had cereals and toast. No doubt some would have been too nervous to eat anything at all. The rest of the morning was taken up with preparing weapons, checking radios, issuing ammunition and briefings.

The flight time from Camp Bastion to Nowzad is around 30 minutes, but the troops arrived at their muster stations at least an hour before flying. The troops checked and rechecked their equipment yet again; second commanders briefed and rebriefed their men. Some soldiers smoked a final cigarette. A few soldiers sat in silence, contemplating what the next hours would bring, while others laughed and joked.

The troops eventually embarked in the Chinooks at around 1130hrs and were airborne a few minutes later. Soldiers squatted rather than sat on the chairs. The adrenaline was now surging through the veins of every man. There was one collective thought: get off the Chinook and on to the ground as soon as possible.

It wasn't lost on many of the Paras taking part in Op Mutay that 62 years earlier members of the same regiment had been about to take part in the greatest airborne operation of all time – Operation Overlord, otherwise known as the Normandy landings. The troops climbed aboard and squeezed themselves on to the red cloth seats. Their weapons were held between their legs with the barrel pointing downwards – if a shot is accidentally fired it is better that it goes through the helicopter's floor rather than the ceiling, above which are the rotor blades.

Once airborne, communication is reduced to hand signals and mouthing words – the din of the engines makes normal speech impossible, but few of those taking part were interested in small talk. The chances were that for some involved in the operation, this could be their first and last mission. To a man, they privately prayed that whatever happened when they hit the ground, no one would falter under fire.

Thirty minutes into the flight and the nerves began to kick in, at which point one of the air crew stood up and gave the five-minute signal. Everyone began carrying out one final check. Two minutes! One minute! The Chinooks touched down. They had made it, so far.

Up to the point of landing, everything went precisely to plan. Two helicopters landed in the north, another landed to the west and the fourth, which contained the Commanding Officer's party, an air reaction force made up of members of Support Company's Fire Support Group, remained airborne. The two attack helicopters circled the compound, waiting to be called into action to unleash their deadly arsenal on the enemy.

As the Chinooks hit the ground the Paras stormed down the tailgate into a swirling cloud of dust, weapons at the ready and adrenaline pumping. As per the rehearsals, the troops dashed to find whatever cover was available in the desert. Some had the comfort of a rock, while others had to make do with lying prone and vulnerable in the undulating desert. The sense of relief as the men left the aircraft was almost tangible.

With the dust and the noise from the Chinooks twin engines, communication was impossible until the helicopters had departed. Fortunately, every man had either been issued with or bought his own set of ski goggles which prevented his eyes becoming clogged by the fine

Afghan dust which was whipped into a storm every time a helicopter took off or landed. As the helicopters flew off into the distance, the order to move was given and the troops gingerly began moving towards the bocage. The Taliban had heard them coming and were prepared for a fight.

Almost from the moment the troops landed contacts began breaking out everywhere. The first bursts of AK47 fire which punctuated the still noon air were aimed at the Gurkhas and the Patrols Platoon. The Patrols Platoon took the brunt and were attacked by ten Taliban fighters armed with automatic weapons and RPGs. The reaction from the Paras was devastating and the full weight of the section's weapons – which included SA–80 rifles, mini machine-guns and the still relatively new under-slung grenade launchers – were brought to bear on the enemy. Within a few minutes, three of the enemy lay dead. A Forward Air Controller (FAC) attached to one of the Para patrols called one of the circling Apaches which had been itching to get in on the fight. The FAC sent through the enemy's location and his request to fire was acknowledged with: 'Roger, engaging, out.' Just 100m above the troops, the pilot aligned the cross hairs of his helmet-mounted sight on the enemy position. Slung beneath the Apache's nose, the 30mm automatically swivelled towards the target. The pilot pressed the firing button and the gun roared into life.

The burst of fire could barely be heard by the two-man crew enclosed inside their air-conditioned cockpit, but both knew the effect would be devastating. A hail of bullets tore into the target area, felling trees and churning up the dusty desert before ripping into the frail bodies of the Taliban who had been foolish enough to give away their position. They were left in a bloody, dismembered heap.

'I'm glad those fuckers are on our side,' said one Tom to another when the firing from the Taliban position stopped.

While the Taliban were being dispatched by the Apaches, the Gurkhas were simultaneously ambushed by another small group of Taliban from the north. The Gurkhas returned fire and were keen to launch a bayonet charge into the Taliban position – every Gurkha wants to use his kukri, a long, curved Nepalese knife which when unsheathed must draw blood, according to Gurkha custom. However, once again the Apaches were called into action and the enemy were dispatched with clinical precision.

After 30 minutes under some pretty intense fire, the Gurkhas managed to extract to the west and moved to what was known as the 'shrine area', to the southwest of the town. Almost at the same time, 1 Platoon was ambushed as they landed. The platoon immediately swung into action and brought an intense weight of fire on to the Taliban firing point before moving to their inner cordon location to the south of the compound. Within the compound itself, the search began.

The Patrols Platoon moved south from their initial contact position and, 30 minutes later, they were attacked again. The Taliban attacks were sporadic. Just when the Paras thought the Taliban had retreated, they were assaulted. On some occasions the firefights would last just a few minutes before the Taliban melted away.

Throughout all of these engagements, the Apaches remained on call, ranging their deadly weaponry against the Taliban positions. This was 360° warfare – the frontline was non-existent and the Taliban could, and did, appear from any direction. Consequently, the Apache gunners were repeatedly called on to carry out fire missions at 'danger close' ranges – sometimes less than 30m from the positions of friendly troops.

As the operation continued, it became clear that the terrain was too dense for vehicles to move without ground troops to protect them from Taliban ambushes. The Patrols Platoon was ordered to move southwest to a more open area where it would be more difficult for the Taliban to launch attacks.

At around 1245hrs, the Chinook carrying the Commanding Officer's party, called the CO's Tactical Headquarters and known as 'CO's Tac', landed with the Fire Support Group.

It surprised all who took part in the operation that, despite the large number of heavily armed professional troops on the ground together with the lethal close air support, the enemy attacks continued throughout the day. The Taliban must have known that they could not beat the British, yet they continued to fight and for some in the British ranks this was a concern.

About an hour into the operation, intelligence was received which suggested that a senior Taliban leader was hiding in a location 500m to the west of the compound. Maj Pike ordered 2 Platoon with elements of the Fire Support Group to conduct a sweep of the area in a bid to either kill or capture the Taliban leader. The mission was fraught with difficulties, not least because they had no description of the Taliban leader or what he was wearing. The patrol would also have to move through some pretty close country and the chances of being ambushed were high.

The patrol deployed on its mission at around 1530hrs, but was almost immediately contacted. As the bullets whistled passed the platoon commander's head, the young officer worked out a plan and ordered his men to attack. Snipers were also deployed and the Forward Air Controllers made excellent use of the attack helicopters and the A–10. Using fire-and-movement, the most basic battle-winning tactic, the Paras fixed bayonets and stormed forward. The Taliban were left with two choices: to flee or die. Up above, the A–10 cannon, which makes a haunting groan that would become music to the ears of the Paras by the time their tour was over, shredded vast areas of the orchard where the Taliban were thought to be hiding.

By 1630hrs, the platoon was ordered to move back into the cordon, having killed an unknown number of Taliban. Yet again the Taliban regrouped and attacked. The FAC again called in air support, this time just 50m away from where friendly troops were based. The impact was devastating and immediate. All fire from that area ceased.

One soldier recalled the moment his section was ambushed:

We were moving along an irrigation ditch in single file. The vegetation was quite thick and we could hear firing from virtually every direction. We were moving very slowly because most of us thought, when are we going to be hit? I was up at the front with the minimi [light machine gun] in my shoulder – my one concern was to put a burst down and drop anyone who fired at us. If I fucked up it could be me dead or one of my mates. Then just when I thought we might not be hit, it happened. The ground around my feet and the trees above my head started exploding. We all hit the ground and tried to assess where the fire was coming from. I thought I saw a burst come from some bushes over to my right so I put several bursts into the bush and the firing stopped. Whoever was in there was gone or dead. The adrenaline was pumping through my body and afterwards the only thought going through my head was 'fuck me'. I was pleased I hadn't messed up but I was also aware how vulnerable I was.

Soldiers from 1 Platoon began moving forward and stumbled into an RPG team. Astonishingly, the Paras gave a warning. When it was ignored, the platoon opened fire, killing the Taliban fighters immediately. Another contact erupted in the orchard and this time grenades were used to kill the enemy, who had managed to get within just a few metres of the Paras.

The battle continued until around 1630hrs when the Apaches returned and destroyed the last few remaining Taliban positions. The mission eventually ended at around 1700hrs and the troops, unscathed and with morale sky high, extracted in a series of Chinooks that flew back to Camp Bastion.

A number of valuable lessons had been learnt during the course of the operation, the first of which was that the months of training back in the UK had paid off brilliantly. The Paras responded to the Taliban ambushes with textbook precision, reacting instinctively with controlled aggression and professionalism. The hard hours spent on the Welsh training areas of Sennybridge in sun, rain and snow had paid enormous dividends.

However, it was probably the Paras' ability to call in air strikes from A–10s and attack helicopters which had proved to be the most vital, battle-effective resource at their disposal and had won the day. Every time the Paras had come under attack, they had returned fire aggressively but had also instinctively turned to combat air support (CAS) as being the best way to kill or neutralize the enemy – and it had worked.

As well as congratulating themselves on a job well done, the Paras had learnt a valuable lesson about the Taliban. True, their shooting skills left much to be desired and probably accounted for the fact that the Paras did not take a single casualty during the entire operation, but the Taliban demonstrated that they were brave, well-organized and capable of reacting to events.

Although the battle group escaped without injury, it was a close shave for some. Private Bashir Ali, a member of the Patrols Platoon, was hit twice in the chest by enemy fire but on both occasions was saved from injury when the bullets struck magazines in his chest webbing.

Walking past the dead bodies of the Taliban fallen, the Paras noticed that these men had no helmets or body armour and went into battle wearing flip-flops or sandals. Yet even when the A–10s and attack helicopters arrived and began destroying their positions with consummate ease, the Taliban fought on. The Paras knew that the worst type of enemy is the one who is prepared to die fighting for a cause.

The Helmand task force was not due to reach full operational capability until later in the summer of 2006. At the time, Brig Butler was still completely reliant on the air bridge back to the UK via Kandahar.

On 13 June, A Company was in Camp Bastion preparing for another mission when word came through the operations room that a US logistics convoy had been ambushed and had taken casualties – one soldier had been killed and another was seriously injured.

The convoy was surrounded and pinned down by enemy fire and daylight was fading fast. The US troops were surrounded and were fighting a frantic defensive action against the Taliban. It was unclear whether the US troops would be able to hang on long enough for help to arrive.

A Company were given the task of rescuing the beleaguered US troops and after a series of hasty orders and rehearsals the Paras departed in Chinooks, supported by two Apaches, for the area, which was located between the towns of Sangin and Musa Qala.

Any remote hope that the sight of Chinooks laden with troops heading for the ambush site might have caused the Taliban to flee soon vanished. Almost immediately, the Taliban fired an RPG which exploded beneath one of the helicopters.

The US convoy had managed to stop near some high ground, which made for a good defensive position. By now, the light was beginning to fade fast but the Paras were able to establish a basic defensive position, from which they could help the Americans, who were salvaging equipment from their damaged vehicles. In the lulls between Taliban attacks, undamaged vehicles were moved into dead ground for their protection. At the same time, the Paras began digging four-man shell-scrapes – foot-deep ditches just wide enough to give them protection from exploding mortar and rocket rounds – from where they intended to defend the area until dawn the following morning. They would then move further into the desert to rendezvous with a US unit.

At around 2100hrs the Taliban launched a highly coordinated, sustained attack against the joint British and US position. Fire from AK47s and a heavy machine-gun located in a nearby village rained down on the coalition troops. The defensive position was also pummelled with numerous RPGs. Those troops caught in the open dashed and crawled into shallow shell-scrapes. The attack marked the first time troops from A Company had been in contact at night. The bible-black darkness of the desert night was illuminated by the distinctive green tracer fire of the enemy. Initially, the weight of fire was so intense that the Paras were unable to do little but soak it up like a heavyweight boxer on the ropes, while gradually trying to identify enemy firing points which they could later attack. This tactic appeared to work, for as the Paras returned fire the intensity of the Taliban attack at first faltered and then stopped all together.

Although the Paras were unhurt, the US troops had sustained two casualties from a direct hit into one of their Humvees. One casualty had a gaping neck wound, which had almost severed his carotid artery but, by an astonishing stroke of luck, it had been cauterized by the blistering heat from the wounding piece of shrapnel. The condition of the other casualty was far more serious. The top of his head had been sliced off in the blast and he had lost an eye. He had also suffered significant bullet wounds to his arms and legs.

Both casualties were stabilized by 1 Platoon's Private Peter McKinley, who would later go on to win the Military Cross, and Lance Corporal Paul Roberts, a medic attached to the company. Both soldiers showed immense bravery in the face of the enemy. The Taliban had spotted where the injured men were being treated. Assuming that they would be a soft and easy target, they began ranging automatic and RPG fire at the damaged Humvee. However, the two young Paras never flinched from their duty. In fact Pte McKinley dished out treatment far in excess of that which should have been expected from someone of his relatively limited experience.

At about this time, the enemy began preparing for another attack but were spotted by Corporal Mark Wright, one of the mortar fire controllers (MFC) attached to the company. He called in 35 rounds of high explosive on to a compound where the enemy were forming up. The effect was devastating. The compound was completely destroyed and many of the enemy were killed or wounded. This action had a decisive effect on the battle. Seemingly stunned by the fact that their second attack had been thwarted even before it had begun, the Taliban withdrew. The rest of the night passed off relatively peacefully and the two badly injured casualties were evacuated by a Chinook. Fortunately, both managed to survive.

At first light, as the morning sun began to climb into the cloudless Afghan sky, A Company withdrew from their position into the dusty expanse of the northern Helmand desert to await the US link up.

Low on food, water and ammunition, the Paras requested an emergency resupply but would have to wait another 14 hours before they were picked up and returned to the safety of Camp Bastion.

The Paras had soon learned that life in Afghanistan was going to be extremely tough, but they were up to the job.

5

THE FIRST TO FALL

While the men of the 3 Para battle group were fighting the Taliban, Brigadier Butler was fighting his own private battle with Mohammed Daud, the governor of Helmand.

Daud, a large, bearded man and a qualified engineer, was under pressure. He had been personally appointed by Hamid Karzai to crack down on narcotics problems and corruption in Helmand. The problem was that most of the drug lords were government officials, police chiefs or their relatives.

Daud wanted Brig Butler to permanently deploy his forces into fixed locations inside Musa Qala and Nowzad to prevent them from falling into the hands of the Taliban. Although both towns had sizeable numbers of ANA and ANP, Daud was aware that they were no match for the enemy.

As far as Brig Butler was concerned, this was never part of the Helmand plan. While his experience as an SAS commander told him that flexibility was the key to everything in combat, such a marked change from the agreed course of action, which had been months in the planning, could be potentially disastrous. What concerned Brig Butler most at this stage was that he did not have enough of his 3,150-strong force up and running in Helmand to commit fighting troops to fixed locations.

The basic theory of expeditionary warfare, which is drummed into all British commanders, is to deploy into the theatre of operations, build up your forces and then get into the process of war fighting. And as Brig Butler well knew, those who ignore this rule do so at their peril.

Brig Butler had tried to explain to Daud that a force of 3,150 did not mean that they were all 'bayonets' – combat troops. With great patience and care, using drawings in the sand to reinforce his point, the Brigadier explained that his force was composed of many different types of soldiers, from engineers to medics. However, Daud had been used to dealing with the US and its seemingly inexhaustible resources and he simply was not interested in the British 'excuses'. The differences between the two men came to a head one evening inside a room within the Governor's relatively luxurious compound in Lashkar Gar, the provincial capital of Helmand and the seat of Daud's power.

Brig Butler had repeatedly tried to persuade Daud to accept that he didn't have the forces to undertake the type of operations being asked of him. He also tried to get Daud to trade ground for time by allowing Musa Qala and Nowzad to fall to the Taliban while the British troops built up their forces. Both arguments fell on deaf ears. Daud was adamant that on no account should the black flag of Mullah Omar be allowed to fly over any town in Helmand.

One of those present at the meeting recalled:

I remember Daud storming around a room saying 'if you don't go in there [Musa Qala and Nowzad], I will resign and I will tell my president and I will tell him to tell your Prime Minister Mr Blair and he will tell Mr Blair that you are not doing what we want you to do and you will be held directly responsible for the loss of northern Helmand to the Taliban.

It was an interesting situation to be in at one o'clock in the morning. When you are not fighting a conventional enemy and you are not engaged in all-out war, the rules of the game are very different.

If you are invited into a country to come and help, as we were, in the fight against the Taliban and then you are asked to undertake an operation which is against your practical judgement, then it is very difficult to turn around and say 'no'.

So this was a clear case of strategic imperatives, principally Afghan, driving tactical action. So you can see the predicament that we faced. Either you say 'bog off, we can't do it, it's against our military judgement', and then of course you immediately fail in your mission by not supporting the people who have invited you in, or you do something against your better judgement.

Reluctantly, a decision was taken to send troops into Musa Qala and Nowzad. From that moment, the whole course of Operation Herrick changed. A few weeks later another force moved into Sangin and two weeks after that troops were also dispatched to guard the Kajaki Dam, a key Taliban target and an asset of great strategic importance to Helmand.

Now the fighting men of 16 Air Assault Brigade found themselves in fixed locations, waiting for the Taliban to attack. It was the so-called 'tethered goat' strategy. Brig Butler knew it was a risk but, if the Taliban decided to take on the British in the towns of northern Helmand, it would mean that reconstruction could begin unimpeded in Lashkar Gar – or at least that was the theory.

The dangers of Sangin were already clear to every member of the battle group for this was the place where the unit suffered its first fatal casualty – it came on the day that the UK's new Defence Secretary, Des Browne, arrived in Helmand. Those present recall the cabinet minister being shocked and visibly moved by the news.

Captain James Philippson, aged 29, who was serving with the 7 (Para) Royal Horse Artillery Regiment, was renowned for his zest for life. For him life was one great big adventure. A super-fit sportsman and expert downhill skier, he was one of the few officers in the British Army who had successfully passed not only the Royal Marines' Commando Course but also the Paras' infamous P Company selection test: quite an achievement for someone who had only been in the Army for five years.

In June 2006, Captain Philippson, who came from St Albans in Hertfordshire, was with one of the Operational Mentoring and Liaison Teams based at the District Centre in Sangin. He was training the Afghan National Army and found that he enjoyed life in Helmand, even though the soldiers based in the town had complained that they were short of men and essential pieces of equipment such as night-vision goggles.

On 11 June, a patrol left the base to go and retrieve an unmanned air vehicle (UAV) which had crashed somewhere in the local area. As the patrol neared the crash site, they were ambushed by the Taliban. The patrol was under sustained and heavy attack and had taken casualties. Back in Sangin, the Quick Reaction Force (QRF) were ordered to give assistance and Capt Philippson, in typical fashion, volunteered to go with them. While he enjoyed training the ANA and all the challenges which that tasked posed, like many other young officers he longed to test himself in battle in Helmand – and this was his chance.

Capt Philippson grabbed his rifle, body armour and helmet and sped to the ambush site in a Land Rover, with other troops following behind. Before they could give assistance, the QRF was also ambushed. The Taliban knew that help would be sent and they were ready. The front Land Rover was hit by automatic fire and RPGs exploded around them. The troops debussed from the vehicles and returned fire but, in the ensuing firefight, Capt Philippson was hit in the head by a Taliban bullet and died instantly. His relatively short life was over. The UAV was eventually recovered and both the original patrol and the QRF managed to extract back to the safety of the District Centre without further injury.

Almost 18 months after Capt Philippson's death, the coroner who presided over his inquest would castigate the Ministry of Defence for not properly equipping the British troops fighting in Helmand. Andrew Walker, the assistant coroner for Oxfordshire, said: 'They [the soldiers] were not defeated by the terrorists but by the lack of basic equipment.' It emerged that the soldiers had repeatedly complained about the lack of night-vision equipment and of troop shortages.

By the middle of June, Sangin was virtually under daily attack. Intelligence suggested that the Taliban were convinced that the British and the Afghan National Police were ready to give up Sangin and they intended to fill the vacuum left behind. As far as the Taliban were concerned, they were on the brink of a famous victory. Sangin was the main narcotics centre in Helmand and if it fell into the Taliban's hands then they would hold sway over a large part of the province. There was no other choice but to reinforce the troops already based in the District Centre. Troops from the brigade had already established bases in Musa Qala and Nowzad, but Sangin would be different. Instead of a platoon-strength unit of around 30 to 40 men, Sangin would need to be occupied by a company group of around 150 men – the net effect of this would be that the brigade would lose virtually all of what the Army call 'manoeuvre capability' and consequently any ability to launch offensive operations against the Taliban. Instead of being a highly mobile force capable of conducting intelligence-led, heliborne assault operations against the Taliban, the brigade had become tied to a series of bases across the north that the enemy could, and did, strike at will. Although this 'tethered goat' strategy was high risk, it did have the effect of keeping the Taliban away from Lashkar Gar and the Kajaki Dam.

A Company, who were the first troops from 3 Para to arrive in Helmand, were given the task of reinforcing Sangin and their mission was simple: stop the town falling into the hands of the Taliban at all costs.

The plan was for the troops to travel to secure landing zones on the outskirts of Sangin and then march into the District Centre (DC) base. On arrival, they were under orders to start improving the base's defences, using whatever material they could find. The troops had no idea how long they would remain in Sangin. A figure of 96 hours was initially mentioned, but most of the Paras knew that they would be in Sangin for considerably longer.

The Sangin District Centre lies on the edge of town with the Helmand river and its desert flood plain on the western flank, a few hundred metres away. A so-called 'urban fringe' of buildings and vegetation lies to the south and the north while the town itself spreads to the east. A *wadi* runs through the town from east to west, directly in front of the DC. A fast flowing canal, which is connected to the Helmand river, courses through the area of the base. The main bazaar, where bread, meat, fruit and vegetables are sold, runs virtually the entire length of the town.

The Paras landed at dawn at a secured helicopter-landing site (HLS) adjacent to the Helmand river, 2km from the DC. If the Taliban knew they were coming, they did nothing about it. The Paras were able to patrol unmolested straight into the DC. The relief of not having to fight their way into the compound was tangible. It had been a step in the dark but this was an operation where fortune really did favour the brave. The first priority was to treat those amongst the ANP and ANA who had been wounded during the fighting with the Taliban. While this took place, the non-commissioned officers quickly organized their men to begin fortifying the base. The men worked for hours on end in blistering temperatures, knowing that at any moment they could be attacked. It was a race against time, but still the Taliban seemed content to sit and wait. While the base was fortified, a mortar line of two barrels was dug and GPMG positions were established to fire on probable routes of advance. A ring of Claymore mines was also established which would act as a last ditch defence and would only be detonated if the base was about to be overrun.

In June 2006, the Sangin base was a large complex consisting of several compounds with, somewhat alarmingly, a porous perimeter.

Many of the buildings within the compound were either only half-built or damaged. Few, if any, afforded any real protection against a determined enemy armed with modern weapons.

Lieutenant Hugo Farmer, an officer of 1 Platoon, A Company, who would later be decorated with the Conspicuous Gallantry Cross, was one of the junior officers based in Sangin at the time. He and his men began to prepare their new home for the Taliban's attack, which they knew could come at any moment.

In the heat of the baking sun, with body armour and helmets nearby, the Paras continued to labour on for those first few days, trying desperately to turn their new home into something like a fortress. It could almost have been a scene from the North African campaign in the Second World War: men stripped to the waist or in cut-off shorts, endlessly filling sandbags, a mind-numbingly boring task but upon which each man was aware their very lives might depend. A properly filled sandbag will stop, or at least slow down, a high-velocity bullet, but the same round will pass through a poorly filled one. Shell-scrapes were dug and thousands upon thousands of sandbags were filled.

One A Company section commander said:

It was back-breaking work and a race against time. All of us expected the Taliban to attack and we knew we had to turn the DC into some sort of fortress, our lives depended on it. The Toms were fantastic. Many worked themselves to a standstill. I saw grown men falling asleep standing up, incredible. They should make sandbag filling one of the tests in P Company because it is utterly exhausting.

During those early, edgy days in Sangin, the Paras began to conduct regular patrols into the town, during which time they tried whenever possible to inform the local population that they were there to improve security and to help in reconstruction. To begin with, the locals were intrigued, but friendly. The first week or so went well and the Paras had real hope that their presence had seen off the Taliban and won the support of the locals. Whenever the Paras ventured into Sangin they gave the same message to the locals: 'We are here to help.' It seemed that the Afghans had accepted them.

Then everything changed. A Special Forces operation to capture senior members of the Taliban caused public opinion in the town to move sharply against the soldiers. The locals complained of broken promises of peace and within a matter of hours the bustling streets around the compound began to empty – a clear 'combat indicator' that something was afoot.

The Special Forces operation involved members of the SBS and the relatively new Special Reconnaissance Regiment (SRR). The secret 16-man patrol was returning from a successful operation during which 4 senior Taliban commanders had been snatched from a compound near the town of Sangin in the early morning of 27 June 2006. However, the Taliban were not about to give up their leaders easily and were waiting for the patrol as its two vehicles moved along a rutted track a few kilometres from Sangin. Just after 0330hrs, a force of around 70 Taliban fighters sprang an ambush. A rocket-propelled grenade smashed into the first vehicle while the other was riddled with fierce automatic fire. The troops jumped from their vehicles, which one later said were acting like 'bullet magnets', and made for the cover of nearby fields and irrigations ditches. As they ran, explosions from RPGs erupted around them and the green tracer fire from the Taliban weapons followed them into Green Zone.

While running for cover, Captain David 'Pat' Patten, 38, from Aghadowey, County Londonderry, who was a member of the Special Reconnaissance Regiment, was hit and killed almost instantly. Capt Patten, who served with the Royal Irish Rangers before joining the Special Forces, was also the SRR's first Regimental Sergeant Major. He should have returned to the UK to his wife and 14-month-old daughter just a few days before he was killed. He had volunteered to spend another two weeks in Helmand because his unit was short of men. His colleagues, one of two brothers in the SBS, later recalled at an inquest in February 2008:

Pat got halfway across the field. You could see the round had hit him. He fell face first with the momentum of it. As he lay there in the mud, with just his black rucksack showing, his left leg moved like it was an attempt to stand up. Then he went still. It was too difficult to cross the open field because the enemy were putting down some heavy fire.

There was no other option than to leave Capt Patten's body where it had fallen. The rest of the patrol headed north along an irrigation ditch towards a bridge. The patrol was attacked again by a large force of Taliban. As the bullets whistled overhead, two Taliban prisoners tried to escape. One of the SBS men attempted to grab them but he was struck in the arm by a bullet as he did so. The bullet went through his forearm and passed through his watch. The patrol was now pinned down in a water-filled ditch.

Sergeant Paul Bartlett, 35, turned to his injured colleague and said that he was going to look for an escape route and moved towards the bridge. The injured Marine said, 'Paul was aware of my injury. He said he was going to have a look for a route out from where we were. He took off his rucksack so he could squeeze through a gap in the bridge. That was the last time I saw Paul.' Minutes later, he heard Taliban voices and then 'a tremendous crash of fire. He said: 'I believe that fire killed Paul. It was then that I was able to pick a hand grenade out of my bag, pull the pin, and throw it.'

The grenade killed the Taliban gunmen on the bridge and the patrol eventually managed to escape before being rescued by a Gurkha Quick Reaction Force sent out from Sangin.

A separate mission was launched later the same day to recover the bodies of Capt Patten and Sgt Bartlett. Both men had been killed almost instantly. Sgt Patten had been hit 12 times by enemy fire. The bullet wound to the injured Marine was so severe that he later had the lower part of his left arm amputated. For his actions he was awarded the Military Cross.

Angry locals told the Paras that the Special Forces operation was a breach of trust. As reported by the *Guardian* on 14 October 2006, Lt Andy Mallet, the Officer Commanding 2 Platoon A Company, said:

The civvies in Sangin started to say 'well who was that doing that, all these explosions and noise?' and we just had to say 'well it wasn't us.' All over Helmand Province, all over Afghanistan, there's Special Forces ops going in left, right and centre . . . you just had to learn to live with it. Just on that occasion, that was the catalyst which turned against us.

Just 36 hours after the Special Forces operation was launched, the Taliban attacked the DC. The stillness of the cool night air was shattered by the fizzing of RPG rockets and automatic fire raking the sentry positions. Muzzle flashes from their AK47s illuminated the Taliban's firing positions in and around the various mud and brick buildings that lay across the *wadi*, directly in front of the DC.

The shouts of 'stand to' – the call to arms for those sleeping or not manning sangars (temporary fortified positions) or sentry posts – were drowned out by the enormous weight of enemy fire being ranged on the buildings.

The crack of high-velocity rounds split the air above and the ricochets fizzed into the night sky. The thumping volleys of RPG rockets lit up the compound with a surreal strobe-like effect so that those troops caught in the open or trying to take up firing positions appeared to be moving in slow motion.

The Paras sprang into action, immediately opening up with highly accurate and sustained .50 calibre fire. The GPMG and the mortar units joined in the fray, while the Toms seized the opportunity of notching up their first operational kill with unabashed glee.

The section commanders took control of the battle, steering their guns on to the Taliban firing positions. Eventually, the incoming green tracer was matched and surpassed in intensity by the Paras' red tracer.

The Taliban fire soon died away and the intense but short-lived contact came to an end. What initially appeared to be a fully-fledged attack was merely a probe by the Taliban commanders who were keen to see how the Paras would respond.

As the troops refilled their magazines, replenished their water bottles and repaired the defences, it probably never occurred to any of them that this was just the beginning of a long hot summer which would test the resolve and spirit of every soldier who served in Sangin.

Initially, the plan was to remain in Sangin for just a few days – but then orders were changed and the message came through that A Company would remain in the DC indefinitely and hold out against the Taliban.

The course of action had already been set: throughout that first month in Sangin, the base was attacked on average 5 times in any 24 hours, both day and night.

In the same *Guardian* article, Lt Farmer, then a 26-year-old who had given up a lucrative job in the City to join the Army, said:

This amounted to near continuous combat as the insurgents varied their positions, tactics and initiation methods and weight of fire in order to probe for any weaknesses within our defensive positions. For what must have been two weeks we were being attacked as many as five, six times a day. The majority of the contacts were at night, so it was like a light show, the tracer rounds coming over, the noise of being fired at – it's a bit like somebody getting a wooden ruler and slapping it on the table, and then somebody standing next to them with a couple of boules balls and clicking those together. It's a very odd sound . . . When it's very close, you'll hear a snap and a ricochet.

Life within the Sangin base was made all the more harsh by the squalid living conditions. Initially, the toilets consisted of just a hole in the ground, but they were later replaced by crudely adapted oil drums. The contents were burnt off every day. The risk of disease and infection were ever present and rats remained a constant bugbear. In a single 2-hour rat-hunting session, more that 22 were found in the building where the men lived. It was not unusual for soldiers to be woken by rats which scampered across their faces as they searched for food amongst their belongings.

Over the following days the Taliban repeatedly attacked with every weapon in their arsenal. In those early days of the occupation of the District Centre, the Taliban's accuracy with mortars was appalling, but they gradually improved. Like all soldiers, the Taliban knew that in order to survive they needed to learn from their enemy and adapt. Only once did the Taliban try a frontal assault on the compound when they attacked a sangar on a relatively narrow frontage. The sangar, however, was equipped with a GPMG which fired burst after burst into the charging Taliban force. The result was utter carnage and the attack was repulsed.

Despite the nightly attacks against the base, the Paras continued to conduct both foot and mobile patrols in the town to dispel any notion in the minds of the locals or the Taliban that the British were under siege, even though this was effectively the case. The British Army had learnt through fighting several counter-insurgency wars over the last 50 years of the importance of patrolling into 'enemy territory'. It was a dangerous tactic but it kept the Taliban on the back foot.

Slowly but surely, the soldiers became exhausted. Sleep was snatched between contacts during both the day and night, with many soldiers sleeping – while still wearing their full body armour and helmet – at the feet of a colleague manning a machine-gun. When not on patrol, the troops were always under pressure to improve defences. This involved stressful physical work in temperatures often in excess of 48°C. The difficulties of resupply meant that bottled water could only be used for drinking. Washing of clothes rarely took place. When it did it was carried out, at risk from mortar attack, in the canal which ran through the DC.

One A Company officer later described the daily routine in Sangin for the *Sun* newspaper on 14 September 2006:

Night after night assaults were repelled. Every soldier manned sentry and defensive positions or scurried around reinforcing positions or resupplying others with ammunition and grenades. Throughout the early deployment of 3 Para, the tower and central buildings took numerous direct hits from RPGs, small arms fire and a 107mm rocket. One rocket struck the tower on the evening of July 1st, killing two soldiers and an interpreter, and wounding another six men. The blast threw many to the floor, deafening some yet to recover their hearing.

As the medics did what they could for the casualties, and with the air thick with dust and masonry falling all around, other paratroopers retook their fire positions and engaged enemy targets.

On numerous occasions soldiers were knocked off their feet by RPG and 107mm rocket explosions. The soldiers manned these positions as small arms fire was directed towards them. Tracer fire ricocheted off the walls, passing between them – and fortuitously between the legs of one.

The officer continued: 'Fatigue would often set in only to be banished by the adrenaline flow associated with another attack. These soldiers were often in prolonged contact for hours at a time.'

The two soldiers killed in the 1 July attack were Lance Corporal Jabron Hashmi, 24, a member of the Intelligence Corps attached to 3 Para, and Corporal Peter Thorpe, 27, of the Royal Corps of Signals.

The six soldiers injured in that attack had to wait until the following day before it was safe enough to casevac them back to Camp Bastion for medical treatment.

LCpl Hashmi, who was born just over the Afghan border in Pakistan, became the first British Muslim to die in the conflict. Speaking after his death, his brother Zeeshan said of him: 'He was fiercely proud of his Islamic background and he was equally proud of being British. He went to Afghanistan to build bridges between the East and West. He always wanted to serve his country since he was a little boy.'

Four days later the company was struck by another tragedy when Private Damien Jackson, who was serving with 1 Platoon A Company, was killed during a routine patrol to secure a helicopter landing site.

After Pte Jackson fell, a call for an Immediate Response Team (IRT) was dispatched to Camp Bastion. The operations officer at Bastion was told that Pte Jackson had been hit and was bleeding badly. Medical help was needed urgently. The IRT was scrambled and was in the air within minutes. The Chinook crew were told that they would be flying into a 'hot HLS' – meaning that they would be taking enemy fire as they landed – and the crew warned the IRT to be ready to load a casualty under fire.

Such was the intensity of the fighting that when the helicopter carrying the medical team arrived it was forced to turn back through fear of being brought down by enemy fire. Tragically, Pte Jackson died where he fell, despite the valiant efforts of those in his patrol to keep him alive.

Although he was the sixth soldier to die in the Sangin Valley in just three weeks, his death hit the troops particularly hard and brought home the harsh and bitter realities of war to many in the company and across the battle group. For the first time, the soldiers were now aware that there was no guarantee that they would be evacuated from the battlefield to the field hospital at Camp Bastion if they were injured in a contact with the enemy.

It was now clear, and accepted by all, that Chinooks, which to the Paras were worth their weight in gold, could not always be risked in order to save the life of a soldier – despite this, the Chinook crews flew dozens of missions and took many hits while attempting to rescue injured troops.

Despite the loss of Pte Jackson, the Paras fought on through the early summer with unabashed zeal and determination.

Everyone based in Sangin and in other isolated outposts in northern Helmand was now experiencing an intensity of warfare which quite simply had not been seen for more than a generation.

Troops became adept at calling in close air support using A–10s, RAF Harriers and US F–16s. Bombs ranging from 500lb up to 2000lb were sometimes dropped so close to the DC that soldiers were quite literally blown out of their sangar positions by the shockwave of the blast. But each man picked himself up, dusted himself down and went back to his firing position.

Laughter and cheers nearly always followed a successful air strike, which the troops described as 'awesome' and 'mega'. Shouts of 'fucking 'ave some' often followed the haunting sound of an A–10 as it unleashed its deadly cargo on a Taliban position. As well as taking hundreds of pictures of the battle that raged around Sangin, soldiers also filmed events using helmet-mounted cameras and mobile phones. In some cases, the film clips were downloaded and placed on the Internet. Seeing soldiers laughing when it is quite clear that the enemy have just been vaporized is difficult to accept, but such events have to be seen in context. These men had been pushed further in terms of combat and battle stress than anyone since the Korean War 50 years earlier. Every soldier knew that each day might be his last. They had all seen friends and colleagues injured and killed over the last few weeks and each man was aware that the reason they had escaped unblemished was more down to luck than judgement. Those who died were simply in the wrong place at the wrong time: it was as simple as that. It is really not surprising that the soldiers cheered when the bombs fell, it effectively meant that they had lived to fight another day.

After four weeks, much of it in contact with the enemy, A Company was relieved by B Company. The sense of relief amongst the men who made it back was almost overwhelming. As they walked down the ramp of the Chinook and stepped on to the comforting familiarity of the HLS at Camp Bastion, each man knew that he had changed forever. In four short weeks, they had managed to rack up more battle experience than anyone else in the entire Army, save perhaps for a few seasoned veterans in the SAS.

In uniforms stiff with weeks of dried sweat and stained with the blood of fallen comrades, they made their way back to the air-conditioned tents which would be their new home for a few weeks at least. Those soldiers from the other companies who came to visit them to hear tales of derring-do on that first night back in Camp Bastion were shocked by what they saw. Most of the men were sporting thick beards and hair that had grown long and become caked in desert dust. Many, thanks to a diet of compo, had lost up to a stone in weight. Their jaws were hollow and their eyes tired, but spirits were remarkably high. The general consensus amongst those who made it back was that Sangin was a 'shit hole' but the fighting had been 'awesome' and 'Terry Taliban', as the enemy was now known, was good, but not good enough.

While Sangin had become the main focus of attention to the outside world because of the number of soldiers who had been killed or injured in the area in the past few weeks, life for the troops based in the ANA compound in Nowzad was also becoming interesting.

In January 2006, the 2nd Royal Gurkha Rifles were warned at relatively short notice that they would need to provide a company to reinforce 16 Air Assault Brigade on Operation Herrick. The company was called D (Tamandu) Company and it was given just three months to train, equip itself and be ready for operations by the following April.

Although the company was initially tasked with a protection role at Camp Bastion, it was clear, given the size of Helmand and the duties being asked of the battle group, that the Gurkhas would see some action. And so they did. By the end of May the company had one platoon based in Sangin and another in Nowzad. As has already been stated, the Gurkhas took part in Operation Mutay and they were also involved in the operation in which two members of the Special Forces were killed on 27 June 2006. They soon found themselves back in the firing line.

On 1 July, D Company's 11 Platoon, commanded by Lieutenant Angus Mathers, conducted a relief-in-place operation, known as a 'rip', in which it replaced 10 Platoon in the Nowzad District Centre.

The town of Nowzad is 65km to the north of Camp Bastion and is surrounded by mountains to the southwest and east. The town has a bazaar, a single road that bisects the town to the north and south and a warren of narrow alleys, high-walled compounds and mud-brick houses. Poppy farming has been the traditional stay of the town's economy for decades. The District Centre lies on the southwest edge of the town and is dominated by a hill, 1km to the south, which is known as ANP Hill because it was routinely occupied by members of the local ANP.

The base itself is within a 200m × 200m walled compound and comprises a central office building, which contain the ammo store, the ANP office, the medical room and the Gurkhas operations room, the roof of which became known as the control tower (CT).

For the duration of its stay, D Company was composed of 11 Platoon, members of 216 Signals Squadron, a Joint Tactical Air Controller (JTAC), a doctor, members of the Royal Military Police and 20 members of the ANA.

The troops of 11 Platoon were given the task of manning the CT and the four sangars at the corners of the compound, while the ANA manned the two central sangars under the supervision of their Operational Mentoring and Liaison Team, led by Capt Dougie Bartholomew of the Black Watch.

D Company and its attachments had just enough troops to man the sangars and provide a Quick Reaction Force which could be called on to deal with any emergency. Later, when it was reinforced, the company was able to provide a small protection force for a Fire Support Group on ANP Hill, but there were insufficient troops to proactively patrol and dominate the town. Three groups of ANP also lived in the compound, some of whom repeatedly passed information to the Taliban on the company's position and movements, including those of the company commander, Major Dan Rex.

When the Gurkhas first moved into Nowzad in June, life for the locals was relatively normal and, like every other village and town in Afghanistan, was focused on the bazaar. There was a weekly market, which would be visited by people from miles around. The local population had been largely untroubled by the arrival of British troops in the town but they were concerned that their presence might bring fresh fighting with the Taliban. It was clear that over the course of the next few weeks that the village elders had been informed by the Taliban that they should tell their people to leave. The departure of the locals was monitored by the troops waiting anxiously inside the high-walled compound.

By 1 July, it was clear that beyond the walls of the compound, the town was effectively controlled by the Taliban. Groups of the enemy could be seen openly preparing defences and firing positions from which they could attack the DC and ANP Hill. This period proved to be the calm before the storm.

By the end of the first week of July, as the intense desert heat became almost unbearable, the Taliban began the first of many attacks which would ultimately define the stay of the men of the 2nd Battalion of the Royal Gurkha Rifles in Nowzad. Initially, these attacks were probing in nature and, although highly disconcerting, they were essentially designed to test the Gurkhas' responses, sangar positions and weapons capability.

The first full-scale attack took place in the early hours of 12 July and lasted for almost six hours. The attack was triggered earlier than the Taliban planned when an ANP patrol stumbled into a Taliban team who were trying to move to the north of the town through the bazaar. The Taliban immediately opened fire with rocket-propelled grenades and automatic weapons, slightly injuring an ANP officer. While the ANP managed to extract from the contact without sustaining further casualties, two sangars and the CT came under fire from multiple, well-prepared positions 200m from the compound. The sangars were hit repeatedly by small arms fire, heavy machine-guns and RPGs. The weight of the fire literally left the Gurkhas momentarily stunned. Those troops not on duty ran to their stand-to positions while the RPGs continued to thump on to the sangars and the CT.

D Company was now paying the price for not having sufficient troops to conduct foot patrols into the town. Had they been given extra men – although it should be noted that there was no spare manpower anywhere in the battle group – the Taliban would have struggled to create such effective firing positions.

As soon as the contact started, close air support was requested. It arrived 30 minutes later. The slow-moving but deadly US A–10 Warthogs, supported by Apaches, were directed on to the Taliban firing points in the tree-line and the buildings to the north by the joint tactical air controllers. An A–10 pilot attacked first with rockets and guns, causing the entire tree-line to disintegrate in a series of rumbling explosions. Rolling away from its first attack, the Warthog flew in an enormous arc and returned to deliver the *coup de grâce* – a 500lb bomb, which smashed into the building in the north. The explosion sent a huge cloud of dust billowing into the sky. It was cheered with shouts of 'Jai Gurkha!' – the Gurkha war cry which translates as 'the Gurkhas are upon you' – from the relieved troops sweltering in the sangars and on the roof of the CT. But the battle was not over. The Taliban knew that the aircraft and Apaches could not remain over the town indefinitely. Despite their losses, the Taliban waited until the aircraft departed and then moved in to reoccupy the tree-line and the buildings devastated by the earlier attacks. However, this time the Taliban waited too long and within the hour the A–10s had returned. The enemy fire was silenced with another 500lb bomb.

Despite their losses, the Taliban were still not finished. Demonstrating either extraordinary bravery or battlefield naivety, the Taliban began regrouping close to where the A–10s had bombed one of their main firing positions. One of the pilots reported that two Toyota Corollas, the vehicle of choice for the Taliban, was spotted resupplying their forces.

An A–10 prepared itself for another bombing run and, swooping down from the north, unleashed another 500lb bomb which obliterated the enemy position, killing or injuring the entire group of Taliban. The weight of the attack may have initially left the Gurkhas stunned but they had managed to rally and, with the help of the A–10s, won the day. The six-hour battle had the effect of preparing the troops for more of what was to come. The troops were aware that the Taliban were now likely to redouble their efforts the next time they attacked – and so they did, less than 24 hours later.

What was to become the most dangerous attack during D Company's time at the Nowzad base took place on 13 July 2006. The first inkling that a full-scale attack was in the offing came when a Gurkha non-commissioned officer spotted armed Taliban fighters crawling across an alleyway 100m from his position. In a bid to seize the initiative, he ordered a GPMG to fire several bursts at the Taliban, managing to kill three of the enemy and subsequently foiling the attack from that location. The Taliban were not finished, though. In a huge attack, two of the sangars and the control tower were simultaneously hit with RPGs and automatic fire from multiple firing positions.

The Gurkhas, crouching in firing positions, held on to their helmets as the sangars and the CT started to disintegrate around them. At first, there were fears that the base was about to be overrun and many of those inside the compound prepared themselves for a fight to the death. As far as the Gurkhas were concerned, the Taliban did not take prisoners and they had no intention of surrendering. Then, just as they began to fear the worst, the familiar groan of the A–10 could heard above the compound during a brief lull in the fighting.

Again, the pilot was directed to a target to the north and delivered a 500lb bomb into the heart of a Taliban firing position. With that, the battle ended, some 2 hours and 40 minutes after it began. Despite the weight of fire ranged against the District Centre, there were no injuries. The compound was attacked again on 16 July, when the Taliban ambushed the Chief of Police en route to the DC. As had happened in previous attacks, the sangars were the main target. The Taliban began opening up from dozens of positions around the British base. An officer later said to me, 'It was one of the most intense situations I have ever experienced. It's very difficult to think beyond the moment – you live second by second. It was the only time I thought "is this where we get overrun?"'

The Apaches flew in low and fast and arrived within 30 minutes of being requested. The gunners, with the aid of the JTAC below, carefully identified each Taliban position and began to irradiate them one by one with their 30mm cannon. At one point during the battle the Taliban managed to get within 20m of the compound, forcing the troops in the sangars to throw hand grenades to repel the attack.

Eventually the attack subsided, but not before an Apache was shot at by an anti-aircraft gun hidden in a building. The attempt was witnessed by the Gurkhas who passed on the location to the Apache pilot, who attacked the house using his 30mm cannon and a Hellfire missile. It is not known if the gun was destroyed, but the firing stopped.

Back in Camp Bastion, it was now clear to Lt Col Tootal that the situation in Nowzad was critical. The Taliban had made several attempts to overrun the compound, only to be forced back after taking heavy casualties. Despite the Taliban's heavy losses, there was no indication of any let-up and so a decision was taken to reinforce the compound with an extra platoon and a Fire Support Group, consisting of a mortar section and two machine-gun teams from the Royal Regiment of Fusiliers.

The reinforcements, who had been sent to Helmand from their base in Cyprus, were positioned on ANP Hill, where they would be at their most effective. The day after the fresh troops arrived, the Taliban attacked the base again by firing an RPG at one of the sangars. But, by now the Gurkhas were ready and waiting. The Taliban attack was met with a wall of fire from the British compound. By the time the Apaches arrived 'on station', the Taliban had fled.

The battle for Nowzad rumbled on for a few more days with sporadic attacks breaking out, usually in the mornings or evenings. On 22 July, though, the Taliban attacked the British base and ANP Hill simultaneously. As in previous attacks, the sangars were targeted but it was the Fire Support Group on the hill which sustained the heaviest onslaught. Again, this was indicative of the Taliban's ability to learn and develop their battlefield skills. The attack was eventually quelled.

Up until 13 July, the Taliban's mortaring skills were limited and ineffective. The periodic targeting of the DC, the helicopter landing site and ANP Hill was relatively inaccurate. That all changed after 13 July, when the accuracy improved significantly and the Taliban mortar teams were able to range their fire directly on to the British positions on ANP Hill. Rounds also landed within 15–20m of the control tower. The Taliban mortar position was eventually identified and destroyed by a 2000lb bomb, dropped by a B1 Bomber, which resulted in a few days of respite before the mortar attacks returned.

On 19 July, the base was struck three times within the compound, with one mortar round landing within 15m of the CT. Although the damage was minor and there were no casualties, the entire company was unnerved by the fact that the Taliban could now drop mortars directly into the compound; if such attacks continued it would be only a matter of time before casualties started to rack up.

The message went out to all the troops equipped with thermal imagery equipment, which allows troops to see in the dark, to try and identify this new mortar position. Up on ANP Hill, soldiers from 12 Platoon reported that they had located the likely firing position and had identified a strong heat source. Maj Rex ordered the machinegunner in the Fire Support Group to strafe the area. The Fusilier's withering gunfire tore the Taliban position to shreds. After that attack, no more mortars fell on the compound during D Company's remaining time in Nowzad.

Snipers also posed a threat to troops inside the base. The Taliban snipers' main targets were the NCOs and commanders of the .50 calibre machine-gun crews. Maj Rex himself was a priority target and his tactical headquarters on top of the CT was regularly pinned down by harassing fire.

Both .50s received direct hits and often had to be fixed during major attacks and thus were temporarily unusable. While this was the case, all movement between exposed positions was banned during daylight hours and troop changeovers had to take place under the cover of darkness. It was highly likely that many of the Taliban snipers may have been members of the mujahideen who had fought the Soviets 20 years earlier. The snipers were clearly trained marksman and knew how to choose a carefully concealed firing position. They also knew how to adjust their sights to account for windspeed and light, a skill which can take years to develop.

The Taliban had managed to acquire high-velocity Dragnov sniper rifles. This was a major worry for the Gurkhas, who were fully aware of the damage that could be inflicted by skilful enemy marksmen. The message was dispatched from company headquarters to all troops to try and identify Taliban sniper positions. Such was the eagerness to neutralize the Taliban marksmen that within a matter of hours three sniper positions were identified. D Company's sniper, Corporal Imbahadur Ghale, became embroiled in a prolonged counter-sniper battle during which he notched up four confirmed kills and only narrowly avoided being shot himself.

The Taliban demonstrated their bravery and determination to take the fight to the Gurkhas when the company was once again engaged from the firing positions which already had been cleared by Cpl Ghale. Rather than deploying the company sniper for a second time, the Taliban positions were engaged by an A–10 which destroyed two more firing points.

During D Company's brief stay in Nowzad, they fired over 30,000 rounds of 5.56mm ammunition, 17,000 rounds of 7.62mm and 2,000 rounds of 12.7mm and they used 21 high explosive grenades in the defence of the base. After 21 July, the Taliban made no further attempts to overrun the base and instead resorted to stand-off attacks with mortars. An estimated 100 enemy were killed in the fighting, with many more wounded. By comparison, D Company suffered just five casualties.

The exhausted but jubilant D Company troops were finally relieved on 30 July by A Coy, 2nd battalion, the Royal Regiment of Fusiliers, who themselves would spend 107 days under attack.

The 3 Para battle group had originally been tasked to conduct peace support operations in Helmand as part of the expansion of ISAF into the south of Afghanistan. The intention had been for the battle group to provide just enough troops to occupy one forward operation base near the town of Gereshk. The remaining two rifle company groups were to be used to provide troops for future operations, an IRT and a number of smaller, platoon-sized QRFs, the majority of which were to be based in Camp Bastion, although some troops would occasionally be based at Kandahar air base.

Both Lt Col Tootal and Brig Butler were aware that it was highly likely their troops would be involved in some tough fighting. In December 2005, Lt Col Tootal had spent three days with US forces based in Zabul Province where he saw for himself the intensity of the fighting. This convinced him of the need for the battle group to be provided with the necessary equipment to fight a counter-insurgency war. After all, it was not as if the Taliban had given any indication that they might be prepared to enter into peace talks with the Karzai government.

However, as has already been seen, within a matter of weeks the Paras found themselves stretched to the very limit when they were deployed into Musa Qala, Nowzad, Sangin and the area of the Kajaki Dam. These additional and unexpected demands meant that it was vital that the battle group was reinforced.

Towards the end of June 2006, General Sir Mike Jackson, the Chief of the General Staff and the professional head of the Army, together with a small staff of senior officers, flew out to Camp Bastion to visit the troops. Within hours of arriving, and following discussions with Brig Butler and Lt Col Tootal, it became clear to him that the battle group needed reinforcements. As has already been mentioned, the battle group had originally been deployed on a peace support mission. While the Paras and their commanders had fully expected to be involved in bitter firefights with the Taliban, they had never expected to be 'garrisoned' across northern Helmand in so-called platoon houses. At a pinch, and providing the battle group did not take too many casualties, there were just enough troops to keep these bases manned at an acceptable level, but that would cease to be the case once the 'R and R' (Rest and Recuperation) programme kicked in.

Gen Jackson was told in no uncertain terms that while the Paras had done a tremendous job in the most arduous conditions, they were very tired and the R and R programme could not be cancelled or delayed without creating a significant morale problem. Therefore, the only solution was to reinforce. The General was also told that the battle group needed more helicopters and more engineers to shore-up the defence of the district compounds, which were being pulverized by Taliban rockets on a daily and sometimes hourly basis.

Gen Jackson and his staff were deeply moved and impressed by the sacrifices being made by the Paras and the rest of the battle group in their conflicts with the Taliban. An official request for more troops was sent back to the UK and Gen Jackson pressed for more reinforcements when he returned to the Ministry of Defence following his short trip.

On 10 July, Defence Secretary Des Browne announced in the House of Commons that an additional 900 soldiers would be sent to Afghanistan in the next few weeks. Of those 900, however, only 300 would be infantrymen. The rest would be engineers and troops trained in providing logistical support. The fighting troops would come from the Royal Irish Regiment, a platoon of which was already fighting in Helmand, while the remainder would come from the Royal Regiment of Fusiliers, who were based in Cyprus and thus were already acclimatized to the searing heat of the Helmand desert.

6

WELCOME TO SANGINGRAD

During the long hot summer of July 2006, the majority of the British public were engrossed in the World Cup taking place in Germany. The English team, said to be the best for a generation, were under-performing and the nation wasn't happy. There seemed to be little room in the newspapers for what was happening in Helmand, where 3,000 British troops were gradually being sucked into an increasingly violent and bloody war.

By the early evening of 4 July, B Company were fully settled into the salubrious surroundings of Sangin which, with the typical black humour of soldiers, had been had been renamed by the Paras as 'Sangingrad'. Within hours of relieving A Company, the soldiers of B Company had become embroiled in a heavy contact with the Taliban. From that moment until they were relieved a month later, they too would be in contact every day.

It soon became clear that the fighting would be even more intense than that faced by A Company. Within a matter of days, B Company needed to be reinforced by another platoon of 30 soldiers to carry out vital repair work on the defences of the District Centre. In the weeks prior to B Company's arrival, the walls and the buildings located inside the DC had taken a significant pounding from the Taliban. The outer perimeter walls were pock-marked with bullet fire and shrapnel splashes, as were many of the walls inside the compound. While sandbag barricades undoubtedly saved the lives of many soldiers forced to take cover behind them, they were at best a temporary measure. If the Paras were set to stay in Sangin, and all the indications suggested that would be the case, then the compound needed to be reinforced with Hesco walls. The repair work began almost immediately and was conducted during both daylight hours and under the cover of darkness.

Engineers in armoured bulldozers worked night and day, often under fire, in a frantic attempt to make the compound both habitable and secure. However, the improved fortification of the compound only seemed to spur on the Taliban to increase the ferocity of the attacks they launched against the DC.

Taliban attacks came thick and fast at all times and were clearly designed to demoralize the troops holed up in Sangin. While some of the contacts consisted of just a few short bursts of fire from a lone gunman armed with an AK47, which would send the Paras scurrying for cover as the crack of the rifle fire passed above their heads, others were highly organized assaults from multiple firing points from where the Taliban attacked with automatic weapons, RPGs and Chinese 107mm rockets.

The intensity of some of these assaults appeared to shake the Paras' base to its very foundations. Walls and ceilings often collapsed on men dealing with casualties. Some of the fire was so intense that it was initially impossible for the troops to raise their heads above the parapet through fear of death or serious injury. Yet the troops remained undeterred and each attack was fought off with unrivalled aggression and professionalism.

Such was the virtual certainty of attack that the troops, like A Company before them, would sleep in their body armour to be sure that they were ready for action at a moment's notice. More often than not, especially during the month of July, the luxury of sleep was restricted to just 30 minutes, such was the frequency of attacks from the Taliban.

Every soldier who served in Sangin, not just the Paras but cooks, signallers, mechanics, military police and even medics, knew that they would be expected to take their place in the sangars and fight when the time came. There was no room for passengers in Sangin: every single soldier had to make their presence count.

Apart from the ever-present fear of death and injury, the soldiers also had to contend with the squalid and primitive living conditions inside the base. In the height of the blistering Afghan summer, the spread of disease through poor hygiene posed almost as much a threat as the Taliban. It was often restated to the troops that more men were lost in the First World War through disease than from enemy fire. Despite the warnings, however, almost everyone based at Sangin in the summer of 2006 eventually fell victim to the dreaded D and V.

Describing the living conditions in the *Sun* newspaper on 14 September 2006, one officer commented:

> They are extremely basic. The compound buildings at least provide some shelter from the sun but they are Spartan, some resembling cave-like chambers. Most are so cramped that the men who occupy them live on top of one another. The issued mosquito nets do a sterling job of keeping away the persistent insect life.

There had been little progress in the quality of living conditions since A Company's tenure. As well as coping with the primitive sanitary conditions, the soldiers still had to survive on basic ten-man Army ration packs and bottled water, all of which had to be flown into the base by Chinook. Despite the heat, fresh water was rationed to just one bottle a day. The rest came from the canal which ran through the base. Before it could be drunk, every bottle of water needed to be treated with sterilization tablets, after which most soldiers added Lucozade powder to make the taste more palatable.

As the days passed, life for the members of B Company in Sangin began to take on an almost surreal routine in which soldiers would spend their hours staving off attacks from the Taliban, patrolling, filling sandbags, weapon cleaning, reinforcing the base's defences, or on the seemingly endless 'stag' or sentry duty in one of the compound's sangars.

In the moments out of contact, or when the soldiers had a few minutes to spare, some would write home. Those who knew the rules played pocket-chess and those who didn't watched or learnt themselves. When time allowed, the soldiers also tried to sleep.

Brig Butler and his staff were fully aware of the Taliban's desire to shoot down a Chinook – ideally one packed with troops – and they had come close on several occasions. This ever-present threat, which was to remain for the entire tour and beyond, meant that helicopters would only fly in to the outstations to collect a casualty or when a relief-in-place (RIP) was occurring. Losing a Chinook would be a catastrophic event for the entire British operation. Apart from the loss of a valuable piece of equipment, the propaganda value for the Taliban would be huge and would also result in a great deal of political pressure being placed on the government, with questions being asked as to the exact nature of the UK's role in Afghanistan.

In order to conduct relief operations, the British Army would have to catch the Taliban off-guard to minimize the risk of losing a Chinook to ground fire. It was decided that each of the three main outposts of Sangin, Musa Qala and Nowzad would be flooded with troops in a so-called 'deliberate operation' in which hundreds of Paras would storm into the town and drive out or kill the Taliban who were housed in the buildings close to the base. Probable Taliban ambush sites were targeted with artillery fire while Apaches or ground attack aircraft provided lethal cover thousands of feet above the Helmand desert.

The tactic was effective, but it was complex and enormously time-consuming. A relatively simple changeover of up to 100 troops suddenly became a 3-day operation in which soldiers faced the real risk of being killed or injured in combat.

By the middle of July 2006, however, the frequency of attacks meant that it had become all but impossible for helicopters to fly into Sangin to resupply the Paras, who were now effectively isolated from the main force back in Camp Bastion. Slowly, but surely, the ration store began to empty; food and fresh water had almost run out. While many of the soldiers thought that the idea of being cut-off and surrounded was 'alley', a Para word for being 'flash' or 'cool', their commanders started to become increasingly concerned.

Hope came in the form of a C130 Hercules. The Paras learnt that they were to be resupplied by the RAF. The drop went ahead as planned in the dead of night but, unfortunately, the much-needed supplies missed the Paras' location and ended up in the welcoming hands of the Taliban – the Paras didn't know whether to laugh or cry. As one officer put it: 'It wasn't the RAF's finest moment. There we were in Sangin, short on food water and ammunition and the RAF managed to drop the lot in a Taliban controlled area – you can imagine the response from the Toms.'

In true 7th Cavalry style, the day was saved by the US Air Force who flew in low and fast to deliver enough 24-hour ration packs before a convoy could break into the town to resupply the beleaguered force.

Throughout that month, B Company used every weapons system available to it, from the SA–80 A2, which after years of bad publicity was finally proving to be a battle-winning rifle, to the 2000lb JDAM bombs. The Apache, which the Taliban had dubbed the mosquito, presumably because it leaves a nasty sting, was also called into action virtually on a daily basis.

By the end of July, the sterling work being conducted by the engineers was complete and the base sported a Hesco defensive wall and a fit-for-purpose set of sangars, each large enough to house a .50 calibre machine-gun. The month-long tour also provided many young Toms, who had been 'green' recruits just a few weeks before, with their first taste of battle. One young soldier later gave this assessment of Sangin:

> That month in Sangin will shape my life. It was awesome, it was what being in the Parachute Regiment was all about. We had contacts every single day. There were many occasions that I was down to just my last few rounds before we were resupplied – you could easily get through 300 rounds in a battle. The Taliban were unbelievable, you have to respect them. They just kept coming, but the more that came the more we dropped but they showed no fear. They must have known they weren't going to beat us but they still kept coming. What amazed me more than anything was the morale of the blokes. We all knew that we could be killed or injured at any minute but morale was high. It was a case of 'we are 3 Para and this is what we do'. That month in Sangin was everything I joined the Army to do.

One month after they arrived, B Company were replaced by A Company in another RIP. To the troops who took part, these changeovers were becoming relatively routine but the dangers associated with this type of mission meant that the soldiers were never complacent. In Helmand, complacency was often punished with injury or death.

By the beginning of June 2006, the Pathfinders, who had been 'stood to' for a series of operations in Helmand only for them to be cancelled, were ordered to prepare for a return to Musa Qala, 160km to the north of Camp Bastion, to relieve a US company who in turn had relieved them a few weeks earlier. At that time, there were just 24 soldiers in the Pathfinders, while the US unit they were relieving was 150-strong. Although there was obvious concern that such a relatively small force should be relieving a larger one, the soldiers took comfort from the fact that they were told that they would only be in Musa Qala for 48 to 96 hours. However, a series of dramatic and wholly unexpected political developments would unravel as the unit returned to the town. The 96 hours turned into 52 days, 26 of which were spent in contact with the enemy.

When the Pathfinders arrived in Musa Qala, they immediately began conducting joint patrols with the ANP and engaged with the town's tribal elders. They were aware from their previous visit to the town that the vast majority of the local people hated the Taliban and wanted to embrace the prospect of real security which was being offered by the British troops.

Both the Governor's office and the ANP were inextricably linked to crime and narcotics, and also to elements of the Taliban. As a result, corruption and mistrust of authority ran very deep.

The Pathfinders soon obtained intelligence that the Taliban were planning to launch a sustained attack against Musa Qala. They wanted to force the Afghan security forces and the British troops out of the town so that they could have a clear run at Sangin. The Pathfinders were reinforced by troops from 9 (Para) Royal Engineers, who were responsible for improving the security of the base, and a troop from 1 Battery, 7 Royal Horse Artillery, who were acting as infantry troops.

By the middle of July, the Taliban were attacking the base daily. Like elsewhere in Helmand where British troops were holed up in isolated compounds, the attacks could range from one-off shoot-and-scoot incidents to full-blown attacks from multiple firing points in which it seemed that the Taliban were attempting to overrun the compound. During one 10-day period, the troops in Musa Qala called in 6 artillery fire missions and 26 air attacks. On the 26 July, a Danish recce squadron managed to break through the Taliban positions and link up with the hard-pressed troops inside the District Centre. By this time, the force had been out of fresh water and rations for five days. The troops managed to sustain themselves by sterilizing water collected from local wells and purchasing food from the local bazaar at hugely inflated prices.

The Pathfinders remained inside the Musa Qala base for another ten days, during which time they went on patrol with the Danish troops and briefed them on Taliban tactics. The Pathfinders tried to leave the base on 1 August, but they were ambushed in a *wadi* and had to conduct a fighting withdrawal all the way back to the compound.

During the attempted extraction, D Squadron of the Household Cavalry were given the task of escorting a battery of 105mm guns from 7 Royal Horse Artillery, which were going to be used to create a diversion. Once the guns were in position, the squadron moved forward in an attempt to get eyes on Musa Qala from the ridgeline to the west of the town. The move forward was almost immediately delayed by minefields and fog, a nasty combination in enemy territory. As the vehicles inched their way towards the ridge, call sign '21', a Spartan armoured vehicle, struck an anti-tank mine. Such was the force of the blast that the vehicle was tossed into the air. The crew, although badly shaken, were unharmed but their vehicle was a wreck. The impact had destroyed the running gear and the gearbox, and buckled the chassis.

The vehicle was beyond repair. In order to 'deny' it to the enemy it was later destroyed by a Hellfire missile fired from an Apache. The Taliban had concealed a huge bomb where the British armoured vehicles were now manoeuvring. The bomb, which was thought to have been composed of artillery shells and old mines bundled together, was connected to a firing point by a long wire. Such devices are known in the British Army as command wire improvised explosive devices or CWIEDs. Overlooking the ambush site were a number of different Taliban positions equipped with heavy and medium machine-guns and RPGs. The ambush design came straight out of the mujahideen handbook of tactics used to defeat the Soviet Army 20 years earlier. One of the command vehicles, a Spartan with the call sign '41', unknowingly moved into the ambush's 'killing zone'. The Taliban watched and waited. As the convoy moved towards the ambush point, the Taliban allowed one of the vehicles to drive over the CWIED before detonating the device beneath the second vehicle. Hidden from view, the Taliban commander flicked the switch and the CWIED was detonated with devastating effect. The enormous explosion echoed around the valley like rolling thunder and sent out a huge mushroom-shaped cloud of dust. Such was the force of the blast that the relatively lightly armoured Spartan was tossed into the air. It landed with a dull thump, its armoured hull pierced, and immediately burst into flames.

2nd Lt Ralph Johnson, 24, of the Life Guards, Capt Alex Eida, 29, of the 7 (Para) Regiment Royal Horse Artillery, and LCpl Ross Nicholls, 27, of the Blues and Royals, were all killed instantly. Trooper Martin Compton, also of the Blues and Royals, survived the initial attack but suffered very severe burns to his body as he crawled from the burning wreckage. Also caught in the ambush killing area were Corporal of Horse Michael Flynn and his crew from the first vehicle, who were blocked from moving either forwards or back. As they attempted to move, machine-gun fire, mortars and RPGs rained down on them. Despite taking numerous hits, they managed to extract themselves back to the relative safety of the other vehicles.

Mick Flynn, 46, from Cardiff, who was on his second spell of duty in the British Army after an eight-year gap, told the *Guardian* (18 November 2006) of the horror and fear of being caught in a Taliban ambush:

> I was in the lead vehicle and the vehicle behind me got blown up. I had driven over the IED. They let me past and blew up the vehicle behind me. I was then trapped and they fired numerous rockets at us. Three RPGs hit us and one went over the top. We took out the machine-gun posts to the front of us and killed them. The Taliban's main killing group was probably about 10m away. There were about 20 or 30 of them. I made a decision to go on through the ambush and I looked behind and saw that there was a lot of smoke coming from the vehicle behind. We turned round and went through the ambush firing phosphorous grenades at them. The bar armour which protected the vehicle had been hit so we had to dismount. The Taliban were coming down the lane towards us. We killed three of them, but the rest kept coming. We had to fight our way along and then jump in a ditch.

Describing the carnage surrounding the damaged British Spartan, CoH Flynn, went on:

> I checked the vehicle behind me. Inside I could see one body. The one outside was blown up and was just a mass of meat. It was just another dead body. Without trying to sound callous, I don't have any feelings. I think I have become immune to it. You can't, they are finished, that's it. I just accept that they are dead. Obviously it went through my brain but my main issue was to get the other two guys out of there alive.

Radders [Lance Corporal of Horse Andrew Radford] came and said there was a body on top of the hill. I said, 'Why don't you shoot?' and he said, 'No, it's one of ours'. We made our way to the body. I could see it was one of the lads. I thought he was dead, but as I moved his leg, which was jutting out at an angle, he screamed. When I first looked at him he had fish eyes and I thought he was dead. I threw him on to Radder's shoulders and we shot our way back. He was really badly burnt, he had 80 per cent burns. To be honest we didn't expect him to survive but he did.

The soldier they retrieved was Tpr Compton who survived the attack despite suffering very severe burns.

The recovery of the dead was a major operation in itself, involving the majority of B Company who crossed the 'line of departure' – the modern phrase for the frontline – sitting on top of Scimitars and other armoured vehicles in what one officer described as a 'scene from another era'. Virtually all of those who took part in the recovery operation were shocked by the carnage of the attack. It was another harsh reminder that the Taliban were a resourceful and determined foe who would exploit any opportunity to attack and kill British troops.

Five days later, a battle group operation was launched and the Pathfinders were eventually able to extract, 52 days after they had first entered the base for a 96-hour operation.

At the end of July, A Company returned to Sangin for the third and final time during Operation Herrick 4. The company consisted of two platoons of around 30 men each, a regimental aid post run by an army doctor and a medic, engineers, an armoured recce troop from D Squadron of the Household Cavalry Regiment and a Fire Support Group composed of Javelin, .50 calibre heavy machine-guns and mortars. Also located within the confines of the compound was a platoon from the ANA and a detachment of seven members of the ANP. The ANP were free to come and go as they pleased, which put them beyond any real control of the British troops. The ANP also refused to wear uniform for fear of reprisals and were therefore impossible to distinguish from the Taliban. Relationships between the ANP and the Army were never good and the vast majority of the soldiers in Sangin believed that, effectively, they were Taliban spies.

During the next four weeks, A Company were under orders to complete three essential tasks: to provide protection to the Royal Engineers who were repairing and adding to the base's fortifications and helicopter landing zone; to disrupt enemy activity, with the specific mission of identifying and destroying them where possible; and, finally, to reassure the local population of the coalition's long-term aim to develop and reconstruct their town, Helmand Province and the wider Afghanistan. Reconstruction was becoming increasingly difficult to sell to the Afghans who, with the arrival of the British a few months earlier, had seen their homes destroyed and their people killed in the inevitable 'collateral damage' that came with fighting the Taliban.

This third and final stay for A Company would last a total of 35 days, 31 of which would involve contact with the enemy.

The company also had a new commander, Maj Jamie Loden, who had taken over from Maj Pike. Maj Loden would later gain a certain notoriety within the Army for criticizing RAF pilots as 'utterly useless' in an email to a friend.

By the time A Company arrived in Sangin in August 2006, it was clear that the battle group's original intention of acting as a peace support force was virtually dead in the water. As far as the troops were concerned, they were at war. It was also evident in the weeks since their last visit that the Taliban had changed their tactics and improved their battle skills. The Taliban appeared to be better organized and were equipped along the lines of a British Army section, with a balance of automatic weapons, namely AK47s, rocket propelled grenades and machine-guns. They had taken many casualties and the mass attacks of 50 to 100 fighters had been replaced by sniper activity and shoot-and-scoot tactics.

The attacks were also becoming more accurate. When A Company first deployed into Sangin at the beginning of the tour, the Taliban were lucky if they could get one round within 200m of the perimeter of the DC. By the end of August 2006, the majority of the mortar bombs were landing inside the compounds.

The nature and ethnic mix of the fighters had also changed. At the outset of the tour they consisted of a few experienced fighters supplemented by hired guns with woeful shooting skills. As the tour progressed, the hardcore had been reinforced by foreign fighters, mainly from the Punjab, who had better marksmanship skills and who were capable of coordinating highly complex attacks from several different firing points while using a variety of weapon systems.

Instead of large mass attacks, the Taliban began to work in ten-man units, which were clearly commanded and coordinated by a senior, experienced Taliban fighter. It appeared that just as the Paras had watched and studied the Taliban, so had they watched the British troops and began to understand their tactics. The passage of information within the Taliban command system was such that when British troops ventured out on patrol the Taliban units were warned and ready to attack. It also became clear that if patrols remained static for ten minutes or more they would be attacked. Thus, vehicle checkpoints were a non-starter and gathering intelligence on Taliban activity by chatting up the locals had become all but impossible.

Another worry was the virtual freedom of movement the Taliban now had within Sangin. Weapons were cached in houses or fields close to likely patrol routes, which allowed the Taliban to move amongst the civilian population, launch attacks and melt away again with impunity.

As in June, the enemy attacked the compound from 360° and any patrol was immediately tracked as soon as it left the base. Attacks against the District Centre were now limited to 30 to 45 minutes – much shorter than the attacks in June. Again, the Taliban's new tactics clearly demonstrated that they had learnt from past mistakes, when scores of Afghan fighters were killed in air strikes.

On 27 July, a patrol into the town sensed the uneasiness of the population, and the troops slowly and carefully moved back towards the DC. Everything went quiet. The locals shut their shops and the population disappeared. The Army described these eerie events as 'combat indicators'. They had seen them before and they knew what was coming. The locals had clearly been told that the Taliban were intending to attack the British the next time they passed through the area and the warning had gone out for the local populace to hide away.

As the patrol inched its way back to base, they were eager to return to the safety of the DC but were determined not to give the impression that they were running scared, as this would only increase the risk of attack. Each man knew what was expected of him. They had been given their arcs of observation and were scanning rooftops, alleyways and likely ambush points when Pte Peter McKinley spotted two gunmen on a roof as the patrol crossed a *wadi*. Acting instinctively, as he had been trained to do, he opened fire with several bursts of automatic fire from his SA–80 A2, at the same time telling his section commander where the gunmen were. The patrol was then immediately engaged with automatic fire from several different firing points. As the Paras took cover and began returning fire, RPGs exploded around them. Straightaway, the patrol sustained a casualty when Pte Neil Edwards was wounded with a broken femur. He was immobilized by the patrol medic and dragged to a relatively safe area in the *wadi*.

Corporal Bryan Budd, a section commander who had previously served in the Pathfinders, quickly assessed the situation and decided to assault the Taliban position in order to push them back. In a desperate but heroic assault, he personally dispatched two of the enemy located in one building with grenades and rifle fire. Cpl Budd's action enabled Pte Edwards to be given more treatment and to be extracted from the battle area by members of the Household Cavalry.

Pte McKinley, who had prematurely triggered the Taliban ambush by engaging the two gunmen, received shrapnel wounds and he too was evacuated from the scene. The rest of the patrol managed to extricate themselves from the ambush and returned to the safety of the DC.

The following day began with another extraordinary incident when the Deputy Chief of Police told the British that he intended to move his officers out of the British base. The decision was yet more proof of the immense psychological pressure the ANP were under. The Paras knew that the ANP, their family and friends were probably threatened every day by the Taliban, some of whom they had probably known for most of their lives.

Over the following days, the loyalty of the ANP, which was at best very shaky, became even more dubious. By 2 August, the Deputy Chief of Police had fled the area. Five days later, a split occurred amongst the six remaining members of the ANP, with three leaving to join the Taliban. It was a classic Afghan switch and, worryingly for the British, it signified that the three who changed sides believed that the Taliban held the upper hand. Within a matter of days, the remaining three members of the ANP also disappeared and presumably switched sides.

On the ground, the tactical situation was becoming increasingly precarious. 1 Platoon became involved in another contact with the enemy on 30 July, while 2 Platoon were ambushed during a patrol through the town. The ambush was particularly intense. It was fought at close quarters and the Paras had to resort to throwing grenades into houses which had been occupied by the Taliban. The Paras were now involved in a level of street-fighting which had not been experienced by the British Army for a generation.

Sangin was proving to be a demanding testing ground for junior non-commissioned officers and young, relatively inexperienced platoon commanders. These were the men who were responsible for ultimately taking the fight to the enemy or extricating their men from a Taliban ambush, something at which they were all quickly becoming adept.

The level of Taliban activity within Sangin meant that any patrol entering the town must be of platoon strength at the very least – a minimum of 30 men. Every patrol deployed with a mortar fire controller (MFC) and a medic. A Quick Reaction Force would also be placed on standby until the troops had returned. The QRF also included a quad bike with a modified trailer which could take a stretcher for immediate casevac back to base.

Each of the three sections which would make up a platoon venturing out into Taliban territory would contain a general purpose machine-gun team, a light machine-gun and an under-slung grenade launcher. Each patrol also carried mouse-hole charges or bar mines, which were used for explosive entry into buildings. The soldiers preferred to use bar mines because they produced a larger hole and the sheer thickness of some of the mud walls often meant that mouse-hole charges were ineffective. The assault ladder, a military tool which had been in existence in a variety of forms since the Middle Ages, was also used on many patrols.

The complex nature of the ground through which a single patrol might pass meant that junior commanders had to have their wits about them. A single patrol might begin by moving through a relatively open area, where the spacing between troops could be quite large. A few hundred metres further on, the same patrol might find itself in an area of dense vegetation where the spacing would have to reduce to a metre or two. Every soldier was aware that there was a very real possibility of a patrol member becoming separated from his colleagues during a fire-fight. The troops knew only too well that if they fell into the hands of the Taliban they would in all likelihood die an unpleasant and painful death which could possibly be filmed and placed on the Internet. Many soldiers had already vowed that they would save their last bullet for themselves rather than be taken alive by the Taliban.

One of the difficulties of daily life in Sangin was the vulnerability of the Helicopter Landing Site. A canal, which diverted water from the fast-flowing Helmand river, split the HLS area from the District Centre itself. Beyond the HLS was a large area of agricultural land where fields of corn grew up to 3m high. This Green Zone area was criss-crossed by irrigation ditches up to 2m wide and hundreds of metres long. The Taliban became expert at using these natural features to launch attacks against the DC.

During August, the engineers constructed a Hesco wall, complete with sangars, and cut back the crops to 100m from the HLS perimeter. Despite these improvements, the HLS remained vulnerable and patrols were often tasked with sweeping the area prior to the arrival of a heli-copter in order to check for cached weapons.

One such operation took place on 17 August 2006 and it serves to underline the complexities facing British troops in Sangin, and Helmand as a whole, during that entire summer. 1 Platoon of A Company was ordered to conduct a clearance of the HLS at the Sangin District Centre. The patrol left the base at 0300hrs, just before dawn, and moved to what is called a Lie Up Position (LUP) close to the location of the HLS. The soldiers were supported by a troop of vehicles from the Household Cavalry Regiment, which included a Spartan and a Scimitar to provide extra firepower if the soldiers were ambushed. Once in position, the 1 Platoon soldiers began to move back to the DC, searching compounds on the way. They were looking for groups of Taliban equipped with RPGs and heavy machine-guns who would be hoping to shoot down a Chinook and, in an instant, achieve a major tactical success against the British.

It became clear almost immediately that the troops were being watched by unarmed locals who were tracking their movements. This was not an unusual activity, for the Taliban often employed locals to supply them with intelligence on troop movements. The suspected Taliban sympathizers were quickly seized by the wary Paras. As the troops were preparing to take them back to the DC, the 1 Platoon commander spotted another seven people moving up a track an estimated 70m away. The men were wearing chest webbing and carrying

RPGs. They were clearly Taliban. The officers turned to warn the rest of the platoon, but he was spotted by the enemy who opened fire. The response from the Paras was immediate and aggressive. Nearly all of the platoon weapons were brought to bear on the Taliban fighters and the MFC called in a fire mission. The weight of fire from the platoon was such that the enemy immediately stopped firing, accepted that they had lost the firefight and withdrew.

To their immense frustration, the troops in the armoured vehicles had been unable to open fire because they couldn't see the position of the Paras and did not want to risk firing on their own side. However, they could see that the Taliban were being reinforced. The message was relayed back to company headquarters and the order was given for the platoon to withdraw northwards. As the soldiers began to move through the thick vegetation, they were ambushed by another group of Taliban on the other side of the canal.

It was clear that the enemy were attempting to cut-off the Paras' escape route. The Taliban opened fire but they were quickly suppressed by the Paras who then moved onwards in the hope of entering the *wadi*, which would afford them greater protection. This choice of route would also allow the Household Cavalry to open fire without fear of hitting their own side. It was now clear that a dangerous situation was developing and that there were far more Taliban in the area than initially had been estimated.

By this stage two RAF Harriers were overhead but in order to allow the RAF to deploy their weapons to maximum effect, the pilots needed to know where the Paras were on the ground beneath them. As a signal to show the pilots the location of the forward line of friendly troops, a smoke grenade was thrown, but this only served to identify the Paras position to the Taliban.

In desperation, the platoon commander ordered a snap ambush. The troops took up position, primed their grenades, fitted a fresh magazine to their weapons and waited for the Taliban to show themselves. When they did so, the 30 or so troops in the platoon fired as one and cut the leading members of the Taliban group to pieces. Shocked by the intensity of the fire, the Taliban withdrew.

The whole of the company was 'stood to' and ready to deal with any eventuality. It was still unclear at this stage whether this was a relatively minor, albeit dangerous, incident or part of a wider attack against the

British base. By now, the Paras had managed to put a clear distance between themselves and the Taliban, allowing company headquarters to bring harassing artillery fire on to the enemy. 1 Platoon began to move back to the DC under the cover of fire from .50 heavy machine guns, mortars and artillery.

The base itself was under fire from small arms fire and RPGs coming from the town, but these attacks were easily suppressed. The enemy had now pushed up to the area at the back of the helicopter landing site, which the engineers had cleared. This proved to be a fatal mistake. Circling high above, the two Harriers had been waiting for the moment when they could attack the Taliban and aid their comrades below. It had now become more obvious that 1 Platoon had managed to clear some distance away from the Taliban. The Harriers were ordered to attack. Screeching in low and fast, the Harriers dropped a 1,000lb and a 500lb bomb. There would have been no time for the Taliban to take cover. Even if they had, the impact of the shock would still have been fatal. Those who were not atomized in the initial blast were either killed or wounded by a mass of shrapnel as it sliced through the air. The explosion was roundly cheered by the exhausted soldiers as they made their way back into the DC. Even though only the 500lb bomb had actually detonated, the necessary effect had been achieved and the enemy fire had ceased.

The contact finally ended at 1100hrs. Remarkably, the company did not sustain a single casualty despite being in contact for almost eight hours. In the process, they had managed to deliver another damaging blow to the morale of the Taliban. Despite the very real and obvious dangers of patrolling in the town, the soldiers knew it was vital. By patrolling into Sangin, the Taliban were kept on the back foot and it reinforced a message to the civilians that the coalition was here for the long run. To have forgone the patrols might have been safer in the short term but it would have had the effect of allowing the Taliban to mass their forces against the British, as well as creating a negative siege mentality within the base.

Three days after the battle to secure the helicopter landing site, the soldiers of 1 Platoon were once again back out on patrol in Sangin. The patrol was moving northwards, with two forward sections providing protection for a rear section, by using bar mines to create a covered route through a series of compounds. One Wmik was with the forward-left section and a second Wmik, supported by a fire team, was deployed into the town to cover approaches to the platoon's right flank.

Corporal Bryan Budd was leading the forward-right section. As he moved forward he saw three enemy positions to his front. Cpl Budd realized there was little else to do but to attack in an attempt to seize the initiative. Taking cover behind a small mud wall, he turned to the rest of the members of his section and told them that they were going to attack the enemy position.

The men listened intently as he spelled out exactly what he wanted each man to do and how to do it. 'Questions?' When no one answered, Cpl Budd, said: 'Good. Then follow me.' As he led his men forward, the Wmik on his left was ambushed. To stall the attack now would have been disastrous and so Cpl Budd pushed on towards the enemy in a bid to regain the initiative. As the section moved forward, an enormous firefight broke out. Almost immediately, two of his men fell. One of the soldiers had been hit in the chest but, although winded and shocked, he had been saved from serious injury by his body armour. LCpl Guy Roberts, the MFC attached to the platoon, was not so lucky and he had been hit in the shoulder. The two casualties crawled towards cover but as they did so the Taliban opened fire on their positions. The ground around them became alive with bullet splashes and the ping of ricochets. Two other members of the section, Pte Stephen Halton and Pte Andrew Lanaghan, fearful that their colleagues were about to be cut to pieces, rushed forward to drag LCpl Roberts into cover but in doing so Pte Lanaghan was hit in the face and arm. Still under fire, Pte Halton managed to pull both of his injured colleagues into cover. Meanwhile Cpl Budd, who by now had also been injured by Taliban gunfire, pushed home the attack on his own. The soldiers watched as he disappeared, firing his weapon as he ran. It was the last time he was seen alive.

The section second-in-command pulled the section back to reorganize and immediately realized that his commander was missing. Amid the rattle of machine-gun fire, the remainder of his section began to call his name. 'Bryan. Bryan.' There was no response. Fearing the worst, the message was sent back to Lt Hugo Farmer, the platoon commander, that Cpl Budd was missing in action. Everyone knew that any soldier captured by the Taliban would die a painful death and so Lt Farmer moved forward with the third section and led two more attempts to reach the position where Cpl Budd was believed to have been wounded. Despite the heroics, both attempts were driven back by enemy fire. Cpl Charles Curnow, the commander of 2 Section, was wounded in one of the assaults; Pte Philip Briggs was hit in the chest plate of his body armour; and Lt Farmer received a shrapnel wound in the buttocks. The attack had broken down into a chaotic mess in which several soldiers had been injured and one was missing.

A message was sent back to company headquarters informing them that the patrol was pinned down, with several injured and one missing in action. It was clear that the majority of 1 Platoon were in a bad way and there was now a real fear that the platoon was in danger of being overrun. The QRF was deployed to secure a casualty evacuation point and Warrant Officer Schofield, A Company's Sergeant Major, retrieved the injured on a quad bike, coming under fire several times himself in the process. Cpl Budd was still missing and the fact that he may have actually been taken prisoner by the Taliban continued to play on everyone's minds. Despite the dangers and the injuries, however, the company as a whole was determined to push on until they found their friend and colleague. One officer recalled:

> The word quickly went around that Bryan was missing. I would have to say that it was one of the low points. We were all hoping that he would make it back, but in our hearts I think we all knew that he was probably dead. Bryan was the sort of bloke who wouldn't be taken prisoner.

In a bid to give extra support to 1 Platoon, a composite force was put under the command of 2nd Lt Andy Mallet and included members of A Company, a sniper platoon, the Household Cavalry, engineers from 51 Para Squadron Royal Engineers and two members of the Royal Military Police Special Investigation Branch. They moved forward to reinforce 1 Platoon and to try and approach what was believed to be Cpl Budd's position from a different direction. Once again, the advance ground to a halt as they became pinned down by enemy fire. The Taliban were now extremely close to 1 Platoon's position. Short on ammunition and with several men injured, the platoon was on the brink of being surrounded. It was clear to all that disaster loomed but the Paras fought on. In the best traditions of the regiment, they fixed bayonets and vowed to fight to the last man.

Such was the close proximity of the Paras to the Taliban that it was simply too dangerous to call in close air support. A 500lb bomb would have seen off the Taliban, but in all likelihood it would have wiped-out the Paras as well. Instead, the Paras sent an urgent request to Camp Bastion and asked for Apaches to be sent immediately.

In the town, the Wmik covering the right flank identified the enemy taking weapons out of a mosque. It was clear that they were going to be used to reinforce the group attacking the platoon and permission was given for this batch of the enemy to be engaged with mortars.

The battle was finally won with the arrival of the Apaches, whose 30mm cannons tore into the Taliban positions and forced them to withdraw. The elation of beating off the Taliban was, however, immediately surpassed by the sad news that Cpl Budd was dead. He had died a soldier's death, fighting to the end and dispatching three of the enemy in the process. Their bodies were found close to his. In a desperate bid to save his injured colleagues, he had attacked on his own, knowing that he was outnumbered and that he faced certain death.

Colleagues of Cpl Budd described him as a thoughtful, softly spoken but highly professional junior commander who was respected by soldiers of all ranks. Throughout the course of a month, Cpl Budd had displayed courage and leadership of the highest standards while under fire. For the events of 27 July and 20 August, he was posthumously awarded the Victoria Cross.

This is the full citation:

During July and August 2006, A Company, 3rd Battalion, the Parachute Regiment were deployed in the District Centre at Sangin. They were constantly under sustained attack from a combination of Taliban small arms, rocket-propelled grenades, mortar and rocket fire.

On 27 July, whilst on a routine patrol, Corporal Bryan Budd's section identified and engaged two enemy gunmen on the roof of a building in the centre of Sangin. During the ensuing fierce fire-fight, two of Corporal Budd's section were hit. One was seriously injured and collapsed in the open ground, where he remained exposed to enemy fire, with rounds striking the ground around him. Corporal Budd realized that he needed to regain the initiative and that the enemy needed to be driven back so that the casualty could be evacuated.

Under fire, he personally led the attack on the building where the enemy fire was heaviest, forcing the remaining fighters to flee across an open field where they were successfully engaged. This courageous and prompt action proved decisive in breaking the enemy and was undertaken at great personal risk. Corporal Budd's decisive leadership and conspicuous gallantry allowed his wounded colleague to be evacuated to safety where he subsequently received life-saving treatment.

A month later, on 20 August, Corporal Budd was leading his section on the right forward flank of a platoon clearance patrol near Sangin District Centre. Another section was advancing with a Land Rover fitted with a .50 calibre heavy machine-gun on the patrol's left flank. Pushing through thick vegetation, Corporal Budd identified a number of enemy fighters 30 metres ahead. Undetected, and in an attempt to surprise and destroy the enemy, Corporal Budd, initiated a flanking manoeuvre. However, the enemy spotted the Land Rover on the left flank and the element of surprise was lost for the whole platoon.

In order to regain the initiative, Corporal Budd decided to assault the enemy and ordered his men to follow him. As they moved forward the section came under a withering fire that incapacitated three of his men. The continued enemy fire and these losses forced the section to take cover. But, Corporal Budd continued the assault on his own, knowing full well the likely consequences of doing so without the close support of his remaining men. He was wounded but continued to move forward, attacking and killing the enemy as he rushed their position.

Corporal Budd's conspicuous gallantry during these two engagements saved the lives of many of his colleagues. He acted in the full knowledge that the rest of his men had either been struck down or had been forced to go to ground. His determination to press home a single-handed assault against a superior enemy force despite his wounds stands out as a premeditated act of inspirational leadership and supreme valour. In recognition of this, Corporal Budd is awarded the Victoria Cross.

Inspired by Corporal Budd's example, the rest of the platoon reorganized and pushed forward their attack, eliminating more of the enemy and eventually forcing their withdrawal. Corporal Budd subsequently died of his wounds, and when his body was later recovered it was found surrounded by three dead Taliban. A post mortem later revealed that Cpl Budd was probably killed by friendly fire. A bullet extracted during an autopsy and later forensically examined was found to be the same as that used by the British Army – a 5.56mm NATO round.

Cpl Budd's death was a devastating blow to the men of A Company, who had now seen several of their colleagues fall in battle. Even though many tears were shed by members of his platoon and others, the embattled Paras were determined to fight on in the spirit exemplified by Bryan Budd.

The high tempo of the operations also meant that it was all but impossible for friends and colleagues of dead soldiers to mourn their passing, for in all likelihood the same soldiers would be back out on patrol or fighting off another Taliban attack in a matter of hours.

The attack in which Cpl Budd died demonstrated that, while the Taliban had taken many body blows and always came off worse when they attacked the British, their morale remained strong and their ability to adapt to an evolving operational situation in quick time was constantly improving. Thus, after 20 August, it was decided that no patrols would enter into the confines of Sangin without air support.

7

THE BLOODIEST MONTH

September 2006 arrived and with it the first signs that the stultifying heat of the Afghan summer was beginning to ease. However, it was to prove to be the bloodiest month for the British military in Afghanistan for more than 80 years.

On Friday 1 September, as will be described later in this chapter, Ranger Anare Draiva and LCpl Paul Muirhead of the Royal Irish Regiment suffered fatal injuries during a contact with the Taliban in Musa Qala.

Less than 24 hours later, on 2 September, 14 servicemen, including 12 members of the RAF, a Royal Marine and a Parachute Regiment corporal, were killed when a Nimrod MR2 spy plane crashed during a routine patrol in the neighbouring province of Kandahar. Initially, it was thought that the plane may have been shot down by a Taliban surface-to-air missile, but later analysis showed that the plane had crashed due to mechanical failure.

On the following Monday, 4 September, Pte Craig O'Donnell of the Argyll and Sutherland Highlanders, 5th Battalion The Royal Regiment of Scotland, was killed in Kabul when a suicide bomber attacked a convoy.

The worst period of the entire tour was underway.

By the middle of that first September, there was a sense that the entire campaign was beginning to unravel. The beleaguered force in Helmand was being hit from every side and the casualties were mounting. On Wednesday 6 September, the situation got a lot worse.

Soldiers now expected to be attacked every day. It might be a mortar, a rocket or a burst from an AK47, but the attack would come. That was now certain. Just about every man serving in the battle group personally knew a fellow soldier who had been killed or injured and just about every man had been involved in combat. Within a few short months, the battle group had been transformed from a highly trained but untested force into a battle-hardened unit of professional fighters. The British Army had seen nothing like the fighting in Helmand for decades. Some senior officers even considered the fighting as equal to that in Korea some 50 years earlier.

By the end of 6 September, even the tough, experienced men of 3 Para were wondering when the fighting would end and some were beginning to question how much more they could take.

In 2006, Kajaki was an isolated but popular posting with the soldiers. The living was hard and the Taliban attacked on most days, but the fighting was often at long range and casualties were relatively light. The Taliban were still primarily concerned with attacking the narcotic centre of Sangin and the towns of Musa Qala and Nowzad. Forcing the British out of one of these towns would represent a major publicity coup for the Taliban and would destroy the credibility of the Karzai government. The soldiers in Kajaki were also away from senior officers and were allowed to get on with the job of patrolling and securing the dam without too much high-level interference.

The dam remains the key strategic installation in Helmand. The dam itself controls the flow of the Helmand river, which effectively bisects Helmand Province from the northeast to the southwest. The generating station enclosed inside the dam is the sole source of electricity to the Helmand region and nearby areas. At full capacity, it was hoped that it would also be able to deliver electricity to the Kandahar region. With electricity would come a better quality of life. Jobs would be created as new factories were developed and hospitals would be able to operate 24 hours a day, 360 days a year. A working hydro-electric power station would demonstrate to the people of Helmand that ISAF were the good guys. Little wonder, then, that the Taliban were hell-bent on destroying it.

The force charged with guarding the dam was relatively modest and consisted of a 30-man group who were split between two observations posts (OPs) sitting high on two hills that dominated the surrounding area. These were known as Observation Post Normandy and Observation Post Arnhem. The OPs had one simple function: to allow the troops entombed inside to report on any movement by the Taliban in the immediate area of the dam. Each OP was a simple structure which had effectively been scraped out of the hillside. They consisted of a bunker, from where the soldiers could spy on the surrounding area, and a place where the soldiers could eat and drink.

Despite their size, the OPs packed a big punch and were more than capable of repelling any attempt by the Taliban to overrun them. They were well-armed: between them they boasted several GPMG, mortars and a new blowpipe anti-tank weapon which could take out a Taliban pick-up from 2km.

Life in the OPs was all about routine. They had to be manned 24 hours a day, so the soldiers in each would split up into different groups. While one group was observing the local area, another would be sleeping, eating or weapon cleaning. Occasionally, the soldiers would patrol out to the reservoir for a wash or a swim – a benefit of being posted to the dam – but, for a lot of the time, Kajaki meant dealing with long periods of inactivity followed by periods of intense fighting. Fresh rations were a rarity and soldiers often survived on 24-hour ration packs and bottled water which, along with ammunition and batteries, had to be flown in to the bases by helicopter.

The soldiers made life as comfortable as they could and by September the broiling heat of the daylight hours was beginning to cool, slightly. At the height of summer, sleep during the day was almost impossible and the night was not much better either. The altitude of the bases meant that mosquitoes were not too much of a problem but the soldiers often woke exhausted and dehydrated. Much of the time was spent inside the OPs' bunkers or living inside the sparse dam buildings. The soldiers did their best with what little they had and even attempted to enliven their army rations with the fresh vegetables that they tried to grow – although this was not one of their most successful experiments.

The two OPs were also supported by soldiers from an Operational Mentoring and Liaison Team who were responsible for training a detachment of the Afghan National Army.

By 6 September most of the soldiers were thinking about the prospect of returning home to their families, wives and girlfriends and Corporal Mark Wright, a tough junior NCO in the mortar platoon, was no different. He was the Mortar Fire Controller in OP Normandy and had proved his worth in battle on numerous occasions. At the age of 27, Cpl Wright had decided that the Army was to be his future. Afghanistan, although it was tough, demanding and dangerous, offered everything he had joined the Army to do. Back home in Edinburgh, however, his parents Bob and Gem were worried, as was his fiancée Gillian, whom he was planning to marry on his return to the UK.

Cpl Wright hoped one day to emulate his uncle, Alec, who had served in 3 Para during the late 1980s and went on to join the SAS, where he eventually became a Warrant Officer 1st Class, gaining a chestful of medals in the process.

Cpl Wright had a calm manner, which made him popular with both junior and senior ranks. He was as strong as an ox and was one of the best Mortar Fire Controllers in the battalion. The job of an MFC is to bring fire down on to the enemy. It is an immensely responsible job for a relatively junior soldier and the decisions of an MFC will save lives or cost them if mistakes are made.

Located in OP Arnhem, 800m due east of Normandy, were Lance Corporal Stuart Hale and Corporal Stuart Pearson, two young NCOs who, like Cpl Wright, were loving every minute of life in war-torn Afghanistan. Cpl Pearson was a 24-year-old trained sniper and was keen to notch up a few more kills before 3 Para returned to the UK, but targets in Kajaki were far and few between.

Then, late in the morning of 6 September, everything changed. All was quiet until around 1130hrs in the morning when a soldier based at OP Arnhem spotted members of the Taliban brazenly setting up an illegal checkpoint in the area of a nearby town. It was a typical Taliban ploy to rob and intimidate the locals but for LCpl Hale and Cpl Pearson it was an opportunity, as one soldier later said, 'to kick some Taliban arse'. However, the Taliban were out of sniper range and indirect fire weapons, such as artillery and mortars, could not be used because they ran the very real risk of causing collateral damage.

If the Taliban were to be attacked, then the Paras would have to go to them. Hale and Pearson quickly cooked up a plan. Hale, the sniper, would lead a three-man patrol down to a position from where they would be able to take out the Taliban.

Hale briefed his team. He warned them about the mine threat and said that they would be using what he thought were 'safe routes'. Their route down would take them past what they believed was one of the largest minefields in the area, but despite not having a mine trace – a map marked with the known positions of minefields – Hale was confident.

Pearson, as the Commander of the OP, knew that permission had to be sought for Hale and the two other men to leave. He assumed that Hale would do this and Hale assumed that Pearson already had. In the event, no one told the neighbouring OP or the Joint Operations Centre (JOC) back at Camp Bastion that a sniper patrol was on the move. Time was critical. The soldiers put on their body armour and helmets and refilled their water bottles. Each man had a full complement of ammunition and a few rations to keep them going in case of an emergency. The patrol would move in bounds, with the distance of each bound dictated by the ground. This was a standard tactic and everyone knew what was expected.

The sun was high in the sky and the temperature was hitting almost 40°C by the time the three men left the OP and gingerly slipped and side-stepped down the steep slope.

Although the soldiers were now used to the scorching heat of the Afghan desert, they all loathed patrolling in the heat of the day. The landscape around Kajaki was hostile and unforgiving. The hills were steep and treeless and there was little, if any, shelter from the sun.

Back in OP Normandy, Cpl Wright scoured the landscape with his binoculars. The day had so far been mercifully quiet and he had planned to write home to his girlfriend and parents. Others within the patrol were lying in their cots or cleaning their weapons. 'Time for a brew,' said Cpl Wright to no one in particular, but the private soldiers were aware that it was a 'request' for one of them to start preparing a cup of tea.

Meanwhile, the three men began their approach. LCpl Hale reckoned it would take 20–30 minutes to reach a firing point from where he would be able to engage the Taliban. If he was lucky, he might be able to drop two or three before they realized that they were under sniper attack and departed. He was hoping to take them out with headshots. The psychological damage of seeing a fellow fighter's head disappear into a pink mist, he believed, would send the rest of them into a panic and enable him to pick them off.

However, as Hale moved into a *wadi*, which he hoped would provide him with a covered route to his firing point, he triggered an anti-personnel mine. In doing so he set-off a chain of events which would ultimately have devastating consequences. 'I'd got about 700m and had reached a tiny, dry river bed. I hopped over it and then found myself hopping back. It was like I had hit a spring and I remember thinking:

"That's strange what's going on here,"' he recalled in the *Daily Telegraph* after the incident.

> I ended up on my arse, looked down at my right hand and noticed that I was missing a finger. Then I looked down at what was left of my right leg. It was twisted at a weird angle at the knee and there was a bloody stump where my foot should have been. I realized immediately that I had stepped on a mine.

Hale had stepped on a mine which had probably been buried by the Russians up to 20 years earlier. With the sound of the explosion ringing in his ears, Hale's mind was filled with a sense of panic and disbelief. His right foot had gone and with it any chance of making it into the SAS, a dream he had harboured for several years. 'Fuck! Fuck! My Fucking leg's gone. Help me,' he shouted loudly. The pain was kicking in. The two soldiers with him initially looked on disbelief.

Back in OP Normandy, Cpl Wright had just brought a hot mug of tea to his lips when the blast from the mine rumbled round the valley. Everyone stopped. Initially, it was assumed that this was just another bout of Taliban harassing fire – but somehow this was different. 'Mine strike,' said Cpl Wright, out loud. The question was, who had triggered it? The answer came a few minutes later when a radio on the battle-group frequency squawked into life: 'Contact! Mine strike.'

The message was followed by a grid reference and a brief description of the injuries sustained. The time was 1212hrs and Cpl Wright knew immediately that for some unexplained reason a British patrol had strayed into a minefield. He quickly briefed his soldiers.

> Right, for some reason, someone from OP Arnhem has been injured in a mine strike and we are going to get them out. You five will come with me to the point of contact and you five will secure the area. Don't worry about helmets and body armour – it's too hot and we haven't got enough time. Just ammo and water. We've leaving in two minutes.

Back in the JOC at Camp Bastion everything stopped. The duty officer, like Cpl Wright, was initially confused – there was no patrolling programme for the Kajaki so in theory no friendly forces should be out on the ground.

Anti-personnel mines are not designed to kill. That would be too easy. Instead, they contain just enough high explosive to blow off a foot or half a leg. The resulting shock caused by the amputation can kill, as can the loss of blood.

Cpl Wright and nine soldiers ran down the hillside and headed towards the area of the blast. LCpl Paul Hartley, a member of the Royal Army Medical Corps who was based at the main Kajaki camp, also made his way to the minefield after he learned that a soldier had been injured.

By the time Cpl Wright's patrol arrived at the scene of the mine strike, LCpl Hale's condition had been stabilized. The blood loss had been stemmed by a tourniquet and field dressings had been wrapped around his bloody stump.

Cpl Wright immediately took command of the incident. He ordered half of his patrol to take up defensive positions while the others followed him. At this point none of the soldiers assumed they were in a minefield. No one carried out any drills to establish whether there were more mines present. Their sole focus was to get LCpl Hale to safety.

'Stu, Stu, don't worry mate,' Cpl Wright encouraged. 'We're gonna get you out.'

Back in Camp Bastion the Immediate Response Team – a Chinook crew and a medical team – were warned that there was a T1 casualty (a seriously injured soldier) in the Kajaki area. The crew were told that he had been injured in a mine strike. The time was 1222hrs.

By 1230hrs, Cpl Pearson had arrived at the scene and was told by Cpl Wright to recce for helicopter landing zones. Cpl Wright also told Pearson to watch out for mines. By now, Hale was being treated on a stretcher. At this stage, some of the soldiers were beginning to get nervous and were starting to believe that they may have walked into a mine area. For the first time, they began to employ the 'look, feel and prod' techniques that they were taught in their pre-deployment training. But the ground was too hard and identification of any mines was proving virtually impossible.

At the JOC in Bastion, the duty officer briefed Lt Col Stuart Tootal of the unfolding emergency. He also explained that he had asked the US for help and to send a medical evacuation helicopter fitted with a winch. Unfortunately, none of the RAF Chinooks have winches – all three winches which came out on the operation had been returned to the UK after a fault was discovered during routine maintenance. The time was 1236hrs.

Seven minutes later the US informed the British that they were tracking the incident but added that they would require high-level authorization before their helicopter could be deployed. Back in the JOC, nerves were beginning to fray. A British Para was lying critically wounded in a minefield and the Americans appeared to be more concerned with the formalities of proper procedure rather than saving the life of a fellow soldier.

At 1305hrs, almost an hour after LCpl Hale had first triggered the mine, the Chinook with the IRT team on board took off. At 1310hrs, the US finally gave permission for a Knight Hawk Combat Search and Rescue Helicopter, fitted with a winch, to be sent to the incident. Ten minutes later the JOC was informed that the US helicopter had broken down on the runway.

As Cpl Pearson returned from his HLS recce, he tried to follow the footsteps of his original path. In doing so, he slipped and stepped on a mine. The blast shredded his leg and left Cpl Wright peppered with shrapnel. Cpl Pearson's foot had disappeared and blood was gushing from the wound. No one moved. Cpl Wright dragged himself towards Cpl Pearson and applied a tourniquet to his damaged leg while Cpl Pearson self-administered morphine into his thigh. 'No one fucking move,' shouted Cpl Wright. 'We're in a minefield.' Silence descended, only to be broken by the groans of the injured and the whispered words of encouragement from Cpl Wright.

Then, amid the chaos and agony, the distant but distinctive sound of the IRT Chinook could be heard and the soldiers' flagging morale soared.

'Don't worry lads,' shouted Cpl Wright, 'We'll soon be out.'

But there was confusion. The pilot could not communicate with the soldiers on the ground because they didn't have the correct radios and when he tried to land he could only manage to get the rear wheels on the ground. The pilot had been told that there was a second casualty who has also been injured by a mine strike. It was too clear to the pilot that the injured soldiers were trapped in a mine-field. If he landed he risked detonating more mines and killing his entire crew as well as those on the ground. There was no other option than to abort the rescue mission. He ordered that no one should leave the aircraft and pulled away. What happened next has never been fully explained.

As the Chinook pulled away, a cloud of dust billowed across the minefield. A third mine exploded, severely wounding Cpl Wright and further injuring Cpl Pearson. Cpl Wright's arm was virtually severed. His nose and chin had been lacerated by shrapnel and his body was now riddled with blast injuries. However, despite being in terrible pain his prime concern was for his injured colleague.

At least one soldier who was at the incident claimed that, as the helicopter pulled away, an object hit Cpl Wright in the shoulder and exploded. An Army Board of Inquiry into the incident, however, decided that in all likelihood Cpl Wright probably detonated the mine while trying to shield the wounded Cpl Pearson from the dust and debris kicked up by the departing helicopter.

There were now three severely injured soldiers in the minefield. For the time being, at least, they were beyond rescue.

By this stage, LCpl Paul Hartley had arrived at the scene and could barely believe his eyes. Two men were lying close together, both clearly severely injured. One had lost a leg and the other was bleeding profusely from his arm.

LCpl Hartley was warned not to enter the minefield but he believed that those trapped inside would soon die unless they received urgent medical care. Resorting to desperation, he took off his large bergen and threw it in front of him. Using this technique, he cleared a path to Cpl Pearson and Cpl Wright and treated them both. Despite being severely injured, Cpl Wright remained in control of the situation and encouraged the other injured men to remain positive. Fusilier Andy Barlow, who was also trapped inside the area and had sustained some blast injuries, triggered another mine as he picked up a water bottle. The blast blew his leg off and floored LCpl Hartley, leaving him suffering from a condition called 'blast lung' which occurs when the force of a blast enters the lungs through an open mouth. Hartley said,

Initially I thought I might die. I had extreme difficulty in breathing due to blast lung. I could hear the other lads screaming and thought that if I could stand I knew I was still alive. For some reason I felt I wouldn't die that day and got across to Cpl Wright.

At the same time as treating Cpl Wright, he threw morphine to the other injured soldiers and told them how to administer it.

By this time there were seven injured soldiers caught in the minefield and three of them had lost legs.

LCpl Hartley attempted to stem the blood flow from a gaping wound in Cpl Wright's chest, but it was proving ineffective. After running out of bandages, he took off his own tee-shirt and used it as a makeshift field dressing.

Despite this horrific situation and the serious injuries he had himself sustained, Cpl Wright continued to command and control the incident. He remained conscious for the majority of the time, continually shouting encouragement to those around him, maintaining morale and calm amongst the many wounded men.

It would be another three-and-a-half hours before the men were hauled to safety by a replacement US Knight Hawk helicopter fitted with a winch. The injured were later transferred to the IRT Chinook which landed close to the camp's hospital. As the helicopter's tail gate was slowly lowered, the soldiers waiting to take them to theatre were greeted by a scene out of a horror film. Three of those on board had lost legs, while three others had sustained blast injuries. Cpl Wright was dead. After hanging on for so long, his shattered body finally gave up at the point of being winched from the minefield.

LCpl Hartley later described Cpl Wright as:

> the bravest man I ever knew. He exercised command and control throughout the incident giving direction and outstanding leadership in dire circumstances and was a calming influence on those who were severely wounded, even though he was fatally wounded himself. His presence contributed significantly to the eventual rescue and survival of those who were injured and prevented others from becoming casualties.

For his actions in the minefield, Cpl Wright was posthumously awarded the George Cross. Cpl Pearson received the Queen's Gallantry Medal.

The day was not yet done. Elsewhere in Helmand, British troops were under attack. Before 6 September was over, another soldier would die.

LCpl Luke McCulloch, a member of the Royal Irish Regiment, had volunteered to serve in Afghanistan. When the call went up for extra troops, he was one of the first in line to offer his services. He was one of that rare breed of men who excel on the battlefield. His relatively short life came to an end in an orchard in Sangin. The 21-year-old Lance Corporal had taken off his helmet during a briefing as he and a few other soldiers took shelter from the harsh early afternoon sun amongst the trees, just beyond the perimeter of the Sangin DC.

Corporal Trevor 'Speedy' Coult, who had won a Military Cross a few months earlier after fighting insurgents in Iraq, was a few feet away from LCpl McCulloch when he was killed. As reported in the *Sunday Mirror* on 22 October 2006, he recalled:

We were being briefed in an orchard just outside our small base in Sangin. Luke was there, tucking into some rations as we listened. There was no warning as the mortars began coming in. One landed just 2m away from me and Luke. Incredibly, I wasn't touched but he was hit in the head. I looked down and for a split second I was too shocked to move. There was a lot of blood. Then my training kicked in and I was down next to him applying a field dressing and trying to get him up. The mortars were still coming in as we got him on to a stretcher and ran through the explosions towards the base medical station. His pulse and his breathing were weak but he was still alive at that point.

The explosions had also caused LCpl McCulloch's windpipe to become blocked and in a desperate bid to save his life the base medics were forced to cut a hole in his neck.

'The medics were incredible,' said Cpl Coult, 31, from Belfast. 'We were still under fire. They got him breathing again but we had to get him on a helicopter and back to the main base. This meant getting to the helicopter landing zone and we were still under heavy fire.'

Badly injured but still breathing, LCpl McCulloch was loaded on to a Scimitar armoured vehicle to give some protection against the mortar bombs exploding around them, and driven to the landing zone (LZ). Cpl Coult continued:

He was still alive but we were taking a huge amount of fire. We went round and round the LZ, firing and trying to clear it. But it was incredibly hot. I heard the Chinook coming in and when it got close the Taliban started pouring fire in towards it. They must have known we had a casualty and this was a perfect opportunity to bring down a Chinook. They were firing RPGs, small arms and machine-gun fire but it still came in. The pilot and crew were incredibly brave.

LCpl McCulloch was loaded safely aboard, but in the 30 minutes in which it took the helicopter to fly to Camp Bastion he had stopped breathing. 'They tried to revive him in hospital but there was nothing they could do. He was only 21.'

It was one of the worst days in one of the worst weeks of the entire operation. As the news of the deaths of Cpl Wright and LCpl McCulloch and the various injuries began to circulate through the camps strung across northern Helmand, many men broke down and wept openly. Both men were hugely popular and both were due to return to their families in the UK in the next few weeks.

As many of the events in Helmand have made clear, one piece of military equipment which was vital to the success of the mission in Afghanistan was the Chinook transport helicopter. Without it, many missions would have been impossible. Right from the early planning stages of Operation Herrick, it was obvious to the commanders and staff officers in 16 Air Assault Brigade that the over-arching limiting factor was the shortage of Chinooks.

The Paras were used to working alongside the RAF Chinook crews and had established procedures for operating with helicopters in combat zones. Prior to their deployment in Afghanistan, all NCOs were trained to talk to Chinook pilots and direct them into landing zones. Each unit deployed on operations had a sufficient number of troops trained as Helicopter Handling Teams (HHT), who were able to rig under-slung loads at day or night to enable the resupply of patrols or outposts to be conducted quickly and efficiently.

Prior to the deployment in Afghanistan, the brigade became used to integrating the capabilities of the awesome Apache helicopter in ground operations. It was clear to the troops that a time would come when their survival would depend on their ability to communicate effectively with Apache pilots during combat. If troops were unable to give the Apache pilots accurate and timely information under the immense pressures imposed by combat, vital seconds would be lost, possibly resulting in the death or injury of colleagues.

Training rules meant that the Apaches could only fire their weapons at targets which were at least 1,800m away from friendly troops. The realities of daily life in Helmand, however, meant that the Apaches were often attacking targets just 30m away from friendly forces.

The management of all helicopter assets were conducted by the Air Cell, which was commanded by Captain Mark Swann, the Air Operations Officer. Capt Swann and his team were responsible for the resupply of all combat outposts, the movement of troops during routine changeovers and the regular movement of troops from the main base areas of Kandahar, Camp Bastion, Lashkar Gar and Gereshk. The team was also responsible for the planning, coordination and execution of all air-manoeuvre aspects of deliberate and reactive operations. The Air Cell also had to manage the battle group's Immediate Response Team, which consisted of an eight-man section and a four-man medical emergency team, which included a doctor. To enable this to be on permanent call, one of the battle group's Chinooks was designated as the IRT aircraft and placed on a reduced 'notice to move'.

At the beginning of the tour, the tempo of operations was relatively easy to handle but after the first month, when the number of engagements with the enemy began to rise and the area of operations began to expand, the pressure on the Air Cell, the helicopters and their crews became almost unbearable.

In the months from May to September 2006, all five outstations in northern Helmand were considered as Amber Land Zones. This meant that there was a very real risk that the Chinooks would be attacked and possibly destroyed either on landing or take-off. The knock-on effect of this meant that even the most routine of journeys, a fresh water resupply for example, would require support from Apaches and ground attack aircraft, while ground troops would need to be deployed beyond the base in a large-scale operation to counter direct and indirect attacks from the Taliban.

As the months progressed, the Chinooks were regularly attacked when they attempted to conduct RIPs, resupplies or casevacs. By the start of July, the attacks which occurred in Musa Qala were so intense that every time an aircraft landed it was fired upon, so a decision was taken to make it a Red LZ. This meant that an aircraft could only go in there to collect a priority T1 casualty, i.e. someone who was very seriously injured. Troops in Musa Qala were often critically low on supplies and when an IRT deployment was required to collect a casualty, the aircraft would be filled with bags of mortar ammunition and medical equipment. The threat was so high at the outpost that Lt Col Tootal ruled that aircraft would only spend 20 seconds on the ground before the pilots lifted off. To achieve this, the IRT became practised in unloading the equipment from one side of the tailgate of the Chinook while the troops loaded casualties into the other side. The risk to the aircraft was huge and it was only directly due to the bravery of the load-masters and the pilots that no aircraft were lost and that many of the resupply missions could take place. It was also critical that rifle companies rehearsed their exit drills prior to an operation so that they could offload up to 43 troops in full fighting order and a quad bike in less than 20 seconds.

The troops on the ground in Musa Qala became aware of the threat to the aircraft and had to accept that if they were injured their casevac could not be guaranteed. At the time, the level of the threat facing troops in Musa Qala was never made public. It became the standard procedure during an IRT pick-up for the doctor in Camp Bastion to speak to the doctor at the outstation to ascertain how much time the casualty had before he became critical.

Such were the dangers facing helicopter crews entering Musa Qala that Lt Col Tootal was forced on several occasions to delay casevac operations until the threat posed by the Taliban had either been neutralized or dissipated. This was also the case in Sangin. It was therefore up to the medical staff at the District Centres to keep injured troops alive until rescue came. The RAF Chinook pilots showed immense bravery on many of these rescue missions. Aircraft were often hit with small arms fire or shrapnel but time and again the pilots flew into the British bases to retrieve the wounded.

Helicopter operations were also restricted by RAF rules which dictated that air crews needed 10 hours rest in every 24 and that 8 of these rest hours needed to be undisturbed. This was at times immensely frustrating for the Army commanders who often found the attitude of the RAF pilots exasperating. However, the consequence of breaching this rule could be the loss of a Chinook packed with 40 soldiers, which would be catastrophic.

Such was the importance of flying time that it became essential that both Apache and Chinook helicopter hours were scrutinized prior to the planning stage of a deliberate operation to ensure there would be enough aircraft available to transport the troops and provide them with air cover.

After months of denying that more troops were needed in Afghanistan, and obfuscation over the real level of fighting and the number of casualties being sustained by the British, Des Browne, the Defence Secretary, finally admitted that the military planners who sent the Paras into Afghanistan had seriously underestimated the tenacity of the Taliban. In a speech to the Royal United Services Institute in London, Mr Browne said, 'The Taliban's tenacity in the face of massive losses had been a surprise, absorbing more of our effort than we predicted it would and consequently slowing progress on recon-struction.'

During the speech the Defence Secretary called on other NATO coun-tries to shoulder some of the load being faced by British troops in Helmand. He called on those countries that had yet to send troops to supply an additional 2,500, and he called on those countries with troops already in Afghanistan to change their rules of engagement to allow them to fight. As we shall see in later chapters, Mr Browne's call fell on deaf ears.

The original plan devised by Brig Butler, Lt Col Tootal and 16 Air Assault Brigade's planning staff had been predicated on the assumption that just one company group of around 120 men would be deployed to a single outstation called Forward Operating Base (FOB) Price, which was located on the outskirts of Gereshk. The increasing commitments imposed upon the brigade, following the arrival of the Taliban in a series of strategically important towns in northern Helmand, meant that an additional five outstations had to be manned and the net effect of this was that the brigade had virtually lost its 'manoeuvre capability'. In simple terms, this meant that Brig Ed Butler and Lt Col Tootal could no longer attack the Taliban at the time and place of their choosing. Instead, they had to wait for the Taliban to come to them.

However, British Army officers are encouraged to turn every devel-opment on the battlefield, including both successes and failures, to their own advantage. With his Special Forces background, Brig Butler knew that it was vital to take the fight to the Taliban if the long-term strategy was to be successful and so the concept of the Manoeuvre Outreach Group (MOG) was developed. Essentially, the MOGs conducted long-range reconnaissance patrols in the areas between the outstations, principally between Nowzad and Musa Qala but later down to Garmsir in the south. The patrolling included visits to local villages so that the brigade could engage with the elders whilst at the same time interdicting or attacking the Taliban's lines of communication and threatening their flanks.

The MOGs were formed around 3 Para Patrols Platoon, an Estonian attached platoon mounted in armoured personnel carriers and half a squadron of the Household Cavalry Regiment. The force was bolstered by a Fire Support Group consisting of 10 to 14 Wmik Land Rovers, each mounted with a 7.62 mm GPMG and a .50 Calibre heavy machine-gun. The Fire Support Group would also be equipped with Javelin and Milan rockets. MOGs were supported by three 105mm light guns and an Unmanned Air Vehicle detachment provided by 7 Royal Household Artillery and 32 Royal Artillery Regiment. The Patrols Platoon was organized into five patrols, supported by medics and engineers. Additional infantry were also attached, when available, and were used to secure choke points in complex or close country where the risk of ambush was high. However, the pressure to man the outstations which were under attack virtually every day meant that the additional manpower was rarely available. The platoon occasionally went on operations with the Household Cavalry when they were not working independently and when this occurred it was not uncommon for 30 to 35 vehicles to be deployed on operations at the same time. MOGs were also often supported by a variety of different aircraft including Apaches, Chinooks, A–10s, B1 Bombers and the Harrier GR7s based at Kandahar.

Overall command of the MOGs rested with Captain T.D. Fehley, Officer Commanding 3 Para patrols, who answered directly to the Commanding Officer of 3 Para. Manoeuvring an organization of this size in difficult and complex terrain was fraught with difficulty and the biggest problems that the MOGs faced, apart from being attacked by the Taliban, were communication or vehicle breakdown. Where possible, the vehicles would be repaired in situ. If this could not be achieved, the vehicle would either be extracted by Chinook to Camp Bastion or simply destroyed.

The MOGs were also used to conduct the more mundane, but equally important, task of convoy escort duties through the desert to resupply the outstations. These were complex operations in themselves and were often attacked by the Taliban, resulting in several British casualties.

A 500lb bomb dropped by an RAF Harrier in late August 2006 explodes close to the British base in Sangin. During the late summer of 2006, the base was under almost constant attack and air strikes were called in virtually every day.

A captured Taliban suspect flanked by two members of 3 Para on board a Chinook helicopter, Helmand 2006. The individual would have been taken to a holding facility in Camp Bastion before being passed over to the Afghan authorities.

A smiling Para guards the approaches to the Sangin base in August 2006 with a .50 calibre heavy machine-gun. Spent cases below the weapon are testimony to the heavy fighting which took place in August 2006.

A dead Taliban gunman killed during a firefight with the Paras in the Green Zone. August 2006.

The telescopic sight of a .50 calibre heavy machine-gun is trained on two civilians as they approach the British base at Gereshk. Summer 2006.

Sean Rayment (second from right) on Operation Palk Ghar. To his left is Lt Matt Fyjis-Walker, the company's Forward Air Controller.

Major Phil 'Angry' Messenger, Commander of C Company 1st Battalion The Royal Anglian Regiment during the operation to 'clear' the Taliban out of the Green Zone.

An exhausted British soldier at Operation Palk Ghar. September 2007.

(above) A makeshift memorial to the British soldiers killed at FOB Inkerman. August 2007. (right) Poem dedicated to Guardsman Tony Downes, 1st Battalion Grenadier Guards, who was killed on 9 June 2007 when his vehicle was hit by an Taliban IED.

POPULATION ...... TALIBAN

GET IT UP YOU TERRY

· Behind a sanger in Jusalay we sit,
Waiting for another RPG or Mortor hit.

· Sometime today it'll happen again for sure,
Terry Taliban will finish second once more.

· We'll man our guns and hit him back,
Hoping to put him in a black plastic sack.

· GMG, Javelin and ·50 cal,
You'll learn right quick your not our pal.

· When Mortars land around you and above your head,
Your filthy skinny little bodies it will shred.

· With you your evil, your cruelty and hate will die,
I promise you now one will ever cry.

· Your bullies, your cowards, like a digusting pest,
When your all in a grave thats when we'll rest.

· Your bastard IED took our mate Downesy; life,
But all that did was create you a world of strife!

· Not even Allah will be able to help you out,
Cause all you'll hear is INKERMAN's victory shout!!

R.I.P.

'Downesy'
Gone but never forgotten!

Soldiers washing in the Helmand River, Sangin District Centre base. September 2007.

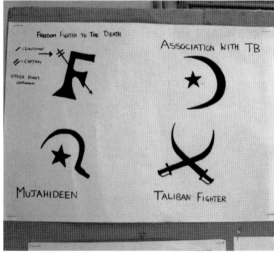

(left) Sergeant Simon Panter of 1st Battalion The Royal Anglian Regiment poses with a captured AK47 just hours after he killed three Taliban fighters in the Green Zone in August 2007.
(above) Poster showing tattoos warn by Taliban fighters. Sangin, September 2007.

The Killing Zone, Helmand Valley, September 2007.

3 Para could sustain one MOG deployed in the field indefinitely, but could also 'surge' to have three MOGs deployed simultaneously for limited periods. The MOGs were resupplied by Chinook helicopters and would typically spend up to 14 days in the desert, returning to Camp Bastion for a 2-day maintenance period before redeploying on another mission. However, the more complex the vehicles, the more time would be spent in Camp Bastion. Thus, when the Household Cavalry Regiment units returned from a 14-day mission they would invariably spend longer in Camp Bastion, a situation which was further exacerbated by the poor provision of spares.

Movement by vehicle in Helmand is never a simple exercise. Despite the vast numbers of patrols conducted by the MOGs, many which occurred without incident, they could never allow their guard to drop or become complacent. Potential choke points on routes had to be treated with extreme caution. If additional troops were not available to dominate the ground around a so-called 'Vulnerable Point' – any piece of ground which might be exploited by the Taliban to attack British troops – then the patrol would have to break into smaller, more versatile packets to over-watch and clear an area of Taliban or hidden IEDs.

Engineers became a vital addition to the MOGs and were frequently used to clear crossing-points that may have been mined. Although the threat from old Soviet mines was ever-present, the real risk was from mines laid deliberately in the vicinity of the crossing-points. Wherever possible, the MOGs adopted a 'soft' posture, meaning they would enter villages in daylight and make a concerted attempt to seek out and engage with the village elders.

Such tactics were less demanding on manpower and also meant that patrols had the ability to demonstrate that they could 'escalate' their response whenever needed, something which was bound to unnerve the Taliban. Patrol commanders soon learnt that it was vital to establish a meeting with a village elder as soon as possible so that they could assess any Quick Impact Projects (QIP) that the provincial reconstruction teams might be able to provide. These could vary from building a well for fresh water to giving children pens and colouring pencils.

During their tenure of operations, MOGs experienced numerous contacts with the Taliban and made a significant difference in terms of distracting the enemy away from the outstations. Intelligence indicated that the Taliban were unsettled by their presence, as they were unpredictable and more difficult to observe.

Manpower pressure on the 3 Para, even before they departed for Operation Herrick, meant that a call went out far and wide across the brigade for volunteers to form an extra platoon of men. The Royal Irish Regiment was an obvious choice. The 1st Battalion based at Fort George, near Inverness in Scotland, had proved its worth in Iraq just a few months earlier and was full of tough and well-trained soldiers. Ranger Platoon was formed in early 2006 and joined 3 Para in April of that year.

Such was the intensity of the conflict, however, that by July 2006 Lieutenant Colonel Mike McGovern, the Commanding Officer of 1 Royal Irish, had been asked by Brig Butler whether he could find more volunteers. Lt Col McGovern, a straight-talking professional officer, simply replied: 'How many do you want and when do you want them by?'

Somme and Barossa Platoons were formed from the 1st Battalion's D and B companies respectively. A mortar section was attached and the men left for a brief but intense period of training and acclimatization in Oman. The soldiers left in no doubt as to what to expect when they arrived in Helmand. They were warned that they would be fighting a brutal and confident enemy and that there was every chance some of them might not be coming home.

When the Royal Irish soldiers arrived in June 2006, such was their eagerness for the fight that they were disappointed to learn that their first role would be to help with the reinforcement of Camp Bastion's security. 'All this way and all that training to stag on in a sangar', one Ranger noted at the time.

However, just four days after they arrived in theatre, the Royal Irish were told to prepare for operations. Somme Platoon and the mortar section were given orders to reinforce the Danish recce platoon which had taken over from the Pathfinders at Musa Qala.

Within three days of arriving in Musa Qala, the Royal Irish sustained two casualties with gunshot wounds. From the moment they arrived inside the District Centre, the Royal Irish troops knew that they were going to be in for a tough fight, but taking two casualties in such a short space of time was unexpected. If the fighting continued with such ferocity and casualties were sustained at such a rate, it would be just a matter of weeks, if not days, before the reinforcements themselves needed to be reinforced.

Like elsewhere in Helmand, the soldiers came under fire every day and night with RPGs, mortars and rockets in a series of well-planned and coordinated attacks. Yet, as the Pathfinders had already found, life in Musa Qala could be even worse than in the other locations where British troops were based. The helicopter landing zone could not be secured because of its position and every time Chinooks came in to extract casualties or deliver supplies it came under fire. As already described, Musa Qala had been declared a Red landing zone: helicopters would only be dispatched as a matter of extreme necessity. A Chinook was worth more than the life of a British soldier – and every man knew it. Those troops based in Musa Qala had to live with the fact that Lt Col Stuart Tootal would not risk losing a Chinook, even if it meant that an injured man could die because he could not get to an operating table.

On 24 August, the Danish squadron was extracted and was replaced by Barossa Platoon and a headquarters element from 3 Para. Composed of around 65 members of the Royal Irish and a dozen Paras, the new unit was called 'Easy' Company. Within hours of the Danish soldiers leaving, the base came under a fierce and sustained attack. Either the Taliban thought that the whole base was about to be abandoned or they had assumed, wrongly, that those inside had thrown in the towel. For weeks on end, the battle raged around Musa Qala. Close air support was called for on a daily basis. Bombs were dropped and rockets were fired at 'danger close' ranges of less than 30m.

The sense of isolation felt by those troops based in Musa Qala only served to make them a more solid and durable unit. They viewed themselves as being 'cut-off' from the rest of the brigade and they revelled in the challenge. And the troops really were effectively cut-off due to the landing zone situation. For weeks, the troops had to survive on ration packs and drank well water which had to be purified with sterilizing tablets.

For many, close combat fighting was exactly what they joined the Army for but they never thought they would be given the opportunity to experience it. During some of the battles in Musa Qala, hand grenades had to be thrown over walls to stop the Taliban gaining entry into the base. Such was the intensity of the fighting that nearly a quarter of all the link ammunition for the 7.62mm GPMGs used during the entire Operation Herrick 4 was spent at Musa Qala, as was nearly 50 per cent of grenades.

Like Sangin, 20km further south, Musa Qala was now effectively a ghost town. Weeks of non-stop fighting had forced the vast majority of locals to leave. The fighting died down at night – a lack of night-vision equipment meant that Taliban attacks in the hours of darkness were either rare or uncoordinated – when a comforting quiet would descend on the DC, during which time one soldier said:

> Looking up at the stars on a hot August evening, it was sometimes possible, for a few minutes at least, to imagine that you were some-where else. The night sky was beautifully clear. It was inky black and you felt as though you could see the whole of the galaxy – it was quite awe inspiring. It was my own way of escaping the madness that was beyond the walls of our compound.

Such was the intensity of the fighting that it was only a matter of time before the beleaguered force was to sustain its first fatal casualty. At around 1600hrs on Friday, 1 September, during a particularly ferocious attack on the base, Ranger Anare Draiva, a 27-year-old Fijian, was killed when a mortar round landed directly on a sangar. LCpl Paul Muirhead, 29, was seriously injured in the same incident and died five days later.

The deaths were a devastating blow to the men within the DC. Both men were popular members of the company and many felt as though they had lost a member of their own family.

Of Ranger Draiva, Lt Col Michael McGovern, his Commanding Officer said:

> He was a superb, strong and courageous soldier. He performed brilliantly well in his recent tour of Southern Iraq and was one of the first to volunteer for the tour of Afghanistan. His contribution in Helmand Province in extremely challenging conditions has been second to none and those that know Draiva will not be surprised that he was killed in action, in the face of the enemy, defending his comrades and base.

His body was returned to his parents in Fiji, via the UK, and was accom-panied by a detachment of his colleagues who ensured that he was given a military funeral – a fact that was never reported by the British press.

As well as these deaths, a further 12 soldiers were injured in Musa Qala at around that time. During one battle in August 2006, Lieutenant Paul Martin and six other soldiers from an eight-man section were injured when a mortar round exploded close to their position. The soldiers had been attempting to secure a rooftop vantage point known as the Alamo. Lt Martin told the BBC:

I didn't know how many were injured at that point because there was a lot of smoke and noise. I didn't know I was injured. It's that old cliché about the adrenaline going. I felt very winded and, with all that was going on, quite disorientated. I got down off the roof to get stretchers.

With blood seeping down his left side, the officer ended up being carted away from the scene on a stretcher he had originally been carrying. Lt Martin found himself in a frantic fight to save his life. He said, 'I had a ruptured spleen and a collapsed lung. I was drowning in my own blood.' One piece of shrapnel, about the size of a thumbnail, remains very near his heart. Others of a similar size are lodged on the edge of a bone in his left arm and in his left lung.

After he recovered from his injuries, Lt Martin said:

I've been told that the piece of shrapnel, 1cm from my heart, is cocooned in human tissue and looks stable and looks fine. 'Will it shift?' is a question that crosses my mind. What would happen if I was in a car accident, or someone punched me, or a grenade goes off near me? Will it shift to the right? I'm told that for it to move would take another explosion like the one I was in and if that happens then I reckon I pretty much deserve it.

While most of 16 Air Assault Brigade started to return to the UK in late September 2006, to be replaced by 3 Commando Brigade, soldiers from the Royal Regiment of Fusiliers based in Nowzad were ordered to stay firm while events unfolded in nearby Musa Qala. The locals in Musa Qala were fed up with the fighting which had raged around them for months on end and so they brokered a ceasefire in which they gave assurances that no Taliban would be allowed to enter the town. The locals told Governor Daud that they would police the ceasefire themselves and so they did, for 35 days. The initial success of the peace deal led to a further round of negotiations in which the elders would guarantee the stability, security and governance of the region, providing the NATO troops withdrew. In many respects this was exactly the type of solution Brig Butler and the NATO chiefs were after. They wanted the tribal leaders and village elders to tell the Taliban that they were not welcome – it would take courage on their part – but at least this was a start. It later emerged that the British actually agreed to the deal just 48 hours before they had planned to abandon the base at Musa Qala anyway because it was simply too costly to hold.

It was agreed that the troops would leave by vehicles, rather than by helicopter, but the only vehicles available were the so-called 'Jingli' trucks, a type of flat-bed lorry seen around Asia which is decorated with bright colours and ornaments. And so, in the early hours of Tuesday, 17 October 2006, truck-loads of British troops left the base, which they had spent countless hours defending. It was a high-risk strategy. The trucks afforded zero protection and made the soldiers inside incredibly vulnerable to ambush by the Taliban. One by one, the trucks left the District Centre, each one packed with soldiers with their weapons pointing out. Each man was surveying the buildings in front of him with eagle-eyes, waiting for the attack they all expected to start. Many locals lined the streets as the trucks drove out of town. There was waving, but no cheering or jeering. Gradually, the trucks moved off into the distance, full of relieved men, looking forward to a comfortable bed, a hot shower and some fresh food, all three of which had been in short supply for many weeks. Many of the locals were no doubt delighted to see the backs of the British troops, for that would surely lead to peace. But who would fill the vacuum? Could the tribal elders really keep the Taliban out of the town?

Many within NATO's high command, especially the Americans, were uneasy with the truce. They thought that it would demonstrate to the Afghans and the Taliban that NATO was weak and did not have the stomach for a fight. Those same complaints resurfaced a few months later when, following the death of a leading Taliban figure in a US air strike, the Taliban retook the town. The town was still in the hands of the Taliban by the end of October 2007 and looked as though it would remain so for some time to come. When I was in Helmand, in September 2007, there was much talk of the taking of the town being the next big push for the British troops in Helmand, an operation which was due to take place in the spring of 2008 with the return of the Paras of 16 Air Assault Brigade. However, as will be described later, the town actually fell to NATO forces in December 2007 when a large-scale operation involving soldiers, marines and US troops and Special Forces pushed the Taliban out after an air bombardment lasting several days.

As a footnote to this chapter, it must be said that the volunteers from the Royal Irish Regiment were some of the many unsung heroes of the Afghan mission in 2006. Many of them had only just returned from six months in Iraq when they volunteered to serve in Afghanistan. Their contribution was huge and without them it was likely that some of the outstations would have fallen. Despite their incredible heroics, they received little official recognition. While honours and awards were heaped on the airborne forces, the men of 1 Royal Irish received just one Military Cross and a single Mention in Dispatches, and that was for LCpl Luke McCulloch who was killed in action in Sangin.

Towards the end of September 2006, the Pathfinders and the soldiers of A Company became the first members of 16 Air Assault Brigade to return to the UK, for they had been the first to deploy.

It had been a long and bloody tour. No one who took part in the tour will ever forget it. It is fitting to remind ourselves of the Defence Secretary's ambitions when he announced that British troops would be going to Helmand: he hoped British troops would return 'without firing one shot'. In the six months that followed, the men and women of 16 Air Assault Brigade fought in more than 500 contacts, with half a million rounds of small arms and over 13,000 artillery and mortar rounds being fired. The Apache was used for the first time and RAF Chinooks were involved in more than 100 casualty extraction missions. Almost 200 soldiers were injured and 33 were killed in action. At times, it seemed like the mission was doomed to fail, but the indomitable fighting spirit of the British airborne soldier kept it alive. Paratroopers, the average age of whom was just 19, lived and fought in atrocious conditions where temperatures could often reach 50°C and where there was no guarantee of being resupplied with food, water and ammunition.

In short, it was one of the most remarkable six months in British military history in the last 50 years.

8

WINTER WAR

Having been pipped at the post by the Paras – their historical rivals – as the lead unit to enter Helmand in early 2006, the Commandos were itching to get their feet into the dust of the Helmand desert. Their initial desire to do battle with the Taliban may have been slightly dampened, however, as the news began to gradually emerge that the campaign in Helmand was like no other in recent memory.

As the Paras departed Camp Bastion, relieved that they had survived the incredibly intense conflict, so the Marines arrived after a lengthy and tiring journey, via Kabul, from the middle of September 2006 onwards.

For the Paras, the mission had largely been a step into the great unknown, but the Marines, courtesy of press reports and daily intelligence reports, more or less knew what to expect. Yet, despite all of the preparation, recces and training, the daunting reality of the harshness of the Helmand desert still came as an unpleasant shock.

Peering through the small windows of the RAF Hercules as it flew into Camp Bastion, the Marines were awestruck by the land beneath them. One young marine described the scene as a 'biblical, barren land' which reminded him of the film, *The Life of Brian*.

The changeover of units, such as was taking place between 16 Air Assault Brigade and 3 Commando Brigade, is described as a 'roulement', a period of time which may take up to a month as the units replace each other in theatre. In theory, the replacement troops should spend at least two weeks learning the ropes from those who have spent the last six months in theatre, thus sustaining operational continuity. For the soldiers handing over a base or undertaking a specific task, such as training the ANA and ANP, it can be as challenging a period as it is for those taking over. The prospects of leave, seeing family and friends, and the safety of the UK are beckoning on the horizon, while at the same time it is clear to all that the amount and quality of information which can be passed on will help to save lives. Consequently, units briefly merge together so that joint patrols can be conducted and soldiers at the very basic level can pass on small but hugely significant pieces of information, such as 'Every time we leave the base, the children run up to us. The only time they didn't was when we were attacked with an RPG.' So, if the same thing happens again, the fresh troops will know to expect trouble.

The first Royal Marines to arrive were members of L Company, 42 Commando, with elements of M Company. After a period of 'Reception, Staging and Onward Integration' (RSOI) training, the M Company elements deployed to Kajaki and L Company relieved 3 Para in Sangin. Members of M Company had learnt that they were going to be deployed to Kajaki just two weeks before they left the UK.

When the Marines arrived the accommodation was sparse and consisted of just a few sangars, but within a matter of weeks the new incumbents had built a gym and a shower. The troops lived off ten-man ration packs and drank purified water from the dam. Slowly but surely, the base became the Marines' home.

The Marines also discovered a house which they christened the 'Honking House'. The building dated back to the Soviet invasion. Local legend in the area claimed that it was the scene of barbaric torture. It served as a grim reminder of the brutal history of Afghanistan.

Throughout September and into October, the Marines continued to arrive at Camp Bastion. Everyday, awestruck young Commandos stepped off the tailgate of a Hercules after it touched down on to the base's makeshift airstrip and into the unknown – many were scared and they were aware that not all of their number would be returning to their loved ones in the UK.

The K Company advance party arrived on 23 September 2006 and was rapidly followed by K Company main body under the command of Major Neil Sutherland. The Marines spent the next few days getting used to life in Helmand and there was a lot to get done. First they were given the latest intelligence picture and then there followed a series of talks on everything from snake bites to driving in Helmand. Most of these took place in tents with little or no air-conditioning. The Marines called it 'death by briefing'. Weapons training followed the briefings and the troops began to focus their minds on the dangers of the mission which lay ahead.

A few days later K Company deployed to FOB Price on the outskirts of Gereshk, an area which, although within the so-called Helmand development zone, was increasingly falling under the influence of the Taliban. The company conducted both foot and mobile patrols and had their first taste of battle with the Taliban when they came under mortar and small arms fire.

The Paras had been through tough battles and had seen many of their colleagues become casualties of war. However, the Commandos were keen to take a different approach to the Paras, whom many believed had adopted an over-aggressive posture. One member of the Commando Brigade described the Paras as 'airborne and furious cloud punchers'.

The Commandos were particularly intent on dealing with the ever-present threat from suicide bombers in their own way. They had watched the Paras in action during the handover period and thought that their stance was too antagonistic – this was especially the case amongst those members of the UK Landing Force Command Support Group based at Lashkar Gar.

Such considerations changed dramatically on 19 October when 22-year-old Marine Gareth Wright became the first member of the British armed forces in Helmand to be killed by a suicide bomber. Mne Wright was providing top cover for a mobile patrol as it passed through the centre of Lashkar Gar when the vehicle was attacked by a lone member of the Taliban wearing a concealed suicide vest. The vest contained several pounds of explosives into which had been pressed dozens of small, steel ball bearings.

The attack was a classic ambush. The two-vehicle Marine patrol slowed as it approached a junction. None of the troops in either of the Snatch Land Rovers noticed anything suspicious about the young man chatting to children at a roadside foodstall. His skin was slightly darker than that of the locals in Lashkar Gar, but as the town is on one of the main transit routes up from the Pakistan border, his presence prompted no real concern. The unknown bomber, accompanied by several children, walked up to the side of the vehicle and detonated the vest. The bomber died instantly, as did two young children who had been standing nearby. Mne Gareth Wright, a Glaswegian, caught the full blast of the bomb. He died immediately. It was a scene of utter carnage, with body parts littering the streets. Two of Mne Wright's colleagues were also injured in the attack, one seriously. Medics rushed to the scene which was about 2km from the British base in the town, but nothing could be done to save the life of Mne Wright.

His death had a devastating impact on the Marines based in the town. On learning the news, many men, including some seasoned campaigners who had seen action in Iraq just a year or so earlier, openly cried and hugged each other for comfort.

During my first visit to Helmand in 2006, LCpl Rob Woods, who was a friend of Marine Wright and was also based in Lashkar Gar, told me of the moment when he learnt of his death:

I cried my eyes out. I'm not ashamed to admit it. He was a friend. We both loved motorbikes and I was devastated. One of the sergeants came over to me and just gave me a hug. A lot of blokes cried but it's odd because I don't really feel anything now. The older guys who have experienced this before tell me that the grief will kick in when we return home.

The attack was a defining moment for the Commandos in Helmand. The threat they had all feared – an attack by a lone suicide bomber – was now a reality. Intelligence reports suggested that there were at least six suicide bombers in the town waiting to attack the Commandos. The troops' attitude changed immediately and questions over the suitability of the initial 'softly, softly' tactics were raised. Had they invited the attack by attempting to interact more closely with the locals? Had the Taliban spotted this approach and viewed it as a weakness which they could exploit? Whatever the answers, the Marines, to their credit, were back out on the streets of the town within hours of the attack. This time, however, they were firmly focused on keeping their distance from the locals. People driving cars or riding motorbikes and even bicycles were warned to keep their distance. Anyone foolish enough to ignore these warnings risked being shot dead. A public information campaign was launched in which the Afghans were told to keep their distance from British patrols, especially when driving cars.

The Marines were taught the Pashto word for stop, *drezh*, which would be shouted with aggression and often fear as a vehicle approached. The troops would also raise a clenched fist, another sign to stop. If these actions were ignored, a mini-flare would be fired into the air, followed by shots into the ground. If time allowed, troops were briefed to then fire into the engine block and, if the driver still failed to stop after all of these measures had been employed, troops were cleared to use lethal force by firing directly at the driver. These rules were, however, only to be used as a guide and troops were expected to treat each incident separately and open fire as and when they suspected they might actually be under attack.

Imagine the scene: you are the point-man of a patrol slowly walking down a narrow back street in one of the slum areas of Lashkar Gar. The street is bordered by thick mud walls 7m high. The sense of being boxed in is very real and there is nowhere to hide if someone decides to drive a car bomb into your patrol.

You have been on patrol for three hours. It is the second patrol of the day and the fifteenth you have completed that week. Dusk is approaching and there is no street lighting. As point-man, your job is to provide the commander with an early warning of anything that appears suspicious. You are his eyes and ears and as such you are likely to be the first person to open fire or killed if attacked. One mistake could result in your death, that of a patrol member or even of an innocent civilian. Oh yes, and you are 19 years old and this is your first operational tour – 12 months ago you were a civilian working in an office. Curiously, you note, the children who were playing in the same street at the same time a few days ago are absent. Suddenly, a car turns a corner and is heading towards your patrol. The headlights are on full-beam and the driver is travelling far too fast for the road conditions. Your mind tracks back to the intelligence brief you received a few hours earlier when you were warned that there were thought to be half a dozen suicide bombers in the town planning attacks against the British.

The driver is now just 100m away. Surely he must have seen us, you say to yourself. You stand in the middle of the street, raise a clenched fist and shout 'Drezh. Drezh.' The index finger on the hand holding your SA–80 assault rifle flicks off the safety catch. A colleague fires a mini-flare into the air, which momentarily lights up the darkening sky. The driver fails to stop. Has he seen us? Is he drunk or high on hash? Or is he a suicide bomber about to wipe out the patrol? At best, you have three seconds to decide. There is no time to ask for advice. You have the best view of the situation: you have to make the call. You bring your rifle up into the firing position and fire two rounds into the road ahead of the car. The first is a tracer round and it ricochets skywards. The car continues, and appears to be accelerating. The next two bullets go straight into the engine block but you know in your heart he is not going to stop. You fire an automatic burst into the windscreen, which explodes as the car bumps from side to side before coming to a rest just 10m in front of you.

The whole patrol takes cover waiting for the imminent detonation, which never comes. You wait two minutes, then three. Whimpering can be heard coming from the car. Slowly, you approach, your rifle still fixed on the car. A torchlight reveals a driver who no longer has a face and is obviously dead – you have killed him. In the back of a car, a woman dressed in black is lying across the back seat. Slowly, she lifts her body to reveal a young girl, possibly five years old, who is alive but clearly very sick. Your interpreter asks if she is okay. Barely able to talk, the woman says she thinks her daughter is has appendicitis and asks whether her husband is okay. It is at that point you realize that the street you are on is a shortcut to the local doctor's house.

An innocent man is shot dead and the Taliban have a major publicity coup: 'British Marine kills father trying to save girl.' You, as the person who opened fire, now have to account for your actions, under caution, during an interview with the special investigation branch of the Royal Military Police. If you have acted incorrectly, you could be charged with murder.

This is the reality of life for troops who patrol the streets every day in the towns and villages of Helmand.

Early in January 2007, Brigadier Jerry Thomas, the commander of the United Kingdom task force in Afghanistan, along with his staff officers in the headquarters of 3 Commando Brigade, began planning for Operation Glacier. By now, the headquarters had relocated from Kandahar airport to the military base at Lashkar Gar.

At its most simple, the mission of the NATO forces in Afghanistan was to secure the country from the threat being posed by the Taliban. The military's purpose was to halt the advance of the Taliban, while at the same time trying to turn the Afghan National Army and the Afghan National Police into organizations which one day would be capable of securing and policing the country without the need for outside assistance.

Once the country was secure, then the Karzai government would begin to flourish and Afghanistan would hopefully emerge from 30 years of war, death and destruction as a secure and functioning state capable of taking its place on the international stage.

The basic plan of establishing security across Afghanistan was to create secure zones where the local population could get on with running their daily lives, their businesses, schools and local government, free from intimidation by the Taliban. To achieve this in Helmand, a security zone had been created in more of less the centre of the province. The zone was gradually being pushed outwards and at the same time, hopefully, the Taliban were being expelled from the areas under British control.

By the beginning of January 2007, the time had come for the security zone to start pushing south towards the strategically important town of Garmsir, a once-thriving trading post that sits alongside the Helmand River.

British commanders from General David Richards, the then NATO Commander in Afghanistan, downwards had always stated that the Taliban could not be defeated by military action alone. The British needed to demonstrate to the local population that the Karzai regime, with the help of NATO, could offer the Afghan people much more than the Taliban. Garmsir provided a near perfect opportunity to prove the point. The area around Garmsir had been occupied by the British since the arrival of the Paras several months earlier, but it was widely accepted that it was a key objective for the Taliban. While every attack had thus far been thwarted, the Taliban remained a persistent threat.

Operation Glacier was designed to deliver a devastating blow to the Taliban and send a clear message to the organization's leadership that the British would never let the town fall into their hands. Garmsir was of vital strategic importance to both the Taliban and NATO forces because it sits on one of the main gateways into Helmand from Pakistan. The once busy town had been deserted for months following intense mortar and rocket attacks by the Taliban hiding in the surrounding area. Although the Royal Marines' MOGs had reaped some success by conducting hit-and-run operations, they had effectively failed to dislodge the Taliban from the area.

The aim of the operation was simple: British Commandos, supported by the US Air Force and the Army Air Corps' Apaches, backed up by close support from the Light Dragoons' Scimitars, would gradually push the Taliban south towards the Pakistan border and thus allow the Afghans to return to their town and start to lead normal lives.

The Operation Glacier mission was given to 45 Commando based at Camp Delhi, a ramshackle collection of stone sheep huts which was located on the edge of Garmsir. The companies involved were the India Company, a unit composed of Marines from 3 Commando Brigade Royal Marines Command Support Group, and Zulu Company.

Living conditions inside Camp Delhi were at best very basic. At that point, toilets were communal and consisted of a bench with a series of holes. The showers were also rudimentary, but the food was always good and plentiful. The Marines are rightly proud of their chefs, as all are trained Commandos.

Although Camp Delhi had only existed as a military outpost for a few short months, it was already pock-marked by the scars of battle. The Marines had already gained a great deal of experience of the enemy prior to Operation Glazier. Bullet holes and the scars of RPG strikes riddled the outer walls and shell-holes were visible both inside and outside the camp, where numerous Taliban mortar bombs and rockets had landed.

Despite the heat, the dust and the ever-present threat from Taliban harassing fire, morale remained exceptionally high. The Marines based in the camp, although bearded and bedraggled after weeks on operations, were emboldened by the fact that they had been blooded by battle.

Their state of mind at the time is best summed-up by a quote inscribed on a wooden plaque on a wall: 'For those who have not had to fight for it, life has a flavour to it which they will never know'. Variations on this quote are often attributed to an anonymous soldier in Vietnam. A more common version is, 'For those who fight for it, life [or freedom] has a flavour the protected will never know'.

The Taliban knew the British would come to Garmsir – at just 120km from the Pakistan border it was simply too important to be ignored. To enable them to move around the area out of sight of the Marines, the Taliban copied a tactic used with great success by the Viet Cong and began digging a warren which was used to move men and weapons.

Throughout their tour, the Marines came to realize that Taliban attacks could appear out of the blue without any real warning. Such was the level of enemy activity in and around Garmsir that minor contacts took place almost daily. One such event occurred on Christmas Eve 2006, when the Taliban launched an attack against a series of Marine positions forward of Camp Delhi, the southernmost British base in Helmand.

Mne Eddie Cain, a member of India Company, had already experienced several contacts with the enemy and a few close shaves. His matter-of-fact description of events is testimony to the intensity of war fighting in the area:

During a fairly routine morning, some small arms fire was exchanged, but nothing unusual until, finally, 51mm mortars were dropped on to a Taliban position, followed by some 105mm shells which seemed to finish the contact.

Having just been instructed to head back to Delhi at around 1.30pm, the Taliban opened fire on us out of nowhere with rocket-propelled grenades, RPGs, and impressively accurate small arms fire. They had managed to sneak within 200m of our position using the dried up canals and trenches. Immediately, we jumped behind the foot-tall sandbag wall to return fire, only to be beaten back by the bullets ripping through our protection. Rolling back from the trench I realized a round had gone through my shirt, just missing my shoulder – for the second time in three days! We then laid down a heavy weight of machine-gun fire, giving us the chance to regroup and re-assault the Taliban as they appeared again. I looked to my left and saw our vehicles taking fire and raced down to provide them with some cover. Jumping into our WMIK – a Land Rover with Weapons Mount Installation Kit – I shunted back another vehicle so that I could bring the .50 calibre machine-gun into good position. All the while, more RPGs and small arms fire were being fired at us.

As soon as there was a lull in the firing I jumped into position and fired into the compound that was protecting the Taliban fighters. We were relieved around 3.30pm so that we could go back to camp.

Although the Marines had been involved in fierce fighting with the Taliban, they had also been patrolling surrounding villages, trying to reassure the locals and gain their confidence, explaining to them the reason for the UK troops being deployed. Captain Tom Evans-Jones, Officer Commanding Multiple 1, said:

> The way the men conducted themselves throughout the fighting was a testament to the rigorous training they undergo to become a Royal Marine Commando, but I was particularly impressed by the control they displayed. They were able to immediately switch from aggressive actions to winning the hearts and minds of locals, which is essential to what we are trying to achieve. We have to provide security and stability so that the local population can rebuild their lives in this previously thriving town without fear of the Taliban.

Prior to the battle of Fort Jugroom on 15 January 2007, the Marines knew that some sort of operation was in the offing. The only details that remained unclear were the exact timing and the nature of the target.

Unbeknown to the rest of the troops in Helmand, the Brigade Reconnaissance Force (BRF), an elite unit of Commandos trained to work deep behind enemy lines, had been covertly observing a Taliban stronghold, known as Fort Jugroom, which sat alongside the Helmand river, close to Garmsir. The fort was ringed by watchtowers where Taliban sentries, armed with AK47s, RPGs and heavy machine-guns, kept a look-out for anyone approaching. The fort was composed of high mud walls which, the Marines had learnt, were extremely difficult to penetrate – even though in many cases they were hundreds of years old.

The troops from the BRF had built up a detailed intelligence picture of the activity inside the fort and had managed to identify a number of high-ranking Taliban personnel. The intelligence seemed to suggest that the Taliban were preparing to launch an offensive against NATO forces in the area. A decision was taken by Brigadier Jerry Thomas, in conjunction with his superiors at the NATO head-quarters in Kabul, that an operation would be launched to either capture or kill the Taliban inside the fort and thus disrupt any plan by the Taliban to launch their offensive. D-Day for the attack was chosen as 15 January and H-Hour for the main assault on the fort would be around dawn.

The military planners decided that nothing would be left to chance. The size and power of the force was designed to overwhelm the Taliban. The troops would be supported by Apache gunships, Scimitars from C Squadron of the Light Dragoons and a battery of 105mm Howitzers from 29 Commando The Royal Artillery. Engineers from 59 Independent Squadron, who were rapidly emerging as the unsung heroes of the campaign, would also be on hand to clear any obstacles. Air support would be provided by B1 Bombers from the US Air Force.

The Marines were under no illusion that they were in for a tough fight. Their own experience had shown them that the Taliban were well-armed and courageous fighters who should never be underestimated and, although they were nearly always out-numbered and out-gunned, they were still prepared to die fighting for their cause. The Taliban based inside the fort were armed with medium machine-guns, the ubiquitous AK47s and RPGs, as well as mortars and rockets.

The plan was relatively straightforward. The BRF was to secure a crossing-point across the Helmand river, through which Marines from Zulu Company 45 Commando would pass in their armoured and amphibious Viking vehicles. Both India and Zulu companies would also be supported by the Scimitars. The commanders decided that the operation would begin with a diversionary attack from the north, which was designed to confuse those inside. The main force would then assault the fort with close air support provided by the Apaches and Scimitars. On paper the plan looked foolproof.

As with all major pre-planned operations, the battle procedure can begin hours, if not days, before D-Day. The commanders issue their orders to their subordinates and they in turn issue their orders to their subordinates and so the process goes on until, in theory, everyone taking part understands exactly what the aim of the mission is and what part they will play in it. After the orders process is complete, the rehearsals begin. Troops will practise everything from how to evacuate a casualty from the battlefield to how to blow a hole in the wall of a heavily defended compound. Under the stress and fear of modern combat it is vital that every soldier is trained to react 'instinctively' to a variety of different scenarios if an operation is to succeed.

In the final few hours beforehand, troops would try to sleep, some would play cards or volleyball, while others would take the opportunity to write a letter home to loved ones. Absolutely everybody, from the commander downwards, would ensure that their personal weapons were in perfect working order. No one wants to hear the so-called 'dead man's click' – when the trigger is pulled but the weapon fails to fire – on the battlefield.

The operation began with the diversionary attack from the north, involving troops from India Company and the Afghan National Army. At around 0200hrs, the first of many artillery barrages were unleashed by the 105mm Howitzers. The B1 Bombers and strike aircraft were also involved in the onslaught.

By this stage, troops from Zulu Company began gathering at their rendezvous point on the eastern side of the Helmand river. The crossing-point had already been covertly secured by the BRF.

No one spoke as the flash from 2,000lb bombs and artillery illuminated the desert around them. As H-Hour for the dismounted attack approached, the Marines stormed across the river in their amphibious Viking armoured vehicles.

The Marines debussing from the Vikings were greeted with ferocious automatic fire from the Taliban positions. The troops made slow progress as they moved closer to the fort. Bullet fire cracking above their heads often forced the Marines to crawl from one piece of cover to the next.

The Marines had been told by the Paras, and had become aware for themselves, that the Taliban were resilient fighters. That day proved to be no different. As a team of Marines from Zulu Company reached the walls of the fort they were raked by automatic gunfire. Within minutes they had suffered four casualties, mostly with gunshot wounds.

It soon became apparent to the commanders on the ground that such was the weight of fire coming from the compound that the Marines would have little choice but to withdraw. The main aim of the mission – the disruption of the Taliban's plans to launch an offensive against NATO – had already been achieved. Dragging the wounded with them, the Commandos made for the relative safety of their armoured Viking vehicles and began to pull back across the river with the assistance of covering fire from the Apache gunships hovering above.

Out of range of the Taliban guns, the troops rested, some bleeding, all sweating and all exhausted after more than five hours of battle. The troop sergeants automatically began to conduct their post-battle drills including reorganizing the distribution of ammunition so that each man had his correct share and checking to make sure none of the men were carrying injuries – adrenaline has been known to numb the pain of serious wounds. The non-commissioned officers also carried out a head count. This left them in a state of horror: someone was missing.

The news immediately buzzed around the resting troops and was met with a mixture of disbelief and anger.

The whole of Zulu Company realized that in attempting to rescue their colleague they would be endangering the lives of others, but there was never any doubt as to what course of action they would take. If he was injured or hiding, time was quickly running out. As far as the Marines were concerned, the Taliban do not take prisoners. The troops had also heard all of the rumours that the Taliban mutilate the dead bodies of their enemies and no wanted that to happen to Lance Corporal Mathew Ford, the missing Marine, who was one of the most popular NCOs in the company. A message was sent back to the unit's headquarters in Garmsir that the Commandos were going back in. Then, out of the blue, one of the Apache pilots hovering overhead, who had been listening in to the conversation between the commander on the ground and his headquarters, came up with a highly brilliant but potentially dangerous plan.

Pilot Mark Rutherford, a 39-year-old Army Air Corps Warrant Officer, told the commanders that there was another possible solution rather than risking the lives of dozens of British Marines. He and Staff Sergeant Keith Armatage, the pilot of another Apache, consulted each other and believed that they could extract the missing Marine by using the same technique that is used to rescue 'downed' Apache pilots.

Mark Rutherford told the ground commanders: 'Time is ticking away and we are getting low on fuel. I know how we can get four Marines out on the Apaches and we could be in and out in five minutes.'

The Warrant Officer explained that the Commandos could sit on the Apaches' small wings and strap themselves to the side of the aircraft using ropes and metal clips. Two men could be strapped to each of the two Apaches while a third helicopter provided covering fire.

When the request for volunteers went out every man, without exception, volunteered. One of the four rescuers who rode in on an Apache was Regimental Sergeant Major Colin Hearn, 45, of 3 Commando Brigade's Land Force Command Support Group. He had watched the battle unfold via a real-time visual link provided by an Unmanned Air Vehicle loitering over Fort Jugroom. When the Army Air Corps offered to take four men in using Apaches, RSM Hearn did not hesitate to put himself in the frame. 'I'm a Royal Marine, I'm the RSM of the unit, he's a Royal Marine, the same as me – there's no way we were ever going to leave him, or anyone else, on that battlefield,' he said at the time.

The three men chosen alongside RSM Hearn were Marine Gary Robinson, 26, from Fife, Signaller Chris Fraser-Perry, who at 19 was the youngest of the group, and Captain David Rigg, an officer in the Royal Engineers, from Newton Ferrers in Devon.

While the three Apaches rumbled towards the forts, just 30m above the parched, flat lands of southern Helmand, it soon dawned on the men that they had virtually no protection from the Taliban sharp-shooters apart from the element of surprise and the awesome firepower of the helicopters' 30mm cannons.

Rutherford was blinded by furls of black smoke billowing from the fort as the Apaches landed in a hail of fire. The pilot of the other Apache made the decision to land within the pock-marked walls of Jugroom, close to where Mat Ford's prone body lay outside the compound's perimeter defences, and raised a wall of dust.

'I thought that we'd probably got about two to three minutes at most with the element of surprise before they [the Taliban] would realize what was happening, and it was after we'd been on the ground for about three minutes that we were engaged,' said Rutherford.

The four volunteers ran towards where LCpl Ford lay. They reached his lifeless body but expelled from their minds the thought that he might already be dead.

Gunfire came from a building to Rutherford's right, prompting him to radio his helicopter gunner, who began targeting the enemy snipers with his 30mm cannon. Moments later, the pilot watched the second Apache rise above the outer walls. Under a withering stream of fire, Signaller Fraser-Perry and Capt Rigg managed to retrieve Ford, tie him to their Apache and strap themselves to its fuselage before taking off.

Hearn and Robinson escaped on the wings of Rutherford's Apache soon after. They had no time to tie themselves on and were forced to cling on to the helicopter as it made its escape. The pilot remembers being exhausted: 'I was too out of breath to speak into the radio.'

But it could have been worse. When the pilot landed at Camp Bastion, he had enough fuel remaining to fly for just two more minutes.

Later that afternoon, the men heard that Matt Ford had died from his injuries. Those who helped to reach him have admitted they could not sleep in the nights that followed. 'The first night I was thinking if we could have done anything quicker, but I've had a word with the surgeon and his wounds were fatal. There wasn't anything we could have done,' said Warrant Officer Rutherford.

Gary Robinson offered the soldier's typically sanguine response to acts of heroism: 'I don't think it was heroic or dangerous in any way. I personally knew him, I served with him, but in my position any one of my colleagues would do the same.'

A memorial service for Mathew Ford was held the following morning, just after daybreak, close to where the Apaches that tried to save the 30-year-old took off. Plymouth-based Hearn said: 'There was a 10-minute service with a couple of readings, then a two-minute silence and some prayers, which I think was closure for the men.'

Explaining the rationale behind the initial attack on the fort, Lieutenant Colonel Rory Bruce, the official spokesman for the Royal Marines, said.

Our intention was to show the insurgents that they are not safe anywhere, that we are able to reach out to them and attack whenever and wherever we choose, even where they think they are at their safest. To that end, the mission was a success and the insurgents now know we can and will strike at any time. By conducting operations on this basis we do not allow the Taliban to regroup and rearm during the winter period.

Despite the 'success' of the operation, only the soldiers and pilots involved in the rescue mission received official recognition in the form of medals for the gallantry they displayed. The two pilots received the Distinguished Flying Cross, while the two co-pilots and the Army officer – Captain David Rigg – each received the Military Cross. The Marines, however, received nothing, which led to claims of double standards and the suggestion that the senior Marines commanders had failed to recognize the bravery shown by their men.

The following are extracts from the citations:

WO1 Rutherford demonstrated selfless gallantry and leadership as he helped inspire a hastily drawn together team to recover Lance Corporal Ford. Rutherford's courage, quick thinking and determination to find and recover Lance Corporal Ford, with complete disregard for his own safety, were an outstanding act of valour and leadership.

During the mission to recover Ford's body Staff Sgt Armatage was unable to land where planned. The rescuers were disorientated and, seeing this, Staff Sgt Armatage armed only with a pistol, got out of his aircraft to lead them to the casualty. Almost immediately, they came under enemy small arms fire. Throughout this audacious mission, Armatage's flying was impressively courageous and skilful. However, the fact that he evacuated his Apache armed only with a pistol to bring coherence to Lance Corporal Ford's recovery was truly extraordinary.

Captain Rigg, despite thinking he was about to be thrown into a deliberate enemy ambush, volunteered immediately to take part in the rescue of Lance Corporal Ford. He knew that he would be returning to face an aggressive, determined and lethal enemy, who were already alert to the company's presence and were very likely to anticipate their return to find Lance Corporal Ford. In the ensuing action Rigg displayed outstanding valour, clarity of thought and purpose to recover Lance Corporal Ford and return him to his comrades, in the face of a lethal and determined enemy, with deliberate disregard for his own safety.

9

THE BATTLE FOR KAJAKI

Throughout the Christmas and New Year period prior to the attack on Fort Jugroom on 15 January 2007, the British Commandos had been involved in daily battles with the Taliban.

At the time that the British mission began in Helmand, the hydro-electric dam at Kajaki was the single most strategically important structure in southern Afghanistan. Once complete, it would bring electrical power to more than 2 million people. The construction work on the dam was being carried out by civilian contractors, a number of whom were consequently kidnapped and murdered by the Taliban. The British troops were stationed at Kajaki to protect the dam and to provide a safe and secure environment for the contractors. The dam's importance was not lost on the Taliban who realized that its destruction or delay would be a significant coup. The Taliban attacks on the civilian contractors and the troops guarding them had been sporadic, but that began to change dramatically in late October 2006.

The threat being posed by the Taliban forced Brig Thomas to reinforce the coalition presence in the area. This vital task was given to M Company 42 Commando. From the moment they arrived in early December, they found themselves embroiled in a series of deadly battles with the enemy. The dam was surrounded on three sides by a strong and well-equipped Taliban force. Gun battles became nightly events, with the darkness illuminated by tracer rounds and mortar fire.

'Nightly engagements using heavy machine-guns are very much the norm, along with mortars being exchanged by both sides,' noted Captain William Mackenzie-Green, the Officer Commanding 10 Troop, M Company.

The first priority for M Company was to limit the freedom of movement of the Taliban who had until now been able to attack the dam at will. To achieve this, elements of the company, including a section from the Reconnaissance Troop, took up positions on three hilltops which dominated the surrounding area.

The majority of the attacks came from an area lying 3km north of the dam, which had been dubbed 'Nipple Hill' by the British troops. The Taliban had established a mortar position on the hill and were using it to bring increasingly accurate mortar fire on to the Marines' position.

As the frequency of the Taliban attacks increased, repair work at the dam all but stopped. The Marines needed to demonstrate to the locals that they, and not the Taliban, controlled in this part of Helmand and so Operation Clay was launched.

On New Year's Day 2007, over 100 Marines of 42 Commando's M Company attacked several different Taliban positions, including a training camp and a cave complex. One Marine was slightly injured in the operation – a gunshot wound to the hand. However, the attack resulted in the deaths of an estimated 20 Taliban fighters and one of their commanders.

Less than two weeks later, in the early hours of 13 January, troops from M Company launched part two of Operation Clay. In the previous attack, they had forced the Taliban out of their hiding places but, because of a shortage of men, the Marines had been unable to hold the ground they had taken from the Taliban. In a matter of days, the enemy positions had been reoccupied. The Marines were right back at square one.

Once again the laborious process of preparing for battle took place. Orders and weapon and equipment checks were followed by seemingly endless rehearsals. By now the Marines were battle-hardened. They had learnt from hard-won experience that the Taliban were tough and canny fighters, and every man knew it would be a dangerous mission. The Taliban would have learned from their mistakes in the 1 January attack. The second battle for Nipple Hill would be much tougher.

The lead up to H-hour was a nervous time. By this stage of the operation, virtually all of the Marines had been in combat and many had seen friends and colleagues become casualties on the battlefield. Every one of them knew that surviving was as much down to luck as it was to being a professional Marine.

The troops formed up in their assault positions as dawn slowly approached from a far eastern mountain range. Each man was silent and thoughtful, his bayonet fixed, waiting for battle to commence. Slowly and silently, they moved up the steep and rocky slopes of Nipple Hill, waiting for the first sounds of gunfire which would indicate that battle had commenced.

As the first streaks of daylight caught the top of the hill, two enemy sentries were spotted – it was the signal for the 'mortar stomp' to begin. Round after round fell amongst the Taliban, causing death and panic in equal measure. As the first shell-burst erupted amongst the Taliban sentries, the lead troop launched a series of attacks on the enemy trench and bunker system. The enemy was 'cleared' with bullets, bayonets and grenades, a brutal but effective tactic that has stood the test of time and was as successful in Afghanistan as it had proved to be in the Falklands 25 years earlier.

'Fixing bayonets for the first time was awesome. As soon as the first mortars went in we fixed bayonets – the feeling of adrenaline was awesome,' said 20-year-old Mne Ash Hore, recalling the feelings of going into battle for the first time.

The two assaulting sections pushed forward using fire-and-manoeuvre – this is where one section sprints forward for 20m or so while the other section provides covering fire. The forward section stops and provides covering fire for the rear section to move forward. The sections continued this exhausting process for 300m up to the top of the hill. As they reached the summit they located a recently abandoned bunker. Inside was a handheld radio. As the Marines carefully entered the bunker, the radio squawked into life. It was passed to an interpreter and the Marines listened carefully. One man said: 'The Brits are coming . . .' while another replied, 'How many?' '. . . I think they have sent all of them for us.'

After cresting the hilltop, the troops began to inch their way forward, but they immediately came under heavy and accurate fire from Taliban small arms and RPGs. Within a short space of time, the majority of the company was engaged. With the aid of two troops of marines, around 70 men, acting as fire support and two attack helicopters firing on the Taliban from the air above, the lead section broke into the compound. The Apaches circled above the battlefield, destroying the Taliban as and when they showed themselves, while the troops on the ground engaged the enemy with every weapon at their disposal.

One Junior NCO gave his view of the battle:

I was in one of the lead vehicles when I saw about ten blokes dressed for battle and armed with a variety of weapons. I immediately assumed they would be Taliban, not because of the clothes that they were wearing, but because they were in the middle of a battle and they had decided not to leave. That was their first mistake. Their second was to open fire on us. I ordered my blokes to dismount from our vehicle and we immediately set about returning fire. We immediately engaged them with a general purpose machine-gun firing bursts of 30 to 50 rounds. I went into an automatic mode, choosing my targets carefully, while at the same time trying to listen to instructions from my section commander. The noise was deafening and you could barely think straight, I was filled with a mixture of fear and exhilaration. In the back of my mind I was thinking 'this is it, this is what all the training is about.' The weight of fire we unleashed was awesome and we accounted for several dead Taliban fighters.

The fire now levelled at the Taliban positions broke the enemy's will to fight. After suffering many casualties, they fled. Having won the initial firefight, the Marines were ordered to push on. It was painstaking, exhausting and dangerous work, with small firefights erupting over the course of the next six hours, but the troops from M Company pushed on with relentless and lethal efficiency, methodically clearing each compound in turn and killing any Taliban foolish enough to open fire. It was during one of these engagements that Mne Tom Curry was shot and killed whilst leading his troop in an assault.

His section had come under enemy fire from a compound and were closing on the enemy. Two Marines, Matthew Bispham and Tom Curry, were ordered to go forward and clear a series of building where it was believed the Taliban had gone to ground. The two men immediately knew what to do: one would move forward while the other would cover him, ready to shoot any enemy who appeared.

The pair were moving through the ruins when a teenaged Taliban suddenly appeared from behind a mud-walled building and shot Mne Curry through the head. The 21-year-old Marine from London, who had joined the Commando in May 2005, did not even have enough time to bring his rifle into aim.

Mne Bispham said in a newspaper interview (*News of the World*, 28 January 2007):

We worked forward as a pair and as we approached a building a young Taliban came round a corner and almost bumped into us.

What happened next came in a split second but the Taliban shot at Tom with an AK47 and Tom was hit in the head. Because he aimed at Tom I had time to raise my rifle and shot the Taliban as quickly as I could. He was only about three feet away. I don't know how many rounds I fired at him or how many times I hit him but he went down.

Suddenly there were Taliban everywhere. The fighter who shot Tom was a young lad, I was quite surprised by how young he was.

He had a beard but he was only in his late teens, I just remember thinking how young he was and how I knew in my heart of hearts that he had killed Tom. We reckon he was from Pakistan and not even an Afghan. He was wearing a sort of Arab dish-dash [full-length clothing] but a very plain one. The lad was not a rich man.

Six medics rushed forward to help me and Tom, but their progress was slowed as more Taliban opened fire but in my heart I knew he was dead, I knew he had been killed instantly. The Taliban were everywhere – it was real 360° fighting, you just didn't know where the next attack would come from.

Although now on his own and in the full knowledge that a close friend had just been killed, Mne Bispham pushed on and killed a second Taliban fighter who emerged from another compound.

Lt Bertie Kerr, who led Matthew, Tom and other men from M Company's 11 Troop, said in an interview with the *Daily Telegraph* on 17 February 2007:

The order went out to all the lads to fix bayonets, so we knew the fighting could get very personal.

We cleared the resistance on top of the hill fairly quickly, then stormed on over the other side and came across a series of mud-walled outbuildings. I've only been with 11 Troop a month or so, but I know Tom Curry was always the first to step forward when a tough job needed doing.

This was no exception and Tom and Matt went ahead to start

clearing the outbuildings and ran across this Taliban. Then all hell let loose, with Taliban everywhere. In all we ended up killing about 20 of them, including a senior commander.

Tom, known as 'Vinders' (meaning Vindaloo) to members of 11 Troop, was just 21 when he died. Just a few weeks earlier, on Christmas Day, he had secretly proposed to his girlfriend Carla during a telephone call from Camp Bastion. The pair had intended to surprise the rest of the family with their news when he returned from operations. Although he had only been a Commando for 18 months, he had become one of the most popular and respected Marines in the company.

After his death, his Commanding Officer, Lieutenant Colonel Matt Holmes, Royal Marines, said:

The tragic loss of Marine Curry is felt deeply by all, a reflection of what he brought to life and all those who knew him. Tom died displaying the qualities so typical of him that had rapidly earned him the respect of his colleagues.

He was at the front, courageously closing with the enemy, with no thought for his own safety, just that of his colleagues who were close by. He was a glowing example of what a Royal Marine represents: courageous, robust and highly professional. That he carried these qualities as a young man into the dangers of battle speaks volumes, and we are all immensely proud of him.

Tom was also a self-effacing, utterly unselfish and cheerful individual, never slow to have a laugh at his own expense. His country has lost a brave, selfless servant who contributed much in his short time. In the close-knit community that is his Company and Commando unit, we feel his loss deeply, but our thoughts and prayers right now are with Tom's family and girlfriend at this difficult time.

For his actions during the battle, Mne Curry was awarded a posthumous Mention in Dispatches.

Without thought for their own safety, and in the knowledge that one of their number had fallen, the Marines pressed home their attack. Eventually, the fighting stopped. The remaining Taliban fled.

After almost seven hours of constant fighting, the Marines pulled back, shattered and exhausted. After the battle Cpl Scott gave the following description: 'Faces lighting up with tracer – that is some-thing I will never forget, the redness of the tracer round as it passes between you and your "oppo". It was like *Star Wars* with tracer going everywhere.'

For his actions during the battle of Nipple Hill, Matthew Bispham, who had been with the Royal Marines for less than three months, was awarded the Military Cross.

His citation reads:

On January 13 2007 Bispham's company conducted a deliberate attack on to a hill and compounds. The enemy fired machine-guns and RPGs from a group of compounds and all troops were pinned down by the accuracy of the fire. Bispham's group was tasked to assault. He and another Marine (Mne Curry) had over 50m of open ground to cover before reaching the first building to be cleared. Fearlessly and with absolute disregard for their own safety, they dashed forward. As they reached the building, an enemy emerged and shot his colleague, killing him instantly. Fighting almost hand-to-hand, Bispham engaged and killed a second enemy. His company's deliberate attack addressed this situation and regained the initiative from a bold and cunning enemy. His fighting spirit, resolve and his unflinching courage contributed directly to his company's success.

On hearing that he would be receiving the award Mne Bispham said: 'I was completely gob-smacked! It is humbling to work with lads who are willing to fight and die next to you. They become part of your family and it makes everything you do worthwhile. Every man I served with deserves recognition in my eyes.'

On their return to FOB Robinson, the Marines took with them a badly injured Taliban fighter who had been wounded in the battle. The Taliban recruit, who was in his 20s, died after British medics fought to save him. When later asked by locals why they had tried to save a member of the Taliban, a Marine replied, 'That's what makes us different to them.'

Despite the victory, within a matter of days the Taliban had returned to take up their old positions and once again began attacking the Marines guarding the dam. This was to become a recurrent theme: the

Taliban would attack the Marines who would in turn attack them, forcing them out of the area around Kajaki. Unable to hold the ground they had seized, the Marines would withdraw, only for the Taliban to move back to their old positions.

Tragically, Mne Curry would not be the last British serviceman to die on combat operations in Kajaki during the Marines' tour.

Two days earlier, on 11 January 2006, Royal Marines from 42 Commando captured a key Taliban headquarters in the south of Helmand during a daring night-time raid. More than 100 men closed in on the compound in the early hours, supported by Apache attack helicopters and NATO aircraft. The compound, with between 60 and 100 Taliban fighters inside, was in the area of Kostay, south of the town of Garmsir, and was considered to be one of the main headquarters for Taliban forces in the south of Helmand Province. The operation began when troops from the Brigade Reconnaissance Force, supported by the Light Dragoons, crossed the Helmand river and took up positions around the compound. BRF snipers targeted the first of two compounds before the building was attacked from the air and destroyed. The troops then switched their attention to the second building, which was also destroyed by the air support.

The BRF Marines, the soldiers of the Light Dragoons and the others involved in this attack are both mobile and, for a Commando unit, heavily armed. They form what is known as Mobile Operations Group South – MOG (S) – which aims, in the spirit of the Long-Range Desert Group of the Second World War, to keep the enemy off-balance by lurking in the desert wastelands of Helmand, watching and waiting for an opportunity to strike before swiftly melting away again. It must have been most unsettling for the Taliban to face a foe that is effectively using insurgent tactics against them.

There were many acts of astounding heroism carried out by the Royal Marines during their six-month tour in Helmand, many of which either went unrecorded or unnoticed by senior commanders and thus were never officially recognized. This is not a criticism of the Royal Marine commanders, but simply a fact of all wars.

One Marine rightly singled out for a special mention is Corporal John Thompson, who received the Conspicuous Gallantry Cross after saving the lives of many of his colleagues and friends by frequently drawing Taliban fire away from them.

One of the 30 actions he was involved in was a 4-hour fight on 10 January 2007 in a remote area of Helmand, when he and his men were surrounded by up to 50 Taliban. While he and his men were not in control when it started, by sheer determination and bravery they took the fight from the enemy, firing everything they had from grenade launchers to machine-guns.

Corporal Thompson's citation reads:

He displayed exceptional bravery and leadership, particularly under fire. His open and un-armoured vehicle led the company group throughout, and as such he was always at the forefront of over 30 fierce firefights with the Taliban. On numerous occasions his vehicle was hit by small arms fire and shrapnel, including rocket-propelled grenades. He constantly put himself in harm's way as he sought to fight the enemy. His indomitable spirit was truly inspirational to the remainder of his company and he was invariably the last to disengage from a firefight. He displayed gallantry, determination, outstanding professionalism and exceptional junior leadership and skills far beyond anything expected. Universally respected and revered, he was key to the success and morale of his company and through his actions many lives were saved.

Cpl Thompson's only injury was a perforated eardrum caused by the noise of constant machine-gun fire. Speaking of one incident, Cpl Thompson, said: 'I had just turned to my driver and said I felt we were going to be ambushed. Sixty seconds later two rocket grenades landed 50 metres away and within seconds more were fired at us, followed by machine-gun fire.'

The Marine repeatedly rearmed as he expended the ammunition from his machine-gun. In just four hours, he managed to fire 4,500 rounds from his vehicle mounted machine-gun, launched two Javelin missiles and laid down further fire with another weapon, expending some 5,000 more machine-gun bullets.

Cpl Thompson added, 'The reason I am here today, and why we all came through that alive, was the training and the teamwork. Everyone played their part. It's not about what I did, it's about the people of J Company – it's about the team.' Notification of the award of the UK's second highest gallantry medal still came as a surprise. 'I opened the letter and all I saw was my name and the words "Conspicuous Gallantry Cross". I was shocked and honoured. Everyone does their best in the Marines and I had done my best.'

Below are extracts from the citations of Marines who were awarded the Military Cross for their actions in Afghanistan. It gives an idea of the type of action the Marines routinely experienced in their six-month tour in Helmand.

Marine Daniel Claricoates:

Claricoates displayed outstanding courage and determination on three separate occasions. Every time he demonstrated remorseless and unerring gallantry in the face of the enemy. In January 2007, whilst manning an observation post he was attacked. He carried his machine-gun across open ground to a point where he could engage the enemy. Subsequently he ran back for more ammunition, exposing himself again. Were it not for his exemplary gallantry, there is little doubt that casualties would have been inflicted on his position.

Corporal Michael Cowe:

On 14 February 2007, during a company level mobile operations group long-range desert patrol, a Viking hit an anti-tank mine, which resulted in two friendly casualties. At the time Cowe's section was in contact 100 metres away. However, without hesitation he led his section into the known mined area, with little thought for his own safety, to help recover the casualties from the smoking hulk and assist with the evacuation; this he did whilst receiving continuous small arms fire from the enemy. He made a significant contribution to the operational effectiveness of his company.

Marine Paul Danby:

On 17 January 2007, a patrol from Danby's company was transiting north of a forward operating base. With no notice three men fired rocket-propelled grenades into the patrol approximately 30 metres away. Just as the grenades exploded, the lead Land Rover, containing Danby, and a Pinzgauer vehicle extracted themselves from the killing area and headed into a fire support position. Danby provided accurate and sustained fire support, engaging a large number of enemy from 30 to 500 metres away, allowing the remainder of the patrol to move away. Danby's selfless and tireless efforts at the expense of his own safety enabled the commander on the ground to extract the patrol.

Marine Daniel Fisher:

On 6 March 2007 Fisher's section was tasked with providing intimate fire support to clear a Taliban stronghold. His section commander wounded, Fisher stepped up to the role and retrieved the command equipment. The assault continued. He led his section through a myriad of compounds for seven hours. This required him to exercise careful command and control, which would have tested the most experienced of section commanders. Having suffered four casualties across the company, his leadership inspired the section to continue what had already proved to be a dangerous task. Despite no formal command training and with less than two years' experience as a Royal Marine, Fisher's performance under these extreme operational circumstances was above and beyond that expected of a Marine.

Corporal Alan Hewett:

On December 2006, Corporal Hewett's section came under sustained small arms, rocket-propelled grenade and heavy machine-gun fire, from multiple, well prepared enemy firing points. Had it not been for Hewett's personal bravery and the self-lessness of his actions, there is no doubt that the patrol would have sustained significant casualties. Hewett's courage and personal example were exemplary.

Corporal Simon Willey:

On March 6 2007, Willey was involved in an operation to clear a Taliban stronghold. Willey, showing complete disregard for his own safety over a prolonged period under effective enemy fire, enabled the break-in and alone was pivotal to success. The company went on to kill over 20 Taliban. Though in danger of becoming isolated and under accurate small arms fire, Willey demonstrated outstanding gallantry and determination in ensuring that this task was completed to enable mission success, saving further casualties in the process.

March 2007 was a bloody month for the Commandos. After almost six months in Afghanistan, the troops were looking forward to a well-earned rest. The prospect of being killed or injured just days before they were due to leave Helmand weighed heavily on the shoulders of most men.

A double tragedy hit the brigade on 3 March when Lance Bombardier Liam McLaughlin, 21, and Lance Bombardier Ross Clark, 25, who were both members of 148 Forward Observation Battery, 29 Commando Regiment Royal Artillery, were killed in an attack when either a rocket or mortar bomb scored a direct hit on the sangar which the two men were manning in the Sangin District Centre. The death of the pair, who were friends as well as colleagues, hit the Commandos particularly badly. The two men, who were soldiers rather than Marines, were immensely popular.

LBdr McLaughlin, known as 'Paddy', was said by Army friends to have 'only one setting and that was throttle fully on'. The Commando, who turned 21 while serving in Afghanistan, had been in the Army for four years. With his 'ready smile, indomitable spirit and boundless energy', LBdr McLaughlin was superb company and 'much loved for it', the regiment said.

'His ability to get into scrapes was both hair-raising and legendary,' colleagues said. 'Above all, he was fiercely loyal – all you could wish for in a colleague, and he won friends and admirers in equal measure, accordingly.'

The gunner spent his weekends 'coaxing a barely functional campervan' around the UK in search of surf and drove sergeant majors to distraction with 'pointedly non-regulation sideburns'.

LBdr Clark was described as an 'exceptionally gifted soldier' who had proved his mettle on operations. 'Enormously strong and physically capable, he took the harshest of conditions in his stride, and strove resolutely to complete any task to the absolute limits of his ability,' regimental colleagues said.

Originally from Zimbabwe, LBdr Clark was brought up in South Africa before leaving to join the British Army in 2002. He successfully passed the arduous Commando course and joined 29 Commando Regiment, Royal Artillery in March 2003, just in time for the regiment's push up the Al Faw Peninsula during the invasion of Iraq.

Very high standards of professionalism meant that the soldier was destined for a promising career, with promotion a certainty on return from operations. In Afghanistan the accomplished triathlete 'performed exactly as expected' being 'utterly reliable and generous in spirit,' the regiment said. He would be 'sorely missed'.

Five days later, on 8 March, Warrant Officer 2nd Class Michael 'Mick' Smith, a Battery Sergeant Major in 29 Commando Regiment and one of the units' 'living legends', was killed in an attack on the Sangin base.

The 39-year-old Commando from Liverpool, who had served in operations around the world, died as he ran up on to the roof of the Sangin base. Just as he moved out from the doorway, he was struck in the face by a 40mm grenade. Although the grenade failed to detonate, the force of the impact was devastating. Medics fought to save the Sergeant Major's life but he died a few minutes after being injured.

A couple of days earlier, on 6 March 2007 – just before the Commandos handed over to 12 Mechanized Brigade – Operation Silver was launched. It formed part of a wider NATO push called Operation Achilles. The operation, like many before, was truly multinational in character and brought together more than 1,000 soldiers, marines and paratroopers from British, US, Canadian and Estonian forces.

The mission's aim was to push the Taliban out of the strategically important town of Sangin and begin what would be the start of a long campaign to force the Taliban out of the entire Sangin Valley, allowing vital repair and rebuilding work to continue on the dam at Kajaki. By this point, the Taliban's attacks on contractors had bought the work on the dam to a halt. The British forces had long been aware that there could be no better demonstration of their good intentions towards the mainly peaceful people of the Sangin Valley than through repairing the dam and supplying electricity to the area.

In the early hours of 6 April, a force of 250 Marines in 33 vehicles were all set to provide an armoured thrust from the north, something the Taliban did not expect. Not since the Falklands War, some 25 years earlier, had so many Royal Marines come together for such a large-scale operation. It was, however, a big risk. The route was virtually unknown to the British but it gave the coalition forces the significant advantage of taking the Taliban by surprise.

As the British pushed along the valley from the north, the plan was for other coalition partners to drop by helicopter close to the town once the battle had started.

As the Marines' huge convoy made its advance to contact, Apache gunships and Harrier ground attack aircraft kept watch above. Within a matter of hours contact had been made with the Taliban and the British artillery sparked into life. The Harriers soon joined the battle as they were called in to attack compounds occupied by the Taliban.

US paratroopers from the 82nd Airborne joined the fray. They were dropped into the Sangin Valley to confront a force of around 400 Taliban fighters which intelligence reports suggested might have entered the area. Marines from Lima Company 42 Commando took the bold decision to push south on a route they had used before. There was a possibility that it might have been mined or booby-trapped by the Taliban but it was a risk Lt Col Matt Holmes, 42 Commando's CO, was prepared to take. As he later said, 'Fortune favours the brave.'

The battle proper began just before dawn when a Hellfire missile slammed into a Taliban position located on the outskirts of Sangin. The Commandos, supported by an awesome array of air power, began to push through the area. As the day wore on, small pockets of Taliban resistance were identified, isolated and then destroyed, usually by a hovering Apache or by one of the many coalition combat aircraft on standby some thousands of feet above the battlefield. The shock of the attack left the Taliban stunned and, thankfully, coalition casualties were minor.

As noon approached, Taliban resistance melted away and the Commandos seized many of their objectives. It had earlier been decided that once the area had been cleared of the Taliban that Sangin should be handed over to the ANA and ANP, primarily because the British did not have enough troops to defend the whole of the town. This was a risky strategy and many British officers believed that neither the ANA nor ANP had the capability to hold on to the town on their own. It was feared that in a matter of weeks the Taliban would creep back in and all the good work that had been achieved on Operation Silver would be lost.

Although the ANA had made excellent progress while being mentored by the British, they were still very inexperienced. However, the ANP were a much worse prospect. The police were widely despised by the local population. Then, and perhaps even now, large elements of the police force were known to be corrupt, many of its officers were heroin addicts and few had little if any training. It was clear that the British would need to have a presence in Sangin for months, if not years, to come.

Once Sangin had been secured, the mopping up operations began. Every compound in the area needed to be searched and cleared. It was a massive operation. While the Taliban could be temporarily forced out of the area, the commanders were aware that it was just a matter of time before they would begin to return, not least because some of them actually lived and worked in Sangin.

The battle had been fierce. NATO troops and the ANA had engaged the Taliban on six separate occasions since the start of the operation. The Taliban knew that to lose Sangin, the major narcotics base in the area and thus crucially important to their financial structure, would be a severe blow. For months, the Taliban's leadership had been telling the local population that NATO was weak and would never defeat the Taliban. Operation Silver was a huge blow to the reputation of Mullah Dadullah, who was one of the most senior leaders of the Taliban until his death in battle in May 2007.

Those Taliban who escaped capture and were not killed in battle were understood to have fled to the town of Musa Qala, which was once held by British troops. As discussed in Chapter 7, the British had encountered difficulties holding the town and pulled out in October 2006 following a shady deal with the local population, who wanted ISAF to leave. Local elders had given the British an assurance that they would not allow the Taliban back into the town, but the Taliban had soon re-established a stronghold there.

3 Commando Brigade had finally completed its task. It had been a tough fight. Twelve members of its force had been killed during the six-month mission and dozens more had been injured. Its troops had been

involved in more than 700 contacts with the enemy, some of which occurred at the rate of 15 a day. Like the Paras before them, the fighting in Helmand had transformed the lives of many Marines.

10

VIKING WARS

Private Chris Gray, a fit, bright and happy teenager with an infectious smile, joined the Army in March 2006 at the age of 18. As he walked through the gates of the Combat Infantry Centre in Catterick, North Yorkshire, he had fulfilled his life's ambition. Also on the same basic training course was Private James McClure, a tough teenager who too had spent much of his brief life looking forward to the day when he would become a member of the Royal Anglian Regiment. A month later Private Robert Foster, also aged 19, arrived at the Catterick Camp and the three fresh-faced recruits became close friends. It was soon confirmed that, once they had passed their training, they would be posted to the 1st Battalion of The Royal Anglian Regiment. The Vikings, as the 1st Battalion were known, were part of 12 Mechanized Brigade which was due to take over from 3 Commando Brigade in Helmand in April 2007. Within 18 months of their first meeting, all three privates would give their lives while showing a brand of heroism which was to become typical of the Royal Anglians.

While they were taught the basics of drill, field craft, tactics and weapons training during their intense 24-week course, the three teenagers were under no illusion that for the next six months they would be fighting for their lives. Within four months of starting the course, they were involved in some of the toughest fighting experienced by British soldiers for many years. Men were being killed and maimed every week in Helmand. The instructors at Catterick made it clear to all of those who were destined to join the Vikings that what they learnt on their training course would help to keep them alive when they were thrust into the heat of battle.

Pte Gray, a keen snow-boarder who was raised in Leicestershire, had particularly impressed his instructors at Catterick and continued to do so when he joined 3 (Coruna) Platoon of A Company in Pirbright, Hampshire, where the battalion was based. By the time he arrived, in September 2006, the battalion was already preparing for Afghanistan. The following month Ptes McClure and Foster also arrived, but they were posted to 7 Platoon in B (Suffolk) Company.

The training was tough and arduous. They soon learnt that their section commanders and platoon sergeants were every bit as uncompromising as they had feared. Each of the three grew into excellent soldiers during early 2007 when they spent three weeks in the Sennybridge training area in South Wales in what was to be the final live firing exercise before the battalion left for Helmand.

On arrival in Helmand, A Company were dispatched to Nowzad where they spent a few days on patrol with the Royal Marines before conducting a relief-in-place. The few days the two units spent together in Nowzad were absolutely vital. It was during this time that the Vikings would have to get a feel for the town and the people. Taliban suspects and sympathizers were identified and the most likely ambush points were pointed out to the Royal Anglian soldiers before the Marines departed for good.

One member of Pte Gray's platoon recalled:

We knew the Taliban would have a pop at us, but we were ready for them. Chris was really up for it. He had the minimi in our section and he like the rest of us really wanted to get stuck in. We all knew we were going to be hit at some stage and we wanted to get a feel for what a real firefight was going to be like. Chris was one of the youngest in the section but he was a real inspiration, a great soldier and very professional for a 19-year-old.

Meanwhile in Fire Base Price near Gereshk, Brig John Lorimer, the Commander of 12 Mechanized Brigade, was having trouble sleeping. For the past two weeks he had worked almost non-stop as he put the finishing touches to the battle plan for Operation Silicon, which would see the Taliban routed from the area north-east of Gereshk – one of their former strongholds.

Now, while his body craved sleep, his mind refused to rest. He sat at his desk and wrote: '3.00am. Still awake.'

Restless, he went outside. Sitting on a stool outside his tent and dressed in his favourite 3 Para green tee-shirt and desert combat trousers, he stared into the distance and sucked on a Benson and Hedges. He made patterns in the sand with his feet and went over and over the plan in his head. 'Would it work?', he asked himself for the thousandth time. 'Was the preparation right? Would the Taliban fight? Had the pre-deployment training been rigorous enough?' The questions kept coming.

In 2007, Lorimer was unique in the British Army in that he was the only brigadier commander to have been deployed on two operations. Sleep was impossible with the endless thoughts rushing around his head. This was the first time his organization had launched an operation at Brigade level – it was complex stuff. His commanders were happy with his plan and in the modern British Army few subordinate commanders would hold back on criticism if they thought a mission was potentially flawed.

He had been here before, questioning his actions and his planning, but he had always been sure in the past that his plans would succeed. But Afghanistan was different to Iraq. The Taliban were highly moti-vated, reasonably well-equipped and natural warriors. Many expected to die in battle and few feared death – and that was the key weapon in their armoury. Lorimer knew that his brigade would take casualties. He privately believed that they would lose about one man a week, but that many more would be injured.

As Lorimer pondered the imponderables, a young soldier appeared out of the dark. His rifle was slung over his shoulder and his hair was thick with dust and dried sweat. He had the look of a man who longed for his bed.

The two men made eye contact and the young soldier, a lance corporal who had just returned from a patrol, broke the silence and said 'Alright mate?' with a tired but cheery grin. It was more of a greeting than a question and Lorimer, unused to being greeted with such infor-mality by a junior rank, smiled and said: 'Yes, I'm fine, thanks', and then quickly added, 'What have you been up to?' 'I'm part of the EOD team,' replied the soldier. 'We've just come back from a patrol. What about you?' Offering the soldier a cigarette, Lorimer said: 'I've just sent 2,000 men into battle and I'm having a little bit of trouble sleeping. I'm the brigade commander.'

'Fuck me sir!' exclaimed the soldier, 'I didn't realize'. 'Don't worry', replied Lorimer, 'There's no reason why you should recognize me dressed like this. Now go and get your head down and get some sleep.' As the soldier walked away, he stopped, turned around and said, 'Don't worry, sir, The Anglians are a good bunch. They'll do the business.'

Despite the successes of the Paras and the Marines before them, it was widely accepted that the summer of 2007 would be the make or break period for the British in Helmand. British commanders knew that having been 'tactically defeated' over the past 12 months, the Taliban would throw everything at the British if their credibility was to remain intact.

Brigadier John Lorimer, with whom I had served in the Parachute Regiment some 15 years earlier, took command of the Helmand task force on Wednesday 11 April. The Brigadier had arrived in Helmand two weeks early via Iraq, where he visited elements of his brigade who had been seconded to units fighting insurgents in Basra.

Brig Lorimer has a reputation as a tough and uncompromising officer, who studied Arabic at Cambridge. He was the officer famously responsible for the commanding the operation which led to the release of two members of the SAS who had been taken hostage by the Iraqi police in Basra in 2005.

When the emergency arose in Basra, Major General Dutton, the general officer commanding the multinational division in southern Iraq, was on holiday in the south of France and Brig Lorimer was in command. The SAS troopers had been watching an Iraqi police chief. He was known to the coalition forces as a nasty piece of work who was quite happy to use an electric drill on those unfortunate enough to be arrested by his corrupt police officers and taken to the notorious Jamiat jail.

The two-man SAS team, who were wearing Arabic dress as disguise, had been compromised by a local police unit who thought the pair were acting suspiciously. The two soldiers fled from their vehicle but were later captured and taken to Jamiat.

The divisional headquarters, which was then located at Basra airport, sent a team of SAS men and military lawyers to negotiate with the Iraqis in a bid to free the two men. A cordon made up of soldiers from the Staffordshire Regiment and the Coldstream Guards, equipped with Warrior armoured fighting vehicles, placed a security cordon around the prison but were soon attacked by an Iraqi mob with stones and petrol bombs. British soldiers were seen on live television, engulfed in flames and leaping from their vehicles. Back at the Ministry of Defence in London, senior officers and politicians were demanding to know what was going on, who had been kidnapped and what Lorimer was going to do about it.

The pressure on Lorimer was phenomenal. He was later to tell me during an interview for the *Sunday Telegraph* that it was one of the most demanding few hours of his military career. As well as trying to develop a plan to free the hostages, he also had to deal with an almost endless list of questions from the MoD in London and from the Permanent Joint Headquarters at Northwood in Middlesex. At one stage, staff officers had to tell civil servants that their endless list of demanding questions was beginning to hamper the rescue operation.

The soldiers believed they were about to be executed and that their deaths would be recorded on film which would be released to the world via the Internet. Lorimer had to make a tough decision. He was under pressure from the SAS squadron commander to launch an operation to free the men, but he was also aware that he had to give negotiation a chance. In the end, he made the call to free the men by using Warriors to smash down the walls of the police station and sending in an SAS team to free their colleagues.

The operation made headlines around the world. While the troops in Iraq celebrated, back in London the silence from Lorimer's colleagues was deafening. Lorimer was later to tell colleagues that if his chiefs or politicians were not happy with his performance then he would resign. However, that was not to be. One of the first people to call Lorimer was John Reid, the Defence Secretary, who congratulated him on his brilliant work. Once it was confirmed that Brig Lorimer was in the clear, other colleagues and senior officers also offered their congratulations. However, the operation was a close run thing and even to this day Lorimer believes he waited too long and therefore risked the lives of the two SAS soldiers before ordering their rescue.

Lorimer had already developed a thorough understanding of the challenges facing the British force in Afghanistan prior to taking command of 12 Mechanized Brigade. In his previous job, as a staff officer at Permanent Joint Planning Headquarters, he was one of a team of officers who drew up the plan for the deployment of 16 Air Assault Brigade in May 2006.

Prior to conducting his Afghanistan reconnaissance in September of 2006, he was told by senior officers to 'think big' when deciding what military assets he would need to complete the job.

And that is exactly what Lorimer did. The Brigadier effectively produced a military wish-list consisting of Challenger tanks, Warrior armoured fighting vehicles, AS90 tracked artillery and an extra battle group. When Brig Lorimer returned to the UK, he distributed his plans as widely as possible amongst his brigade staff. While the document sent a flurry of excitement through his staff officers, it also sent civil servants and military officers in the Directorate of Joint Commitments into panic. Brig Lorimer had asked for equipment that was simply not available because much of it was either being used in Iraq or was due to deploy there. Within minutes of the document's arrival at the MoD, Brig Lorimer's headquarters at Bulford in Wiltshire received a phone call from the MoD asking him not to distribute the document to his staff. The panic stricken officers in London were simply told, 'You're too late.'

Brig Lorimer was told by PJHQ that he would have to revise his plans. After having been told to think big, he was now being told to think small and he was clearly frustrated, as were many in his brigade. The fact that Lorimer was told to change his plans was eventually leaked to the *Mail on Sunday* newspaper. It ran a story on 18 November 2006 saying that British commanders were being denied vital equipment just weeks after Tony Blair, the Prime Minister at the time, had 'promised' hard-pressed senior officers that they could have whatever equipment they needed.

According to one officer, the story was 'spot on'. The *Mail On Sunday* contacted the MoD press office on the Saturday prior to publication to inform them that they were running a story saying that a senior British officer was 'angry and frustrated' that his request for extra equipment had been turned down. Later on that same Saturday, Brig Lorimer, a great field sports enthusiast, was shooting with some friends when he received a call on his mobile phone. It was a senior officer informing him of the contents of the story. The senior officer said, 'John, we need to sort out a quote basically saying that you are quite happy with the equipment that you are going to get.' Lorimer replied: 'But I'm not. I had nothing to do with that story being leaked but I am angry and I am frustrated.' The senior officer replied, half jokingly, 'Lorimer, do as you are told,' and so a quote was manufactured by PJHQ and the MoD press office which said: 'Suggestions that I am angry or frustrated are simply not true. I have conducted my reconnaissance and made recommendations. I am perfectly happy that those are being considered in the normal way and I am closely involved in that process.'

The whole of the force generation process surrounding the deployment of 12 Mechanized Brigade was later described to me by an officer, who would only speak on the grounds of anonymity, as a 'shambles'. Over lunch at the officer's home on the fringes of Salisbury Plain, he told me of his frustrations: 'I could never be quoted as saying this but the political interference in this deployment could end up costing the lives of British soldiers. It is completely unacceptable.' The officer complained:

> We had to deal with a situation where one of the Infantry units, the 1st Battalion of the Worcestershire and Sherwood Foresters Regiment (1WFR), was supposed to be going to Iraq and then we were told that they might be coming with us to Afghanistan, but we were sworn to secrecy because no formal announcement had been made in the House of Commons by the Defence Secretary. In the end, Brigade Staff officers told the Commanding Officer that there was a strong possibility that his unit would be going to Afghanistan rather than Iraq, but that he was not to inform anyone. The secrecy meant that while the rest of 12 Brigade began training in earnest for Afghanistan, the commander of the 1WFR had to sit on the sidelines and watch what was going on. It was ridiculous and it was wrong and everyone knew it.

The problem for the commanders and soldiers of 1WFR was that they could not begin to train properly for the Afghan operation and neither could they get their hands on any of the equipment, weapons or uniforms which they would be using on their arrival. The fear was that the battalion would arrive in Helmand woefully unprepared for the challenges facing them. Despite the delays and the prevarication by the MoD, 1WFR arrived in Helmand ready for action, largely thanks to the efforts of the soldiers and their commanding officer Lt Col Richard Nestley, MC, OBE.

Operation Herrick 6 began when the first elements of 12 Mechanized Brigade arrived in Helmand towards the end of March 2007. They underwent a period of acclimatization before joining the Royal Marines on operations at a variety of locations across the province. This handover process occurs with every operational deployment but it is still sometimes a tense and difficult period. Each regiment, and indeed each unit within a regiment, has its own idiosyncratic way of doing things. This, however, was not the case in Helmand. The Commandos had survived a tough tour. They had been involved in more than 700 separate contacts with the enemy, 12 men had been killed and dozens more had been injured. The fighting had been as tough, if not quite as intense, as the Paras had faced six months earlier, yet the Marines had received far fewer headlines. The new troops who would be doing the fighting, the Royal Anglians, the Worcestershire and Sherwood Foresters and the Grenadier Guards, were well aware that they needed to extract every useful piece of information they could from the Commandos in the two weeks they had together – their lives could quite literally depend upon it.

The day after he assumed command, Brigadier Lorimer and his staff flew into the northern town of Sangin, a name that was now synonymous with tough fighting and sacrifice. Sangin was the town where Corporal Bryan Budd won his Victoria Cross for the selfless valour he displayed in July and August 2006. It was also the town where, at that time, 12 British soldiers and Marines had so far died in fighting. The black flag of the Taliban had once flown there, so it had tactical and strategic importance for both sides.

As described in the previous chapter, a week earlier, on 6 April 2007, Operation Silver had involved a bold push up the Sangin Valley, forcing the Taliban out of Sangin and the surrounding villages, through the desert into the hinterland beyond. It was a 'ballsy' operation, as one senior non-commissioned officer said. Lieutenant Colonel Matt Holmes, the Commanding Officer of 42 Commando, described it as an operation into the 'heart of darkness'. The shock of the attack left the Taliban's command and control ability completely paralysed, according to Brigadier Jerry Thomas. Also taking part were troops from US 82nd Airbourne Division who actually conducted much of the fighting. However, the Taliban had been pushed out of Sangin in the past, only to return when the British forces withdrew back to its small base in the town centre.

The success of the operation did provide Brig Lorimer with an opportunity to meet the locals. Having arrived in the town by Chinook, Brig Lorimer, his staff and bodyguards attended a *Jirga* – an Pashtu word for 'meeting' – with 100 tribal elders. The 'stick' had been the operation to rid Sangin of the Taliban, now Brig Lorimer had arrived to offer the 'carrot'.

Sitting cross-legged on intricately woven Afghanistan rugs, the officers and the elders had a traditional lunch of grilled chicken and naan bread, at the end of which Brig Lorimer appealed to the elders for their cooperation.

He told them to talk to the ISAF soldiers and tell them of their needs. 'We need you to talk to military engineers who are currently establishing what reconstruction and development you need and where.' Again he appealed:

> Please help us. Security will improve as the investment in the Afghan National Army and Police Force training comes to fruition. You can already see the Afghan National Army patrol base being built now, with security in place development can follow. We are committed to helping you and in time, and with your continued support, the Kajaki project will provide a fantastic opportunity to bring longlasting security to Helmand Province.

However, the Brigadier also gave the tribal leaders a warning for he knew that some people in their villages and towns had already aligned themselves with the Taliban. 'Senior Taliban and foreign fighters have now been driven from the Sangin District Centre. Our operations against them will continue both in Sangin district and across the province. We will strike them at a time and place of our choosing.'

It was clear that many of the elders who attended the *Jirga* were linked directly or otherwise to the cultivation of poppy and the production of opium, and hence to the Taliban as well. Poppy is the main crop in the area and vast fields flank either side of the Helmand river as it runs through the valley.

It was well known amongst the British that counter-narcotic operations were helping the Taliban to recruit otherwise peaceful farmers or their sons. For many Afghans who lived in Helmand, growing poppy was their only means of making money. If the poppy disappeared, so would their livelihoods, and that was something for which they were prepared to fight and die. Brig Lorimer attempted to reassure those who thought the British troops had come to destroy their crops: 'It's not ISAF's responsibility to eradicate poppy; we are here to defeat the Taliban leaders. We will do all that we can to avoid harming the innocent or causing damage to your property.' In a final warning to the locals, he added: 'If your young men fight alongside the Taliban, however, they will die.'

It was generally agreed that the *Jirga* had gone well. Governor Wafa, a senior local government dignitary, and the police chief both agreed that the tribal elders were keen to make progress and work with the British.

As Brig Lorimer and his staff left Sangin, their smiles soon faded for the following day the brigade suffered its first casualty when a British patrol was involved in a fierce firefight in the town of Nowzad, in the north of Afghanistan.

The Royal Anglian soldiers who made up A Company, which was composed of 1, 2 and 3 platoons, had been in Nowzad for a little more than a week, but in that time they had learnt a great deal about the Taliban and the local area. It was clear to the troops that the best way of keeping the Taliban on the back foot was to be in the town as often as possible, but without setting a pattern.

Friday 13 April began early for the majority of the Royal Anglians housed in the secure compound which served as their base. It was still dark and cold and the men queued for their early morning breakfast of beans, powdered scrambled egg and barely edible sausages. As the soldiers huddled in groups, sipping hot, sweet tea, their platoon commanders and sergeants began to check and recheck that each man was ready for the forthcoming patrol. This was A Company's first large-scale operation. It was important for the morale of the men that the operation was successful. The soldiers rechecked their weapons, the signallers tested their radios and the medics ensured that their life-saving equipment was ready to hand. The tension started to build as the soldiers moved into their patrol formation. Then it was time to go. Slowly and quietly the three platoons moved out of the base and into the empty, dusty town. The majority of the locals were still asleep, soon to be woken by barking dogs and crowing cockerels. Intelligence reports suggested that the Taliban had been monitoring the soldiers' movements but there was nothing to indicate an attack.

The plan was for the company to move through the town at first light, around 0600hrs. The three platoons would move independently but ready to support each other in the event of an attack. The operation was going well. The locals appeared friendly, if somewhat suspicious, and a few even offered the soldiers some fruit and bread. As the sun began to rise into the Helmand sky, the pre-dawn chill began to disappear and the soldiers began to feel more relaxed.

At around 0930hrs, the process began of moving back to the base for a well-earned cup of tea and a rest. The route back to the compound took the company across a piece of open ground – an obvious ambush point. 1 Platoon were ordered to move forward and take up fire positions to cover the rest of the company back on its way to the base. As the troops moved forward, about a dozen members of the Taliban armed with automatic weapons and rocket-propelled grenades launched a surprise attack. The weight of fire was ferocious and initially the soldiers were left stunned, like a prize-fighter caught off-guard by an unseen right hook.

Simon Panter, the Sergeant of 3 Platoon who had served with the Royal Anglians in Iraq and during the 2001 tour in Kabul, described the moment:

> The Taliban were already in the position which 1 Platoon were trying to occupy and as we moved they opened up on us. It was a classic ambush and there was so much fire zipping around our heads that it was difficult to work out where the Taliban were. All hell broke loose. My platoon was on the right flank and we immediately went into a snap ambush. The area was like a jungle. It was thick with orchards, bushes and irrigation ditches. You could barely see 10 metres.

With the Royal Anglian soldiers pinned down, the Taliban began to move into a flanking position. The move was spotted by a soldier who told Sgt Panter that they were about to be outflanked. If the Taliban managed to get into position, his platoon would be caught in a crossfire and cut to ribbons. As the bullets zipped above his head, Sgt Panter assessed the situation and ordered his men to outflank the Taliban.

As Cpl Billy Moore's section headed for a new position, with young Pte Chris Gray leading the move, they came face to face with half a dozen Taliban fighters who opened fire from behind a wall, just a metre or two in front of Pte Gray.

Both Cpl Moore and Pte Gray, armed with the rapid-firing minimi, opened fire. The burst tore into the Taliban and four of them were killed outright. However, a burst of fire from another direction hit Cpl Moore in the arm, while another bullet smashed through Pte Gray's chest armour, leaving him badly wounded.

Cpl Moore's upper arm was sliced open as if it had been hit by a machete but, despite the pain, he stood over Pte Gray and continued to fire while shouting, 'Man down, man down.'

The first that Sgt Panter knew of the casualty was when he heard that dreaded cry:

> I moved forward to help assisting with the casevac. Normally the job of the section is to get the casualty to the platoon sergeant but I thought I had better get to him as quickly as I could. He was about 70 metres to my front so I pushed on. There was a huge battle raging around me, rounds were flying above my head, hitting the trees and branches.

As the fighting continued a third soldier, Pte Craig Fisher, was hit in the leg. The situation was now critical. Unless the Anglian could overpower the Taliban, they ran the very real risk of sustaining even more casualties.

Sgt Panter continued:

> When I got to the guys I could see they were in a bad way with Pte Gray. Cpl Moore had been hit in the arm but he was still managing to fight. He had picked up Pte Gray's minimi and was still firing. He had also managed to throw a grenade even though he had been injured.
>
> When Cpl Moore saw me, he said 'I'm hit, I'm hit,' so I said 'Right Billy, get back into cover and sort yourself out.' I could see that Billy was wounded but my main concern was Pte Gray, I knew he was in a bad way and I also knew that Billy could take care of himself.
>
> I saw that it was Pte Gray who was injured so we got his kit off and I could see that he had a chest wound. We were still getting plenty of incoming at that stage. It was a pretty ferocious firefight. We gave him first aid as best as we could. I gave him mouth-to-mouth and made sure he had a pulse and then got him out of the

killing area. We got him on to a stretcher and then began carrying him back to the Company Sergeant Major, who was about 800 metres away. The guys carrying him were getting exhausted. The battle was raging and the ground was really difficult. I was encouraging and cajoling and swearing, calling them all the names under the sun. At one stage I screamed 'If he fucking dies I will hate you forever.' My only concern was to save Pte Gray.

Sgt Panter drove the section back over 2km of hard terrain. When they arrived at the rendezvous with the casualty evacuation vehicle, all were exhausted.

Sgt Panter continued:

We eventually got him to the Company Sergeant Major who was waiting for us. We strapped Pte Gray on to the back of a Pinzgauer and he was taken back to Nowzad. At that stage I was just hoping that we had done enough to save him. I knew it was touch and go. I knew that the bullet would have done a lot of damage.

Pte Gray was rushed back to the compound and medics fought to keep him alive while a Chinook with a medical team flew in from Camp Bastion. It was a race against time. The medical team also wanted to evacuate Cpl Moore and give him morphine, but he refused to leave his post and remained with his men after his wound was dressed.

As the Chinook landed, six of Pte Gray's colleagues carried him on a stretcher to the aircraft, which then disappeared into a cloud of fine brown desert dust. As the aircraft took off, the medics inside knelt beside Pte Gray and searched for signs of life.

Back on the ground, the whole of A Company was now locked into a ferocious, 360° battle with the Taliban. Sgt Panter recalls, 'The Taliban were around us and amongst us. The soldiers were quite literally bumping into the Taliban. We were getting support from the guys on ANP Hill and we had plenty of air strikes taking place but it was a fucking fierce fight all day.'

A Company finally managed to break free from the Taliban. Short on ammunition and exhausted, the soldiers returned to their base.

When we eventually got back to the base we learned that Pte Gray hadn't made it. I can tell you now that is not a nice feeling, that is not something you ever want to experience twice. I had a lump in my throat and I had to fight to keep it together especially when the CSM said go and lower the flag. We were all physically and emotionally knackered after fighting all day, so coming back and discovering that one of your own had been killed was difficult to take. At the time I thought that if every day was going to be like this – remember this happened in the first week of our tour – then we are going to have a pretty torrid time. But we gave the Taliban a good kicking that day. We had one killed and two injured but we killed 22 of them.

I still think about it quite a bit. For days afterwards my head was doing overtime. I kept asking myself whether there was any more I could have done to keep him alive. I questioned all of my actions but then I was told that his injuries were such that from the moment he was hit he was beyond medical help. He would have died if we had managed to get him on an operating table two seconds after being hit.

Pte Matt Duffy, Pte Gray's best friend from A Company, said: 'Chris was an awesome soldier and a better mate. He loved the job more than anyone and died doing what he loved.'

While on R and R, Sgt Panter visited Pte Gray's parents and told them how he had died and that their son fought like a hero. Although only 19, Pte Gray was mature beyond his years and was a highly regarded soldier. He was the point-man of the lead section. His ability to open fire quickly and kill three Taliban fighters helped save the lives of those behind him.

Friday 13 April was the first time many had fought in combat and the elation of having survived soon melted away when it emerged that one of their own had been killed in battle. The battalion had been in Afghanistan for just a few days and already one of their men had been killed. It was going to be a long tour and everyone knew that more brave young men would die before they returned to the UK. Cpl Moore was later awarded the Military Cross for his actions on that day and Sgt Panter received a Mention in Dispatches.

The success of the Operation Silver, which saw the Royal Marines and other NATO troops push the Taliban out of Sangin, meant that vital reconstruction could finally begin. There was a view amongst senior

FCO officials that Sangin should be handed over to the Afghan National Police and Afghan National Army to control because of the complex nature of the tribal system which existed in the area and which the British military could never hope to understand. Sangin was also a main narco-centre where the influence of drug barons was at least as strong as the Taliban.

Lt Col Stuart Carver, the Commanding Officer of the Royal Anglians, had a different view. He argued that if the British could bring peace and stability to Sangin, start to rebuild the town and keep the Taliban out, the message would start to spread across the north of Helmand that the British bring prosperity. It was a view which won the support of senior British military and NATO figures and so the Royal Anglians remained in Sangin.

'I just thought it was worth the extra effort,' said Lt Col Carver. 'Actions speak louder than words and I wanted the local population to see that we were here to help them.'

Within a matter of weeks local people, seeing that the Taliban had gone, began to return to their shops and stalls within the bazaar area of the town. As more people flocked to the town, so more shops opened up and by the beginning of August the town was thriving again, with butchers, bakers and shops which sold fruit, sweets and music. Even a mortorcycle shop opened. The Anglians managed to secure funding for some 'quick impact projects', such as the repair of irrigation ditches which helped the farmers to return to their fields, and they restored street lighting to part of the bazaar. The projects were small and it will be many years before the damage done to Sangin from the fighting will be repaired, but, for the first time in more than a year, the local people saw that the British troops were there to help.

Confidence grew within the town and more and more of the local men started to attend the weekly *shura*, which was always attended by a British Army officer. These meetings allowed the soldiers to inform the locals what they were doing and how they were bringing security and stability to the area and it also allowed the local elders to voice their concerns. The meetings were also attended by Taliban spies and sympathizers who would report back to their commanders on the activities of the British.

Now that the Taliban had been pushed out of Sangin, the British began to patrol into the Green Zone which sits alongside the Helmand river. No more than 2.5km wide, it is called the Green Zone because of the density of the vegetation, which from above looks like a green carpet in an otherwise dust-brown desert. The actual zone fans out from the area of the town of Sangin and runs north, almost to the area of Kajaki, around 25km in length. Through centuries of working the soil, farmers in this part of Helmand have managed to turn the desert into fertile land by the ingenious use of irrigation channels and streams which feed the patchwork of fields. Today poppies are grown in abundance, as are cannabis, maize and a variety of other crops. The area is littered with compounds, which are home to mainly peaceful Afghans who simply want to get on with their way of life. Bizarrely, at night the temperature inside the Green Zone plummets and, unlike other places in Helmand, a heavy dew forms on the ground, even in the height of the summer.

The Green Zone had long been a Taliban stronghold. The numerous fort-like compounds provided perfect hiding places for the Taliban, who used the area as a refuge and a resting place between raids on the British bases. But that was about to end. Over the summer of 2007 the Royal Anglians, supported by the ANA and ANP, would take on the Taliban in their own backyard – but the fighting would exact a heavy toll on the British troops.

Three weeks after Pte Gray was killed, the battalion suffered another tragic set back in Kajaki, where C Company were responsible for providing security in the area of the dam. The base was isolated and was only visited by helicopter once every five days unless there was an emergency, such as a casualty. The base was also located in one of the most heavily mined areas of Helmand. During the days of the Russian occupation, the dam was a prime target for the mujahideen and, in a bid to fend off repeated attacks, the Russians saturated the area with anti-personnel mines. The vast majority of them still posed a threat to those in the area, especially British troops, as has already been seen in the terrible events described earlier.

Thursday 3 May was a day like any other for the men of C Company in the late spring of 2007. After a cooked breakfast, the men busied themselves in preparation for the forthcoming patrol, which on that day was to provide security for the Royal Engineers who were going to 'deny' or destroy a series of Taliban bunkers which had been discovered in the area. The Taliban had been using the bunkers as a base from which to attack the Royal Anglians. Most patrols took place in the early morning or the evening, when the day was cooler and the strength of the Afghan sun was at its weakest.

The troops left their base and patrolled to the area of the bunkers. The mortar team, back at the base, were on standby for the duration and jets were also on standby, unseen and unheard by those on the ground thousands of feet below.

The engineers destroyed the bunkers with bar mines and within a couple of hours the troops slowly and carefully withdrew back to their base. Unusually for Kajaki, the patrol had virtually reached the point of completion without incident. Then someone stepped on an anti-personnel mine.

Private Matt Woollard, a young soldier from Westcliffe-on-Sea in Essex, had only ever wanted to be a soldier. He often joked that he came from a long line of lorry drivers and wanted to start a new family tradition. As soon as he finished school, he went to his local Army Careers Office and joined up. Two years later, he found himself on the frontline in Afghanistan, fighting the Taliban.

'There is no better feeling in the world than being shot at and shooting back,' he would later say. 'Initially you are obviously scared, then the training kicks in and it's just fantastic.' Although still only 18 at the time and one of the youngest soldiers serving in Afghanistan, Pte Woollard was already a veteran of many firefights with the Taliban.

The blast blew Pte Woollard off his feet and left him poll-axed on the ground, temporarily paralysed by both fear and pain. The other soldiers around him immediately thought they had come under mortar fire. Pte Woollard knew differently. Raising his head and looking down at his leg, he could see that his right foot had been blown off and part of it was embedded in his left thigh. Both of his forearms had been burnt by the blast and torn open by shrapnel, which also peppered his upper legs. At first he struggled to speak, but as the smoke and dust cleared he managed to scream: 'Woollard. I'm hit, I'm hit.'

His colleagues came to his aid and immediately began to give him life-saving treatment. A tourniquet was wrapped around his leg to stop the loss of blood and he was given a dose of morphine. One of his friends held his hands, gave him words of encouragement and told him to think of his family and stay strong.

At the same time a casevac request was sent to Camp Bastion, telling the operations rooms that a soldier had just been involved in a mine strike and was now a T1 casualty. Within minutes of the message being received the Immediate Response Team helicopter was fired up and on its way to Kajaki to bring back the wounded soldier to the field hospital in Camp Bastion.

Speaking after the incident, Pte Woollard said:

> Initially, after the blast, I thought I was dead. I actually said to myself, 'I'm dead.' Then I thought, 'Well, I can't be dead because I'm thinking this.' I could hear the blokes around shouting 'Who's hurt, who's been hit?' I knew straight away that I had stepped on a landmine but everyone else thought it was a mortar attack.
>
> At first I couldn't move or speak. I was in shock and the words just wouldn't come out. It was as though I was paralysed. My arms were burnt and bleeding with shrapnel wounds. Then I managed to move. I looked down and could see that my foot had gone – it had been blown off – and I thought: 'I'm going home.' I was gutted because I wanted to stay with my mates.
>
> I was conscious all the way through the whole thing so I saw and heard everything. I could see the look of concern on the faces of the blokes and I didn't think I was going to make it. I thought I was going to be one of those guys who survives the blast and then dies later.
>
> But then the morphine began to kick in. I kept drifting away and the morphine takes away the fear and I was ready to accept that I might die.

Despite his injuries, Pte Woollard has no regrets. 'Even if I knew I was going to lose my leg I would do it all again. Being a soldier is the best job in the world.'

When Pte Woollard arrived at Headley Court in the UK to begin his rehabilitation, he said the large number of amputees was shocking. 'You hear about the injured but you never really think about them until it happens to you. When I arrived here I thought "Bloody hell, there are so many."'

Pte Woollard was not the only casualty of his injury. Every day his mother, Angela, relives the morning she was told her son had been injured. 'Mum has suffered more than me. She panics when the phone rings and is now having counselling, so hopefully she will get over it in time.'

At the time of writing, more than 40 servicemen have lost limbs fighting in Afghanistan. In all likelihood that number will increase. The nature of their wounds will determine whether they will be allowed to stay in the Army or whether they will have to look for another career. Pte Woollard's leg was amputated below the knee, so he has a good chance of getting back to the level of fitness required for an infantryman. However, his forearms were badly damaged in the blast and were repaired using skin grafts which have reduced their flexibility and may prevent him from properly holding a rifle, a fact which could signal the end of his military adventure. 'I will have to wait and see what the future holds,' he says.

By the end of June 2007, life for the soldiers of the Royal Anglians was beginning to take on a deadly routine. The soldiers would go out on patrol and would invariably face some sort of resistance from the Taliban. More often than not they would be sent back into the same area where they had been attacked 24 hours earlier, leaving the Taliban with two choices: run or fight.

11

FRIENDLY FIRE

On 30 June 2007, 5 and 6 Platoons of B Company of the Royal Anglians were sent back into the village of Kowtayzay in the Upper Sangin Valley to conduct a clearance operation. The village had been the scene of heavy fighting the previous day and B Company were given the task of flushing out the enemy. Everyone knew it was a risky operation. They also knew that by the end of the day several members of the company could be dead or injured. The majority of those taking part in the operation were very anxious. The enemy they had fought on the previous day were clearly highly motivated and well-organized. Everyone knew that on this occasion the Taliban would fight rather than run. Not much sleep was had the night before the operation. The soldiers went to bed late, after hours of planning and kit-checking. Most of the company were awake before first light and few had the stomach for a cooked breakfast.

One of those taking part in the operation was LCpl Levi David Ashby, who in 2007 was just 21. LCpl Ashby was the commander of 2 Section in 6 Platoon. Despite his age, LCpl Ashby had already seen a great deal of action in Afghanistan. He had seen men fall and die in battle and he knew that this operation was going to be tough.

The fighting erupted as soon as the first elements of 5 Platoon moved into Kowtayzay. They were ambushed by a large Taliban force positioned in well-defended compounds. The Anglians were forced to take cover as a barrage of RPGs exploded around them. The Taliban were aware that if they allowed the British to get close to their positions before opening fire, they would be less inclined to use air strikes against them. The fighting was ferocious and at close quarters. The British troops could clearly see the flashes of gunfire coming from the Taliban positions just 50m away. The proximity to the enemy also precluded the use of artillery or mortars. Both platoons were fighting hard to fix the enemy in preparation for an assault.

With 5 Platoon providing fire support to suppress the enemy, 6 Platoon was ordered to destroy the remaining enemy position, thought to number around eight Taliban, which was established in an irrigation ditch to the south of the village. 2 Section, commanded by Ashby and supported by 3 Section, assaulted the enemy position with bayonets fixed. Heavy and accurate fire forced both sections into cover as they broke into the position. Just as the two sections were preparing to launch another attack, an RPG exploded in the centre of 3 Section, severely injuring five of the team, including the section commander.

LCpl Ashby immediately realized the severity of the situation. The injured troops were sitting ducks and were in danger of being picked off by Taliban snipers. It was also apparent that some of the injured might die unless they received urgent medical treatment.

LCpl Ashby quickly issued a new set of orders and his men rushed forward to the irrigation ditch which was occupied by the Taliban. The situation was now dangerous and complex. 2 Section were now being engaged from several different positions but, despite the weight of fire they were facing, LCpl Ashby managed to coordinate the extraction of the casualties. LCpl Ashby was told that he would be reinforced by another section which would be moving up to join him. However, he soon realized that they would be exposed to enemy fire as soon as they broke cover. So, at enormous risk to himself, he grabbed a GPMG which had belonged to one of the injured men and crawled to an exposed area of high ground where he was an obvious target for the enemy. As the reinforcements moved forward, LCpl Ashby began raking the enemy position with automatic fire and he continued to engage the Taliban single-handedly until all of the casualties and his own section were back in the safety of the village. Only then did LCpl Ashby rejoin them. For his remarkable bravery, LCpl Levi David Ashby was awarded the Military Cross.

The Royal Anglians continued to push the Taliban further and further up the Sangin Valley throughout the summer of 2007 in a series of operations which led to the creation of a number of patrol bases on Route 611, the road which links Sangin with Kajaki. Route 611 is really just a rough track, but in this part of Helmand it is equivalent to the M1 motorway,

On 17 July, C (Essex) Company occupied one of these bases, called Patrol Base Inkerman – a dust bowl of a compound on the edge of the Green Zone, around 6km northeast of Sangin. The compound covered an area of two or three acres but there were very few buildings in which the troops could live. The base was horribly exposed and could be observed from several high features in the area. There was no electricity, running water or toilets. Although surrounded by an 8m-high wall, it still needed greater protection if it was to be a secure base for up to 200 men.

Occupation of the base was part of a wider plan to keep the pressure on the Taliban and force them further and further north out of the Sangin Valley. The base had once been home to the ANA and, while the Anglians had some reservations about occupying a compound which was in range of Taliban weapon systems in the Green Zone, the troops quickly set about turning the compound into their new home.

A Fire Control Tower was built to house a new mortar-locating radar system and sangars were built in each of the corners. Viking armoured vehicles soon arrived, as did the much-lauded Mastiff troop carriers which were later to prove extremely popular with the soldiers because of their ability to withstand improvised explosive devices and mine strikes with impunity. Toilets were also built, but these were merely screened-off holes in the ground. An operations room was established in one of the few buildings available, as was a first aid post.

Inkerman Patrol Base had been named in honour of Guardsman Tony Downes of the Inkerman Company, the 1st Battalion of the Grenadier Guards, who was killed on Saturday 9 June close to the area where the base was later established. The 20-year-old Guardsman had been part of the Operating and Mentoring Liaison Team operating in the area. Guardsman Downes, who was single and from Manchester, gained a staggering 16 GCSEs and so was the obvious choice to be the company's intelligence representative, a crucial job within Inkerman Company. Although, he had only been in the Army for three years, Guardsman Downes was already a veteran of the Iraq War and had been earmarked for future promotion.

He was on patrol with the ANA during an operation to widen the irrigation ditches in an area close to the town of Sangin when his vehicle was hit by an IED. Lieutenant Colonel Carew Hatherley, Commanding Officer 1st Battalion Grenadier Guards, said:

Always full of energy and enthusiasm, his intellect and humour constantly shone through the darkest of situations. He was a resolute and steadfast friend to all who knew him. He excelled as a soldier, whether in tunic and bearskin or combats, and was held in the highest regard by all who had the pleasure to serve alongside him.

Over the previous twelve weeks he had fought alongside his fellow Grenadiers and the Afghan National Army soldiers against the Taliban, never once flinching from his duty. He gave his life in selfless service to his country. He will be greatly missed and never forgotten.

Major Marcus J.G. Elliot-Square, the Inkerman OC, described Guardsman Downes as, 'One of the most remarkable Guardsmen that I have had the pleasure to serve with.' He went on:

He was a man of huge intellect. In possession of sixteen GCSEs he was always going to be the Company's choice as intelligence rep. This was a responsibility that he fully embraced, always willing to give informed briefs at a moment's notice. He had developed such a depth of understanding about the areas that we worked in that the Company was always well prepared. Consummately professional in everything he did, he never stopped gathering vital intelligence whilst on patrol in areas such as Sangin, Gereshk and Babaji.

He was completely dedicated to his job and to the men around him, making him both a pleasure and an honour to command. Guardsman Downes loved soldiering and so died doing something he loved and believed in totally. Guardsman Downes added so much to the Company and asked for very little in return. He was a real asset and his loss will be felt keenly within the Inkerman Company and the Grenadier Guards as a whole. His family and girlfriend have our deepest sympathies and our thoughts will be with them always.

The soldier's death was a bitter blow to the company and the men of Inkerman had promised revenge. The following poem, entitled 'Get it up you Terry', was written on a cardboard box and hung on the wall outside the operations room in Inkerman.

Behind a sangar in Jusyalay we sit,
Waiting for another RPG to hit.
Sometime today it will happen again for sure,
Terry Taliban will finish second once more.
We'll man our guns and hit him back,
Hoping to put him in a black sack.
GMG, Javelin and .50 cal,
You'll learn right quick you're not our pal.
When mortars land around you and above your head,
Your skinny, filthy, little bodies it will shred.
With you your evil, your cruelty, your hate will die,
I promise you no one will ever cry.
You're bullies, you're cowards like a disgusting pest,
When you're in a grave that's when we will rest.
You're bastard IED took our mate Downesy's life,
But all that did was create you a world of strife!
Not even Allah will be able to help you out,
Cause all you'll hear is 'Inkerman's' victory shout.
RIP Downesy. Gone but not forgotten.

For civilians such sentiments might be difficult to understand, but it must be remembered that the loss of a close and much admired colleague, such as Guardsman Downes, is the equivalent to the loss of a family member.

Immediately following their occupation of the Inkerman Patrol Base, life for the 150 men of C Company was relatively quiet. Just 1,500m beyond Inkerman's thick mud-baked walls, the Taliban were watching. Their spies in the small hamlet which lay just a few hundred metres beyond Inkerman's gates would inform the Taliban of small but important details, such as the number and times of the patrols which left the base daily and the frequency of helicopters and the duration of their stay. This all helped to build up a detailed intelligence picture of life inside the base. The Taliban were keen to know the compound's weak spots and how the troops inside would respond when they did eventually attack.

Life inside Inkerman changed dramatically in late July 2007, during the second week of C Company's occupation. The compound, and patrols leaving its confines, came under attack almost every day. On some days it would be a burst of machine-gun fire, while on others the compound would come under indirect fire from rockets and mortars. With each day the attacks grew more intense.

Captain David Hicks, C Company's second-in-command, was becoming increasingly concerned for the safety of his men, the majority of whom were living in the open with just a mosquito net protecting them from the outside world. He knew only too well that a mortar round landing in the centre of a platoon's sleeping area would cause devastation. Some protection was afforded by the creation of Hesco walls, which were being constructed by the Royal Engineers, but the size of the base meant that it would be weeks before the camp received the additional defences he had requested. As far as Capt Hicks was concerned, the work was not taking place quickly enough and he made his views known to the chain of command. His main concern, shared by Lieutenant Colonel Stuart Carver, the Royal Anglian's Commanding Officer, and Major Phil Messenger, the Officer Commanding C Company, was that there wasn't a doctor based at Inkerman.

Brigade headquarters and the Joint Force Medical Team had made the decision that the level of threat facing Inkerman was such that the 200 troops based there could be catered for by a small team of combat medics. Although these individuals are highly trained and are more than capable of dealing with gunshot wounds and traumatic amputation – in the sense that they can keep a wounded individual alive until they undergo surgery – their skills are limited. For instance, because they are not qualified doctors they cannot prescribe medicines or carry out surgery, however minor.

As the second week in August approached, Capt Hicks found himself in charge of C Company when his boss, Maj Messenger, left Afghanistan for two weeks R and R. By now, the lack of a doctor had become a major headache for Capt Hicks, who had put in numerous requests, only to have them all turned down. This was not Capt Hicks' only concern, though. According to a fellow officer, he had also made it clear to his battalion headquarters that he needed greater force protection and more air support in the form of Apache attack helicopters.

The dangers facing C Company were tragically illustrated on Friday 10 August 2006. A patrol composed of soldiers from 11 Platoon left Inkerman for the Green Zone to check on an irrigation project near the area of Jusyalay. After arriving at the Green Zone, the troops moved in single file, every man scanning the area around him and knowing that at any minute the Taliban could strike.

The soldiers were just settling into the pattern of the patrol, their early nerves calmed by a lack of human activity in the area, when the peace of a sunny August day was shattered by the unmistakable rattle of AK47 gunfire. The troops dived for cover as the bullets sliced through the vegetation and thudded into the ground around their feet.

One of the soldiers on patrol described the incident:

It was a boiling hot day just like any other in Helmand. We were patrolling through the Green Zone and were just coming up to a small hamlet. We knew that there were Taliban in the area – they're always are around here. They regard the Green Zone as their territory. Then we came under fire. It's not like in the movie, you hear the crack of bullets and they thump when they hit the ground or fizz if they pass above your head. The rounds were coming down amongst us, so instinctively everyone had hit the ground and fire control orders were being shouted out as we tried to locate the enemy position.

The troops located the enemy position and returned fire, which gave way to a short but intense firefight. Then, one of the soldiers noticed that Private Tony Rawson was lying slumped on the ground. He had been shot through the head in the opening stages of the firefight and killed instantly.

One of the patrol said:

It was pretty surreal. One moment he was alive and one of us and the next he was dead. You sit there and think, 'What a fucking waste', and then it dawns on you and you realize that it could've easily have been you and that's when you realize that it's all about luck. Nicey didn't do anything wrong – it was just wrong time, wrong place. His time had come and nothing was going to change that.

Pte Rawson's body was flown back to Camp Bastion and the patrol returned to Inkerman, shattered, exhausted and wondering when the killing would stop.

Pte Rawson was one of the most popular soldiers in the whole of the battalion. His willingness to help those around him, no matter what the task, had earned him the nickname 'Nicey'. He had joined the Army in 2002 at the age of 22 and was dedicated to his regiment. He had already been selected for promotion and, despite still being a private, was working as the section second-in-command when he was killed. He had been in Helmand for a little over a month when he was shot dead. A knee injury sustained before the battalion departed for Helmand prevented him from accompanying his colleagues earlier.

At the time of his death, Captain David Hicks, said:

> Private Rawson epitomized not only the core values of the British Army, but also embodied the spirit of the British Infantry. Selfless, good-natured even in the face of adversity, and courageous under fire, he will be sorely missed by all his comrades within C (Essex) Company. His loss will be felt deeply by all those who knew him. All our thoughts are with his family and friends at this time.

Like any death within a close-knit organization such as C Company the impact was hard and immediate. After Pte Rawson's lifeless body was taken back to Camp Bastion by the medical helicopter, the 27-year-old soldier was pronounced dead at the scene. The soldiers returned to Inkerman, each man lost in thought.

While his friends and colleagues sat around their platoon location under the scorching Afghan sun and swapped fond memories of a soldier they would never see again, his platoon sergeant went through the painful task of collecting his military kit and personal belongings. It is not good for morale for a dead soldier's equipment to lie around for all to see and on which to ponder.

A bad week for C Company was about to get even worse. It had become clear to Capt Hicks that the Taliban had decided that Inkerman was now a priority target. One man under his command had already been killed, and, although Pte Rawson died instantly, Capt Hicks was determined that he would not lose another soldier. After penning Pte Rawson's eulogy, he sent another message to brigade headquarters via his battalion requesting a doctor but the same, negative response came back. For the time being, he was told, there were no spare medical officers available.

At around 1315hrs, Capt Hicks was chatting to his girlfriend on one of the satellite phones which formed part of the 'welfare package' for troops. Each soldier is allotted a certain number of minutes each week, which he can use to call girlfriends, family or friends. Although there was mobile phone coverage across most of Helmand, soldiers were warned not to call home on private phones because the Taliban had developed a means of downloading numbers from soldiers' mobile phones.

As he chatted, the base came under a sustained attack from the Taliban. Capt Hicks told his girlfriend, Nicola, he had to go and would call later. Tragically, they were the last words the couple would ever exchange.

As Capt Hicks donned his body armour and helmet and cocked his rifle, either a mortar round or an RPG flew over one of the compound's walls and exploded near to where a member of the ANA was standing. The impact was devastating and virtually severed the poor soldier's legs at the hip. He would later die in the military hospital in Camp Bastion.

As the battle raged, Capt Hicks ran up the ladder into the Fire Control Tower and began to take control of the ensuing battle. The troops in sangars returned fire with .50 calibre machine-guns and the mortar crew, housed in pits close to the northernmost wall, sprang into life. All over the compound soldiers who had been sleeping or resting out of the heat of the early afternoon were running to their 'stand to' positions or taking cover from the indirect mortar and rocket fire as it landed around them.

By now Capt Hicks was in the Fire Control Tower, firing on to Taliban positions. Although the tower afforded the best view, it was also the most exposed, with the only protection being offered by a wall of sandbags. It was at that point that disaster struck. The Taliban had managed to move a Russian-made anti-tank gun up to a tree-line some 1,500m from the north face of the Inkerman compound. The gun crew managed to fire just one round, but it had a devastating impact. The missile struck the FCT and injured around seven of the soldiers inside, including Captain Hicks. All of the injured suffered shrapnel wounds. Capt Hicks had wounds to his leg, groin, shoulder and head. While undergoing treatment from Corporal Haley Pierce, a 20-year-old female member of the Royal Army Medical Corps, Capt Hicks insisted that he should be allowed to return to the tower so that he could continue coordinating the fight back. It has been claimed that he also refused morphine, although it is highly unlikely that he was offered any as casualties with head wounds are never given morphine.

An Immediate Response Team helicopter was requested but its arrival was delayed by the ongoing battle. Initially, the delay was not regarded as too much of a problem for the injured. Although the wounds were very serious, their conditions had stabilized. However, Capt Hicks' condition began to slowly deteriorate. Unbeknown to Cpl Pierce, Capt Hicks was bleeding internally and his life was ebbing away. By the time the helicopter arrived, some 45 minutes later, he was barely conscious. He died on the way to hospital.

Two deaths in two days had a devastating impact on both the company and the battalion, not least because Capt Hicks had been complaining about the lack of both a doctor and force protection for several weeks. The following day, the battalion second-in-command demanded that the time had come for a medical officer to be sent to Inkerman. Later that day, a doctor finally arrived.

Capt Hicks had decided to leave the Army when his regiment returned from Helmand. According to those who knew him, he loved every minutes of his Army career but, like many soldiers who have tasted battle, he was keen to see what else life had to offer.

Lt Col Carver was told of Capt Hicks' death while he was back home in the UK, relaxing with his family while on R and R. It was the second time in two days in which he had to put pen to paper and write a eulogy for one of his men:

Captain Dave Hicks was an outstanding officer who will be sorely missed by all members of the Battalion. It is typical of him that he had led from the forward position during the attack on his Company, in order to best direct the battle and provide an inspiring example to his men. Even after being mortally wounded his only concern was to get back into position to control the fight. Highly professional with a genuine concern for his soldiers, he typified the highest standards of leadership and commanded genuine respect from all who served with him. Our sincere condolences are with his family and friends at this most difficult of times.

Capt Alex Maclay, the Regimental Signals Officer for 1 Royal Anglians, was one of Capt Hicks' closest friends. The pair had been through the rigours of officer training at Sandhurst together, where they were in neighbouring rooms. After learning of his close friend's death, he said: 'Words cannot describe what the loss of Dave means. Whether it was his shoulder to cry on, as a partner in crime, or just comradeship, we shared many good times, the memories of which I will always cherish.' He later told me that tears were shed by many people of all ranks on the day that Capt Hicks died.

The death of Capt Hicks angered many officers and soldiers within the Royal Anglians. Many of his colleagues believed that his death was preventable and was, in part, due to the lack of a doctor at the base. In reality however, his injuries were such that it may be doubtful that he would have survived even if a doctor had been present, but nobody knows for sure.

The loss of Capt Hicks also brought home to many people in the UK the enormous risks soldiers were now facing on a daily basis in Afghanistan. Prime Minister Gordon Brown was deeply moved by Capt Hicks' death and he personally wrote to the soldier's family to express his condolences.

A bloody month for the Royal Anglians, however, was to get worse still. As with the Marines before them, Kajak was a popular posting for the Royal Anglians. It was true that there was a lot of fighting to be done and it was therefore dangerous, but the ranges of battle were much greater than those in the Green Zone and so it was considered by many to be somewhat safer. Kajaki was also relatively isolated, sitting at the top of the Sangin Valley, and commanders and soldiers alike revelled in the fact that they could get on with the job of securing the dam and killing the Taliban pretty much as they pleased. The accommodation was also relatively good and was now equipped with showers and proper toilets. What lifted morale beyond anything else was the chance to swim safely in the lake. In the height of summer, when the temperatures nudged 50°C, this was an absolute godsend.

It was said that while Kajaki was a plum posting for the British, it was a death sentence for the Taliban. Rumour had it amongst the British troops that those Taliban and foreign fighters who survived the battles in and around Garmsir were posted up to Kajaki, where their life expectancy was very short. It must have been a daunting experience for a young Taliban fighter to be plucked from his village on the Pakistan border and sent to a madrassa where he was indoctrinated by Mullahs bent on destroying the infidels in neighbouring Afghanistan. After a few weeks of military training, he would have been press-ganged into a unit bound for Garmsir, in the south of Helmand, where he might be lucky and escape with his life. These wretched people are quite literally cannon fodder.

At around 1600hrs on 23 August, a company-sized fighting force from B (Suffolk) Company left the base at Kajaki to conduct an advance-to-contact operation. This was an operation which had been conducted countless times before by the men of B Company. They knew the drill and each one of them would normally have been able to predict the sequence of events. The troops leave their base, patrol out into the wide open mountainous area beyond their camp and then contact the enemy. A firefight ensues, cover air support is called, the compound in which the Taliban are hiding is destroyed and then cleared by the Royal Anglians, who then move on and continue with the operation. Only one out of the numerous patrols conducted by B Company had not been in contact with the enemy.

The only difference with this particular patrol was that it took place in the late afternoon rather than in the morning. The patrol was under the command of Major Tony Borgnis, the Officer Commanding B Company, and consisted of the company tactical headquarters as well as soldiers from 7 Platoon under the command of Lieutenant George Seal-Coon.

The patrol pushed north to the forward line of enemy troops, or FLET. Here, the ground was very open with rolling hills. There are four or five major *wadis* in the area, which the troops used to move their longer-range weapon systems into action. By and large, the fighting was at long range, at around 200 to 300m and often much further out. Only once had the men of B Company been forced to fix bayonets in anticipation of a close-quarter battle.

The basic plan was to conduct an advance-to-contact and push up to the area of Merzie and then on to Mazdurak before returning to the base around last light. The Royal Anglians were accompanied by a team of ANA soldiers. Now that the ANA had a few months of operational experience under their belt, it was established procedure for them to accompany all British patrols. As well as supplying additional fire support, they were also responsible for searching and clearing Afghan compounds.

As the troops pushed forward, they would be supported by the troops in Wmiks fitted with .50 calibre machine-guns which could lay down accurate fire up to around 1,800m. As the troops moved on foot, the Fire Support Group moved on to a high feature known as Essex Ridge where they could give the best possible covering fire. The patrol also had close air support in the form of two US F–15 ground attack jets.

The patrol was going according to plan. The company pushed forward to Merzie without any sign of the enemy and the compounds in the area were cleared by the ANA without incident. The patrol continued and moved towards the area of Mazdurak. At this stage 6 Platoon were moving along a *wadi* when they started to take enemy fire. Everyone in the company knew that contact with the enemy would be made. When it came, there was no surprise. Like a well-oiled machine, the company pushed forward to give support to the men of 6 Platoon.

Lt Seal-Coon moved his lead section – 2 Section – into a compound known as 248. Four of his soldiers climbed on to the roof while another soldier, Private Robert Foster, positioned himself inside the building and acted as a link-man, ready to move when he was called. Foster was one of the fellow Catterick trainees of Pte Chris Gray, who had been killed in Nowzad in April. Lt Seal-Coon pushed another of his sections out to one side to provide flank security for his position, some 80m away. By now, his lead section were putting down quite a serious rate of fire on to the enemy position and Lt Seal-Coon climbed on to the roof to join them. The roof was corrugated so the soldiers lay in the dipped sections to give themselves an extra bit of protection from enemy fire. It was at about this time that the Fire Support Group started taking enemy fire. RPGs, mortars and small arms fire began landing close to their position. As this was happening, Maj Borgnis called on the Joint Tactical Air Controller to start talking the F–15s on to the target. Air support is never a problem around Kajaki because it is often the chosen area for coalition jets to refuel. The Air Controller gave the locations of the friendly troops to the pilots – a standard safety procedure.

An F–15 circled high above until the pilot was ready to launch his attack. The pilot told the ground controller that he was about to begin his bombing run and a warning over the radio-net stated that the bombs would hit in 20 seconds.

The soldiers on the roof peered into the distance, waiting for the bombs to hit, when there was a blinding flash, instantly followed by a thunderous explosion. The shockwave tore through the building, followed by thousands of razor sharp pieces of shrapnel. With seconds the whole area was engulfed by a plume of powdery dust. The roar of the bombs rolled around the surrounding country.

Something had gone terribly wrong. A bomb had struck the wrong target.

Speaking to me after the incident, Lt Seal-Coon said: 'All I got over the net was that the bombs would hit in 20 seconds. A short while after that there was a loud bang and the shockwave hit the building which I and the other guys were on. I realized immediately that something had gone badly wrong.'

Private Foster, 19, from Harlow, was still inside the building. His friend, Private James McClure, a 19-year-old from Ipswich who he had met along with Pte Gray while training at Catterick in 2006, was on the roof. Also on the roof were Private John Thrumble, 21, from Chelmsford, Corporal Stuart Parker, the 2 Section commander, and Private Joshua Lee, 19.

Lt Seal-Coon went on:

The bombs landed just 20 feet away. I remember ducking down before they hit. Perhaps I saw or heard something which I can't remember but I ducked down and that reaction probably saved my life. I know I am lucky to be alive. Since that moment I have been left with a sense of disbelief over what happened and the fact that I managed to escape, virtually without a scratch. I can remember the shockwave hitting me, it pushed me down between the two arches of the roof. I knew what had happened, I knew the bomb had fallen short. I can't say that I was angry with anyone at that stage. I knew a mistake had been made but how and why was something that would be dealt with later.

Seconds later, Lt Seal-Coon hauled himself to his feet. The force of the blast had broken his radio, his chest hurt and he sensed that his hearing had been damaged. As he moved along the roof, he saw that a large part of the compound and the building he was on had been damaged. It was then that he saw the injured soldiers lying on the roof in front of him.

It was a scene of utter carnage. I was probably in shock from the effects of the blast and the state of the casualties. I yelled out that we had casualties on the roof. I could see the other company moving down to where we were and I suppose they must have realized that the bomb had hit our position.

Lt Seal-Coon could see from the appalling injuries to both Ptes McClure and Thrumble that they were probably dead. Their clothes and body armour had been ripped from them. Neither of the two soldiers appeared to be breathing.

'We were now totally exposed to the enemy and I knew it was just a matter of time before we would start taking enemy fire but my main concern at that stage was to get the casualties off the roof and get them some first aid,' said Lt Seal-Coon.

As he moved forward, Lt Seal-Coon saw that Cpl Parker and Pte Lee were in a bizarre embrace. Initially, he thought they were also probably dead but as he approached them he heard the men moan. Although both were burnt and covered in deep abrasions, the fact that they appeared to be conscious meant that they had a good chance of survival.

Pte McClure was passed down to the medics below. He was not breathing and there was no sign of a heartbeat. Although medics tried to revive him it was clear to all that he had died.

Seconds after the bomb landed, a soldier turned to Michael 'Woody' Woodrow, the 11 Platoon sergeant, and, pointing to the scene of the explosion, said, 'Your blokes are down there.' Sgt Woodrow, fearing the worst, rushed down to the bomb-damaged building and witnessed the scene of utter devastation.

I saw one soldier partly hanging off the roof. The moment I saw his face I knew that he was dead. I pulled one guy out of the rubble. He looked up at me and said we've got casualties. That's when the boss popped up. He had fallen through the roof. He stood up, looked at me and said we had casualties. I suppose it was at that stage that I began to realize how bad the situation was.

Sgt Woodrow immediately sent a 'Check Air' message over the radio. It was now beginning to dawn on everybody, including the pilot, that a tragic error had been made. Sgt Woodrow said, 'I knew at that stage that we had at least two dead and two were very badly injured.'

Soldiers from 6 Platoon took the bodies of Ptes Thrumble and McClure while Cpl Parker and Pte Lee were carried back by 11 Platoon.

The troops were met by a quad bike which took the casualties to an armoured Pinzgauer vehicle. To cover the extraction, a smokescreen was laid using the 51mm mortar, but this did not prevent the Pinz being fired on as it loaded the casualties into the rear. The Pinz pulled away slowly. The medics feared that those who had survived the blast may have suffered lung damage, which could easily become a very serious problem.

The soldiers eventually arrived at the rendezvous, which was to be used for the IRT extraction. Lt Seal-Coon said:

> The guys did a fantastic job of keeping it together. We all knew at that stage that we had lost some close friends. We had been together as a unit for two years and we all knew each other really well. We were like a family, some of those guys were as close as brothers.

After the injured and dead were extracted by helicopter, the rest of the company moved back to their base. They were shattered and exhausted, with some men in tears. Sgt Woodrow conducted another head count. He was one man short.

He told Lt Seal-Coon and together the pair did another head count and then another. Both men looked at each other and were struck by the realization that someone had been left behind. It was Private Robert Foster. Both men had assumed that he had departed the scene with the soldiers of 6 Platoon when they withdrew with the bodies of the dead. Lt Seal-Coon said:

> I told the OC straight away that we had left someone behind. The building was at least 3km away so we immediately began to draw up a plan to go back out. I was gripped by a terrible fear that he might be taken either dead or alive by the Taliban. It was something that was a very real possibility but which I could barely bring myself to think about.

Soldiers from 6 Platoon mounted in the Pinz with four soldiers from 7 Platoon and a signaller. Together with Lt Seal-Coon and Sgt Woodrow, they left for the damaged and smoking compound. Lt Seal-Coon continued:

> When we got back to the compound I took one look at the building he was in and was 100 per cent sure he was dead. The building had been completely destroyed and he was inside it. We dug with our bare hands at first and then some shovels arrived when troops from the Helmand Reaction Force arrived by helicopter to conduct an RIP with 6 Platoon. We carried on digging until we eventually found him at around 2.30am. He was in one piece but he had died instantly – he didn't suffer and that was a blessing.

Chris Gray, James McClure and Robert Foster, the three privates who became friends while training to become members of the Royal Anglians at Catterick in 2006, were now all dead.

By the time Lt Seal-Coon and the rest of the soldiers returned to the Kajaki base, most of those who had taken part in the battle had fallen asleep, emotionally and physically exhausted. 'I tried to get a couple of hours sleep,' said Lt Seal-Coon, 'but it was too difficult. I had too much on my mind.'

The following morning, many of the soldiers hoped that the previous evening's events had been a horrific dream. Everyone wanted to know how the two survivors, Cpl Parker and Pte Lee, were doing. It was still early days and they were still very seriously injured, but it was thought that both would survive.

Sergeant Woodrow had been trained in Trauma Risk Management, known as 'Trim'. He knew that over the next few days many of his men would start to get angry, have sleepless nights and even feel guilty over having survived. Both he and Lt Seal-Coon encouraged the soldiers to talk to one another about their feelings and to express their anger and cry – and most did. Lt Seal-Coon said:

> Most of the soldiers cried at some stage, including me. We encouraged people not to bottle up their emotions. Everyone was very down. Some of the guys busied themselves getting the

casualties' kit together. We knew that the injured wouldn't be coming back for this tour so we packaged it up.

News of the tragedy broke on the morning of Friday 24 August. The immediate assumption was that the US pilots had messed up. There had been several previous occasions in which so-called 'trigger happy' US pilots, keen to get a kill under their belts in combat, had attacked friendly forces. Although this has been the case in some incidents in Iraq, there is no evidence to suggest that this has been the case in Afghanistan. In fact, many soldiers have told me that they owe their lives to the bravery and skill of the coalition pilots. US jets have conducted hundreds, if not thousands, of bombing runs for the British and have saved many lives.

The tragedy also raised the thorny issue of combat identification. The UK has yet to purchase any form of sophisticated system which will electronically alert friendly troops as to the positions of other friendly troops on the ground. Instead, the British military has what it calls a range of tactics and procedures, using marker panels, various infra-red signals and basic training to avoid 'blue-on-blue' attacks – so-called because blue is the colour used to illustrate friendly forces on a map.

Every soldier knows that the battlefield is a complex and dangerous place where things can go wrong and as a result troops can be seriously injured and killed. Such incidents have probably taken place in every significant war for the past 1,000 years. But this should not be used as a get-out clause by the British Army to make up for the fact that it had not invested enough in combat identification. Privately, many senior officers I spoke to in Afghanistan immediately after the incident were appalled that they were being sent into combat in the twenty-first century without such equipment when several, workable combat ID systems were available on the market. Officially, of course, no one was prepared to go on the record and complain for they knew only too well that such comments could damage, if not end, military careers.

At the time of writing, the incident was the subject of three investigations. The US Air Force was looking into the tragedy to see if its pilot was at fault or whether there was a fault with the bomb. A British Board of Inquiry was also established to discover what went wrong. And, as with all service deaths, an inquiry by the Special Investigation Branch of the Royal Military Police was launched. The reality is, of course, that the accident can only be down to three things: pilot error, an error by the Air Controller or a problem with the bomb. Satellite guided bombs are relatively simple. A sophisticated nose cone, attached to the front of the bomb, uses satellite guidance to steer the bomb, via fins attached to the rear, on to the target. If the satellite or the fins lock then the bomb goes from 'smart' to 'dumb' and it will fall anywhere that gravity takes it.

A few days after the tragedy, the bodies of the three men were flown home to the UK from Camp Bastion in a moving service which almost every member of the base attended to pay their respects. Lt Seal-Coon was one of the standard bearers carrying the regimental colours as the bodies of his three soldiers were loaded on to a Hercules transport aircraft for their final journey home. Lt Seal-Coon admitted that the ceremony was difficult, but he was glad he attended.

After the incident, 11 Platoon were moved from Kajaki to Sangin to provide base security as part of a pre-planned move for Operation Palk Ghar. This period out of the frontline helped the men come to terms with the loss of their colleagues and gave them the opportunity to chat and remember those who died. Gradually, the sleepless nights suffered by some soldiers came to an end and the men were able to remember their mates without tears welling up in their eyes.

Two weeks later, 11 Platoon were back in Kajaki conducting a virtually identical patrol to that in which the three were killed. The patrol ran into a large group of Taliban fighters entrenched in a series of compounds. On this occasion, five air strikes were called, delivering bombs on to the target without incident. More than 25 Taliban were killed.

12

THE KILLING ZONE

As the months of the summer of 2007 progressed, the Taliban were pushed even deeper down the Sangin Valley by the men of 12 Mechanized Brigade and 1 Royal Anglians. The battle against the Taliban in this part of Helmand was difficult and dangerous work which had cost the lives of many soldiers, both coalition and Afghan.

In reality, the push had begun when the Paras entered Sangin in June 2006, as has been described in earlier chapters. Back then, the Paras were satisfied just to hang on in Sangin – in those difficult and violent days, no one who was there could actually conceive of a time when the Taliban would be driven out. The turning point came with the launch of Operation Silver in late April 2007 when the Taliban were left reeling by a series of body blows by the men of the Royal Anglians.

Operation Lastay Kulang took place at the end of May, eight weeks after Operation Silver, when troops from Task Force Fury, the theatre reserve battalion from the US 82nd Airborne Division, were used in a clearance of the Upper Sangin Valley, south of Kajaki. During this operation a US Chinook was shot down by small arms fire after dropping off US troops, killing seven personnel including one British soldier.

Operation Ghartse Ghar followed at the end of June. A force of around 600 troops, mostly Royal Anglians but supported by Danish and Estonian soldiers, went into the Green Zone to clear the Taliban from Jusyalay, which lies between Sangin and Putay. The operation was launched to provide safe conditions so that work could continue on digging essential irrigation ditches to prevent crops from drying up and decaying in the intense Afghan sun.

To maintain the element of surprise, soldiers from A (Norfolk) Company set off overnight on the operation from their base in Sangin. They covered the 16km distance to their starting position on foot, carrying up to 80lbs of equipment such as heavy machine-guns, mortars and under-slung grenade launchers as well as food and water.

At dawn the following day, the Royal Anglian soldiers approached the Taliban positions in a pincer movement from all sides, blocking their escape routes. The Afghan National Army was used to draw out the Taliban so that the Royal Anglians could engage them and push them further north and out of the Sangin Valley area.

The soldiers came under attack from small arms fire and rocket-propelled grenades, which continued throughout the day. At one point during the battle, the ANA soldiers were pinned down by the Taliban and support from a US F–15 was called in to drop a 2,000lb bomb on the Taliban position, killing eight fighters.

Despite the severity of the firefights, A and B Companies continued their advance through the Sangin Valley, clearing the Jusyalay area. The remaining hardcore Taliban were destroyed or managed to escape. During the operation, the soldiers were often helped by the local villagers they came across, who gave them vital intelligence on the whereabouts of the Taliban. It was one of the increasing number of occasions in which the local Afghans demonstrated their hatred of the Taliban.

The operation was the first time the Royal Anglians had marched out from their base in Sangin. On all other operations the troops had left in armoured vehicles. The march into the Green Zone took an exhausting 12 hours. After moving to one of the many compounds for the night, A Company was attacked but the Taliban were quickly repelled. During the operation, troops from A (Norfolk) Company became embroiled in what was described as some of the hardest fighting since the Falklands War.

Three days of heavy fighting followed and many foreign fighters, including Waziris and Pakistanis, were killed. These foreign fighters, according to the Royal Anglians, fought well but did not know the ground and were ultimately destroyed by the British. The operation went on for longer than expected, as the Royal Anglians pursued the Taliban through the Green Zone. A Company, who had expected to be out on the ground for around 24 to 48 hours, remained in the Green Zone for a week. Most of the soldiers had only taken a day-sack containing a spare pair of socks and one or two comfort items. No one had taken sleeping bags or spare clothes in order to save weight. For hours on end the troops marched through the broiling and muggy heat of the Green Zone or lay in stinking irrigation ditches, sometimes for up to 12 hours a day. By the end of the week, many of their clothes had quite literally rotted off their backs.

Brig Lorimer described these excursions into the Green Zone as 'mowing the lawn' because of the frequency at which they had to be repeated. Each time the British attacked, the Taliban would initially stand and fight and then melt away. A few weeks later, they would infiltrate back. It really was a case of two steps forward, one step back, but with each operation the Taliban were pushed further away from Sangin. The repetition was necessary because there were not enough troops in the Helmand task force to hold the ground permanently. Consequently, the patrol bases on Route 611 were set up to maintain a presence.

It was after Op Ghartse Ghar that Patrol Base Inkerman was established in late July. At the time, apart from the base at Kajaki, it was the most northerly and isolated patrol base in the Sangin Valley.

Inkerman was also the location at which I joined the Royal Anglians for three weeks in August 2007 as an 'embedded' journalist working for the *Sunday Telegraph*. Such was the nature of the fighting in Afghanistan at the time that any journalist wishing to cover the war on the 'frontline' had to become embedded with the British Army. As part of this type of deal, journalists have to allow their copy and pictures to be read and censored if they in any way breach operational security. Such censorship issues do not rest easily with most journalists and are on the whole looked upon as a necessary evil.

Justin Sutcliffe, a freelance photographer also working for the *Sunday Telegraph*, and I finally arrived in Camp Bastion after four days of travel and delays. Justin is a seasoned photo-journalist who had covered the conflict in Afghanistan since 2001. He had already visited the country on more than ten occasions and travelled widely in the area. His knowledge proved invaluable, as did his sense of humour which kept both our spirits high at times of stress and danger.

Justin and I arrived at the isolated base on the afternoon of Tuesday 28 August by Chinook helicopter. The aircraft was packed with soldiers laden down with equipment. Most of those on board looked lost in thought as the aircraft, flanked by two Apache helicopter gunships, flew at low level northwards to the Sangin Valley. The helicopter was heading deep into enemy territory, where it would be vulnerable from ground fire. If the helicopter crashed, everyone on board would be killed. Try as they might, I'm sure nobody on board could stop themselves thinking of such an event.

Such are the risks facing transport helicopters such as Chinooks in Helmand that they can only fly when they are supported by two Apache gunships. Most commanders accept that it is now just a matter of time before a Chinook packed with troops will be lost in Afghanistan, either by mechanical failure or by enemy action. Twenty minutes after leaving the relative safety of Camp Bastion, one of the air loadmasters on board issued the 'two minutes to landing' sign. The soldiers prepared themselves for a rapid departure, climbing to their feet and readying the weapons for action. As the Chinook touched down, the cabin was immediately filled with fine, powdery, brown dust, which filled our mouths, noses and, for those not wearing goggles, eyes as well. Everyone ran off the Chinook as quickly as possible; it was impossible to see more than 5m so Justin and I just followed everyone else and hoped we were going in the right direction.

A few minutes later, the Chinook was airborne again, sending up a thick, swirling cloud of dust which left many of us completely disorientated. As the dust cleared and the deafening noise of the Chinook's engines began to fade away, we heard the beckoning voices of soldiers standing by an opening into an inner compound.

Justin and I, wearing helmets and body armour and laden down with computer bags, rucksacks and cameras, sprinted towards the gates. The deep desert dust sucked at our feet so, in reality, we were barely jogging. As we arrived breathless at the gate, a tall, bearded officer stuck out a hand, smiled and said: 'You must be the journalists. I'm Matt Fyjis-Walker. Come with me.'

Dressed in shorts, tee-shirt and sandals, with a rifle slung over his shoulder and his hair thick with dust, the young officer continued, 'Welcome to Inkerman, you'll like it here. It's a bit dusty and basic but you'll get use to it.'

As we walked through the camp to the company headquarters, I was struck by how primitive and basic life seemed to be. Most of the soldiers were wandering around in shorts of cut-off combat trousers, tee-shirts and either flip-flops or sandals. Those who weren't wearing shorts wore swimming trunks or underpants and virtually everyone, apart from the two women in the base, sported a thick beard.

Matt explained that he was a lieutenant in the Light Dragoons and had been seconded to C Company as commander of the Fire Support Group, which meant that his main job was to call in air strikes during combat.

We were introduced to Major 'Angry' Phil Messenger, the Officer Commanding C Company, who like his men was wearing cut-off combat trousers, sandals and a maroon tee-shirt lined with dried sweat stains. He had acquired the nickname of 'Angry Phil' for his brief but explosive temper, of which everyone was wary.

It was abundantly clear that the formalities of barrack life had no place in Inkerman. The only way to stay cool was to shed as much clothing as possible. It was also obvious that any attempt to stay clean would be met with failure.

'I suggest you change into shorts if you have them,' said Maj Messenger, smiling. 'You only need to wear your body armour and helmet when you are moving about the camp. I'll get you a brew and brief you on tonight's operation. After that you'll be shown where you are sleeping and I suggest you get some rest.'

The OC explained in detail the nature of Operation Palk Gar, which was due to begin in the early hours of the following morning. Put simply, it was designed to put a squeeze on the Taliban who were believed to be hiding out in the Green Zone. The first phase of the operation had already begun a few days earlier when a squadron of Scimitar light tanks from the Light Dragoons left Camp Bastion and headed north to take up blocking positions on a series of mountain escape routes on the western side of the Green Zone. To the south, US Special Forces from Task Force 71 were moving in to block a major crossing-point and were expected to be involved in some stiff fighting with the Taliban. Northern escape routes would be blocked by Estonian troops and the Brigade Reconnaissance Force. The actual clearance would be conducted by A and C Companies, who would push through the Green Zone in parallel on an advance-to-contact. Resistance was expected to be tough and Lt Col Stuart Carver was hoping to kill at least 300 Taliban. It was, as the soldiers said, the last 'big push' into territory which the Taliban regarded as their turf. It was also hoped that the operation would give 40 Commando, who as part of 52 Brigade would be taking over from the Royal Anglians as the 'Battle Group North', a week or two of breathing space from Taliban attacks as they got to grips with their new environment.

As Maj Messenger handed me a mug of tea, he explained:

So, basically, we want to box the Taliban in and kill them. All the escape routes will be blocked so that should cut off anyone trying to flee. But we won't get all of them, we never do. A lot will melt away, some will try and get back to Musa Qala – we should get those – but the others will keep their heads down for a few weeks and then return. We're leaving here at around 0130 hours so get some sleep, make sure you have plenty of water and at least one spare pair of socks. Tomorrow will be a long day. Now I suggest you get some scoff [army slang for food] and get some rest.

As we walked through the camp we were shown the Fire Control Tower where Capt Dave Hicks was killed just two weeks earlier. I was surprised at how exposed the tower was. Although it was protected by a wall of sandbags, the observation post sat high above the compound walls and would have been an obvious target. It was clear that Capt Hicks' death was still very raw. One could immediately sense that soldiers were unwilling to talk too much about the men who had been killed or injured in action because it reminded them of their own fragile mortality. After just a few days in a war zone, it is obvious that fate or luck plays a huge part. Time and again, I was told stories of narrow escapes where bullets had hit ceramic body armour plates, of mortar rounds that failed to explode and of RPGs passing through the legs of soldiers coming under attack in a Taliban ambush. Even the most professional of soldiers had been killed or wounded, simply because they were in the wrong place at the wrong time. In the end, survival was all down to luck, and everyone knew it.

It is worth mentioning at this stage the situation concerning Rules of Engagement (RoE) – these are a series of conditions which must be met before a soldier or commander can use lethal force or open fire on the enemy.

Until around the end of July 2007, troops in Helmand were allowed to open fire on more or less anyone who could be 'positively identified' as a member of the Taliban – in essence, this meant any armed person acting suspiciously in a Taliban area. Soldiers would have to exercise discretion because a lot of people in Afghanistan have guns and not all of them are members of the Taliban. However, if an individual is seen running across a poppy field with an RPG on his shoulder, the chances are that he is a member of the Taliban and under 'Rule 421 Alpha' soldiers would have been allowed to open fire. If a mistake was made and an innocent individual was shot and wounded or killed, the soldier would be legally protected providing he could prove that it was a genuine mistake and that he had satisfied himself that he had met all of the correct criteria before opening fire. Failure to do so would mean that a soldier might face prosecution for murder or manslaughter.

In late July, however, the RoE were changed, ultimately at the insistence of President Karzai. There had been increasing problems with collateral damage which were mainly, but not exclusively, caused by US troops taking part in Operation Enduring Freedom. Unbeknown to most of the general public at the time, there were still two operations taking place in Afghanistan: the NATO mission, to secure and reconstruct the country, and OEF, the American-led hunt for al-Qaeda, Osama bin Laden and senior members of the Taliban. OEF was an offensive 'search-and-destroy' type operation and operated under different rules from the NATO mission. It was mainly led by US Special Forces, with some involvement from the British SBS and other covert agencies. Mistakes had been made and a large number of innocent Afghan civilians had been killed. As a consequence of this, Karzai put pressure on NATO. British troops in Helmand were ordered to change their RoE from Rule 421 Alpha to what was dubbed Card Alpha. Card Alpha essentially means that troops can only fire in self-defence. I know from my own experience that it is the same RoE that was issued to troops in Northern Ireland.

For many commanders this was a huge mistake and was described as a 'key concern' by one commander in a briefing to senior officers. RoE are complex issues and commanders are fully aware that some soldiers, in the heat of battle and under the pressure of operating in very dangerous areas of Helmand, need clear and concise rules as to when and where it is acceptable to open fire. The last thing that soldiers want and commanders need is for troops to start hesitating when they are on operations.

According to one officer who I spoke to in Helmand, this is precisely what happened. Soldiers on a routine patrol had come under fire. A few minutes later, an Afghan male was seen running away from the area carrying a weapon but no one opened fire. One soldier later told a commander that he had the suspect in his rifle sights but was not sure whether or not he was allowed to open fire under the recent rule change. The soldier was confused – and who can blame him – as to exactly at which point the armed suspect ceased to be a threat. Many officers I spoke to found the whole business ludicrous and complained that their soldiers were being forced to fight the Taliban with one hand tied behind their backs.

Commanders complained that it would be absolute madness to embark on a dangerous military operation into Taliban territory equipped with little more than Card Alpha. The commander of Regional Command South, Major General Jacko Page, managed to secure an agreement with NATO in which troops could revert to Rule 421 Alpha for a limited period during offensive operations such as Operation Palk Ghar. Most commanders regarded such changes as the best of a bad situation. For the soldiers, however, it was a confusing process which made a hard job even more difficult.

The site of Patrol Base Inkerman had once belonged to an Afghan farmer who grew poppies and probably supplied opium to the Taliban. Now it was in the hands of the British who had paid several hundred thousand US dollars for the site. For the time being, it was home to C Company and a detachment of the ANA. Also based inside the compound were several Viking troop carriers, which are tracked, lightly armoured vehicles that had arrived with the Royal Marines several months earlier. There were also several of the new Mastiff armoured wheeled vehicles. These impressively large machines had gone down very well with the troops, not just because they could withstand the blast of an anti-tank mine, but because they had air-conditioning.

As Justin and I began to get our kit ready for the impending operation, there was a thunderous explosion. It was difficult to work out whether it was behind us or in front, but it was close. Very close. For a split second everyone stopped moving. Then there was another explosion, and another. The Taliban were attacking us. The words 'incoming, incoming' echoed around the camp. Those soldiers who had been trying to sleep under camouflage nets just a few seconds earlier quickly donned helmets and body armour. Justin and I enthusiastically copied them. 'What's the form now?' I asked one soldier as he fixed the chin-strap of his helmet. 'Get under some hard cover and wait for it to stop. It will soon. This is quite a laugh, isn't it? Welcome to

Inkerman – we haven't had this for about a week. I wonder if they know we are coming after them,' he said thoughtfully, referring to the forth-coming operation.

The attack ended as quickly as it had started. The soldiers carried on with their preparations, only mildly irritated that their routine had been disrupted by a hidden enemy trying to kill them. These men had seen it all before. Each one was a veteran of 50 or 60 firefights. They had seen their colleagues killed and injured in action and taken the lives of more Taliban than they could possibly remember. Like the Paras and Marines before them, their average age was just 19.

The main topic of conversation amongst the soldiers was the prospect of returning home. Every single man could tell you how many days he had left to serve. They looked tired and thin, but their morale was still high. To a man, however, they were convinced that their efforts and sacrifices had gone unnoticed by a British public more concerned with Premiership football results than the war in Afghanistan.

'No one cares about us,' said Private Luke Harris, a 20-year-old, whippet-thin soldier with a thick Essex accent. 'The public think this is the same as Iraq. They think we should leave. They have no idea what's going on. Why aren't they interested? Why aren't the papers interested?'

It was a theme I heard time and time again during my three weeks in Afghanistan. The soldiers had a point. The general public were immune to the realities of war and tended to group Iraq and Afghanistan in the same category, even though they could not have been more different. The same could be said of the newspapers. There was a time when the death of a British soldier would make it on to the front page of the newspapers, but now that only happened if two or three soldiers died in the same incident or whether there was some-thing regarded as extraordinary, such as an event involving extreme heroism or the death of a female soldier. It was clear to me that there was no sense that the soldiers were fighting for the British government or even for the people of Afghanistan. They were fighting for them-selves and for their own survival.

As darkness fell, Justin and I, like the soldiers, packed and repacked our kit in an attempt to reduce the weight we would be carrying on the operation. While we were carrying just 6 litres of water, 24 hours' worth of rations and spare socks, the soldiers were laden down with up to 80lbs of weapons, radios, water, rations and ammunition, including hand grenades, smoke grenades, 51mm mortar rounds and 5.56mm rounds of ammunition for the GPMG. On top of this, they would be wearing body armour weighing 30lbs and a helmet. I lifted some of the packs the soldiers would be carrying and they seemed impossibly heavy. It would take a normal, fit man all his strength just to lift one of the soldier's packs, let alone carry it. My small sack, although heavy enough for me, felt pathetically light by comparison

The company formed up at around 0100hrs and moved into marching formation for the first phase of the operation. A Company were already moving towards what the Army calls the 'Line of Departure' – beyond lies no man's land and enemy territory. A Company was tabbing around 16km through the night just to reach the Green Zone. It was likely that many of their number would be on the brink of exhaustion before the battle even started. We all knew that those of us attached to C Company had the easier of the two options.

The order to move came at around 0130hrs. Slowly, under the light of a full moon in a cloudless night sky, we left the safety of Inkerman for the approach march into the Green Zone. The 120 soldiers who made up the C Company group were stretched across the ground to our front like a giant snake silently moving through the alleyways of the hamlet, which lay just beyond the gates of the base.

Shortly after we started out, dogs started barking. I remember thinking to myself, if the Taliban did not know we were coming, they do now. For the first half an hour or so, I was utterly convinced that we would be ambushed or that someone, perhaps myself, would step on an anti-personnel mine. I later discovered that such fears were felt by virtually everyone. Afghanistan is the most mined country on earth. At least a dozen soldiers had already been killed or lost limbs after stepping on mines or booby traps that had been laid by the Taliban. Every few hundreds yards or so we would stop while the point section of the lead platoon would scout forward for potential ambush or booby-trap points. It was during one of these stops that a Taliban message from a fighter to his commander was intercepted. The Taliban use fairly unsophisticated radios known as Icoms, which can be bought on the open market, to communicate with each other. Using an Icom scanner, the British were able to intercept Taliban communications, via the Afghan interpreters. The intercepted message read: 'The infidels are coming. We are ready for them.' It was confirmation, if any was needed, that the Taliban would stand and fight: in the Green Zone, they always do. The Taliban also knew that the British soldiers scanned the radio frequencies they used and in all likelihood they were hopeful that the message would be intercepted in the mistaken belief that it would unnerve the British.

Somewhere hidden in the shadows, Taliban spies, known as 'dickers' by the Army, were watching us. Every time a patrol of any size leaves a base, it will be 'dicked', meaning that details such as its formation, size and direction and whether the troops are moving on foot or in vehicles will be passed to the local Taliban commander, usually via mobile phone.

After two hours of stop–start marching, we finally made it into the Green Zone. Once inside the temperature dropped dramatically and a heavy dew which had already formed on the grass made movement quite perilous in some places. On several occasions, soldiers with heavy packs slipped off narrow embankments and plunged into the irrigation ditches below. At around 0300hrs, we stopped inside a compound a few hundred metres short of the Line of Departure. We were told to relax for a short while prior to first light, when we would move into Taliban territory. Sentries were put out while the rest of the soldiers, already tired from several hours of marching, slept where they sat.

Collectively, it seemed, the entire company woke an hour or so later, shivering from the cold, as dawn broke over Helmand. The haunting sound of the Muslim call to prayer echoed around as we readied ourselves for action. Silently, the troops moved into their assault forma- tions and pushed forward into the patchwork of fields that made up the Green Zone. As daylight illuminated the surrounding landscape, I was struck by the beauty of this part of Helmand, which seemed more remin- iscent of Provence than Afghanistan. Lush, fertile and wonderfully green, in a different, more peaceful age it would, without any doubt, have been a major tourist attraction.

The clever money amongst the soldiers suggested that the Taliban would attack at around 0600hrs, an hour or so after dawn. However, 0600hrs came and went without sight or sound of the enemy. At first I was disappointed and began thinking of what I was going to write for the next edition of the newspaper if there was no attack. Then I recalled one of the favourite maxims of the Royal Anglians serving in Afghanistan: 'Be careful what you wish for.' After all the planning and preparation, it appeared that, for once, the Taliban had done the sensible thing and fled. Slowly, we moved from one compound to another, the lead platoon 'clearing' the houses before the ANA conducted a detailed search.

Then, at around 0700hrs, as we moved into yet another abandoned, mud-walled compound, the Taliban attacked. The lead platoon of A Company, about 500m to our left, were ambushed with a volley of RPGs, immediately followed by a series of sustained bursts of auto-matic fire. The advancing troops sprinted for cover and took shelter in irrigation ditches and behind 30cm-high mud embankments as the bullets cracked and fizzed above our heads. Peering through binoculars and rifle sights, the soldiers searched the ground in front of them for the enemy positions. Gradually, the tell-tale flashes of gunfire and smoke from the grenade launchers gave away the Taliban position.

The previously peaceful countryside erupted into a deadly battle-field. Like everyone else, I assume, I felt the adrenaline coursing through my veins. However, there was no sense of panic or excitement, just one of calm professionalism. The soldiers were quiet, and most seemed to be looking towards the sky as if they were waiting for an RPG to coming flying over one of the walls. 'It's started,' said one of the soldiers. Another hauled himself to his feet, looked at me and said, with a broad grin, 'Here we go.'

The battle raged back and forth, with each volley of Taliban fire being met by the distinctive rattle of a British general purpose machine-gun. Slowly but surely, the Taliban fire began creeping towards our position. RPGs began to explode closer and closer to where we were taking cover. Instinctively, everyone began to move closer to the walls of the compound. As the sound of battle drifted closer towards us, Maj Messenger reminded everybody to switch on and to keep our spacing.

Searching for cover, some other soldiers unwittingly entered our part of the compound but there was little or no room and they are quickly ordered to leave. 'Get out,' shouted Maj Messenger angrily, 'I just said switch on. One RPG over that wall will take the fucking lot of us out.' The soldiers backed away in single file and disappeared. The distinctive crack, crack, crack of bullets flying through the air was now directly above our heads. Every now and again the 'pee-ow' sound of a ricochet could be heard as a bullet pinged off a compound wall and the booms of exploding rockets could be felt in our chests.

Terry Taylor, the diminutive C Company Sergeant Major who was sitting just a few feet away from me, said what everyone was thinking: 'Now that's close. I wonder if the Taliban know we are hiding here?' Although he is looking at me the question is not directed at anyone in particular. He seems to be asking it more out of curiosity rather than genuine concern.

He then told me of the 'bad period' three weeks ago when two soldiers died in two days:

> The day after Private Rawson was killed, we lost Captain Hicks, the company second-in-command. It was a really tough week, it affected us all, but we pulled through. I had to make sure the lads' morale was up, that's my job. Some found it harder than others and we had to send one lad back who was clearly suffering mentally. It was too early, I think, to say whether he had PTSD [Post-Traumatic Stress Disorder] because that usually surfaces a few days after the incident but he was clearly disturbed. It's not surprising, really. Some of the wounds on the injured guys were very nasty. The young lad was just sitting there, shaking and looking very distant. We sent him back to Camp Bastion and I think he's going to be okay. These things happen. Everybody has their breaking point.

Terry Taylor is a classic sergeant major in every sense, apart from his build. He is completely bald and hairless and is relatively short at around 5ft 8in, but he has the physical presence of a giant and one senses that he is liked, respected and feared by everyone, including Major Messenger. Being in his presence automatically makes me feel more secure. He has the air of man who has witnessed such events countless times before.

Gradually, the enemy fire creeps even closer to our position. The banter stops and the soldiers steel themselves for a potential attack. The tension is broken when Steve Armon, the sergeant of 10 Platoon, turns to his men and, referring to the closeness of the explosions, says, 'Don't worry lads, they are not aimed at you, so if they hit you, it won't hurt.' For a few seconds, we all laugh until we are silenced by more bangs.

As the battle rages on our left flank, the order is given to advance to a more secure position. Each soldier dashes across open ground towards covered positions that should be out of sight of the Taliban snipers. The temperature is now beginning to climb and I can feel the sweat running down my face and back. As we sprint across an open field, I'm convinced that the Taliban must have seen us. It dawns on me that having a sky-blue set of body armour is not such a good idea. In recent wars, the colour would single me out as a member of the press and therefore, hopefully, not a legitimate target. It is unlikely that the Taliban would allow themselves to be restricted by such conventions.

As elements of the company move forward, the Taliban are spotted fleeing their positions. The troops have them in their sights but are unable to open fire for fear of hitting A Company. 'There they are, over there. Fuck me, there they are,' said one soldier in disbelief. Maj Messenger explains that because of our position, we cannot engage the enemy without the risk of hitting A Company on our left flank. The soldiers are clearly miffed. It is rare for anyone to get such a good and clear view of the Taliban in the flesh.

The soldiers enter another compound, which has been 'cleared' by the forward sections. This time, everyone moves close to the wall and prepares for an attack. It is clear that there are many Taliban in the area and every compound is now regarded as an enemy stronghold. I can feel my heart pounding beneath my body armour as I flop to the ground and take refuge next to a soldier inside a fireplace. He looks at me and winks. Like me, he is too exhausted to speak.

To sighs of relief, Lieutenant Matt Fyjis-Walker, the company's Forward Air Controller, informs Major Phil Messenger, the C Company Commander, that Apache helicopters are preparing to attack.

Two Apaches, call signs 'Ugly 51' and 'Ugly 5 Zero', arrive 'on station' and begin circling the Taliban compound. Lt Fyjis-Walker ensures the pilots are aware of our position, while his opposite number within A Company gives them a description of the target. A warning comes through that the Apaches are about to fire.

Seconds later and high above, a 30mm cannon growls into action as the Taliban attempt to escape. White smoke can be seen pouring from the gun barrel before the haunting 'brrr, brrr, brrr' of the gun is heard.

'What a nice sound to hear on a warm summer's day,' says Corporal Sean Doyle, 27, the Scottish soldier with whom I am sharing the fire-place in the abandoned compound. 'There's no escape from the Apache – you can run but you can't hide.'

He is wearing white weightlifters' gloves with the words 'Fuck' written on one and 'This' written on another. 'Does that reflect your general feeling of life in Helmand?', I ask with a smile. He laughs out loud and says: 'It was the end of a particularly hard and very hot day earlier in the summer. We had been in contact all day and everybody was hung out [army slang for exhausted]. It seemed very appropriate at the time.'

The Apaches hover over their prey. Burst after burst of 30mm cannon fire slices through the Taliban positions. After a few minutes, Lt Fyjis-Walker, turns to me and says, 'Watch this!', pointing to the helicopters. He then quickly shouts out, 'Rockets in 20 seconds.' High above we see rockets screaming out of the pods on both of the Apaches stubby little wings. There is a thunderous explosion to our front – it is the *coup de grâce*.

It is an awe-inspiring site, but it is difficult not to feel sorry for the Taliban who are now lying dead, injured and dismembered in a smoky ruin. 'Fuck them,' says a soldier when I voice my concerns. 'They don't have to fight us,' he adds.

A message comes back through one of the interpreters that as the Apaches arrived the Taliban began to panic. We are told that the message 'Stay safe, stay safe' was sent just before the Taliban compound was strafed.

During a lull in the battle, I begin chatting to Lt Fyjis-Walker about his role as a Joint Tactical Air Controller. Although this is his first operational tour as an Air Controller, he has already been involved in as many as 60 missions. I ask him what it feels like to deliver death on such a grand scale. 'I don't really think too much about it, to be honest,' he confides. 'I'm more interested in getting the job done properly and as quickly as possible. There's a lot to think about so the last thought going through my mind is "poor sods".' He explains that the US pilots are the easiest to work with and are more willing to bend the rules than the British:

The Yanks are great, very cool, very relaxed. The RAF are good, but there are more US planes so we work with them more regularly. We only occasionally get the French, thankfully. There was one occasion when we had a French pilot who could barely speak English so I was trying to communicate in schoolboy French. It took ages. I was trying to get him to identify a compound with four buildings inside. He was trying to count them but didn't know the English for five so he said "four and another one". It took quite a while before I knew what he was saying. It's not really the way you want to carry out an air strike.

We chat briefly about the friendly-fire incident a few days earlier in which three members of the Royal Anglians were killed.

It's just war. These things happen. No one set out to make a mistake. I think soldiers accept that things can and do go wrong on a battlefield. I know it's not easy for the public to accept but it has always happened and probably will always happen. You can't eradicate human error from the battlefield.

One of the Fire Support Team commanders is Captain Charlotte Peters, one of only two female forward observation officers in Helmand. She is trained to call in air strikes and artillery fire. It is a reflection of the modern era that women now serve on the frontline, even if they are not allowed to fight in infantry regiments.

She, too, is based in Inkerman and attached to C Company. The only other woman in the camp is Lance Corporal Haley Pierce, the 20-year-old medic who had attended to Capt Hicks during the fateful attack on Inkerman on 10 August. I ask Capt Peters how she copes in such a male-dominated environment.

She appears to be slightly offended by my question and says: 'It's not a drama. If anything the dust is more of a problem, like it is for everyone. Being amongst men is a non-issue.' She describes her job as 'awesome' and adds that being in Helmand is a 'fantastic opportunity to put everything you have learnt in training into practice'.

Capt Peters again looks perturbed when, during a lull in the battle, I question her about using Apache or an artillery barrage to kill large numbers of the enemy. 'It's proportionate force,' she says defensively, before adding, 'My view is the destruction of the enemy further secures the Sangin Valley.' A young male officer looks at me and says, 'Charlie knows all the text book answers.'

The operation is going according to plan and the Royal Anglians make excellent progress as we push north through the hamlets and fields of the Green Zone. Most of the dwellings have been abandoned.

Occasionally, some of the farmers come back during the day to work the fields but most are too scared of the Taliban or the fighting to remain permanently. As C Company moves through one of the villages, machine-gun fire again cuts through the air over to our left as soldiers from A Company make 'contact' with the enemy once more. Suddenly, a local man appears wearing a black dish-dash. The soldiers train their weapons on him, fearing that he is a member of the Taliban. He is searched respectfully, and then questioned. The interpreter asks him if he has seen any Taliban. He replies that there haven't been any Taliban here for days, but the soldiers appear unconvinced. 'Yer right,' says one. 'You haven't seen any Taliban. What the fuck's that then?' he adds, referring to the gunfire in the distance.

At around midday the company halts in a compound and the soldiers take cover in the shade of a fig orchard. The temperature is about 35°C and getting hotter. The water I have been carrying around all day is warm but still refreshing. Sergeant Major Taylor tells me that there is a well, which has cold water, in one of the adjacent compounds. I stand, feeling light-headed, and walk into the neighbouring compound. About 30 soldiers are crashed out on the floor. Some are awake while others are dozing on their packs, their shirts drenched in sweat or dirty water. Everyone looks exhausted and I silently wonder to myself whether they have the strength to continue. One of the soldiers fills my water bottle and makes sure that I sterilize it with water tablets. He then hands me a tube of Lucozade powder and says, 'Pour this in, it will take away the taste of the chlorine.' I'm touched by his kindness and we start chatting about the war.

He wants to know why the public are not interested. He then points to the soldiers lying around us and says:

Do they really know what it's like out here? Do they really know how hard it is? We've been involved in so much fighting. Most of us have had around 60 contacts. This is a real war, it's not like Iraq. I was on R and R recently and friends of mine would say, 'So what's it like in Afghanistan?' and I would tell them that it's a war and people are fighting and being killed. But I could see that they weren't interested – they thought I was being boring. It makes you wonder what you are doing it all for.

An hour later, we leave the comfort of the fig orchard and head deeper into the Green Zone. The Taliban, Maj Messenger tells me, are now being squeezed into a tight box. The escape routes to the west have been cut off by the Light Dragoons and the Estonians are pushing down from the north. Intercepted Icom messages suggest that the Taliban leadership is in disarray. British commanders know that many of the Taliban fighters in the Sangin Valley have been recruited from Pakistan and other Muslim countries. Rumours abound that British voices have been heard over the Icom radios but this is mostly accepted as a battlefield myth. Once the leaders have been killed or injured, the Taliban tend to panic. The local fighters simply return to their farms, hide their Kalashnikovs and carry on tending to their opium crops. For the foreign fighters, who are loathed by the locals, such an escape is much more difficult, if not impossible.

As C Company moves through one settlement, we come to a fast-flowing stream about 2m wide. The bridge in the village has collapsed and the only means of crossing is to leap across its ruins. To achieve this without ending up in the stream, we must jump from one narrow bank to another. Maj Messenger goes first and successfully jumps the gap, quickly followed by his signaller. It is then the turn of Capt Peters. She jumps and the signaller grabs her hand but her footing is unsteady and she starts to fall back. The signaller lets go and she hits her backside on the opposite bank before plunging into the stream. She appears to go under and is unable to get to her feet. At this point I jump in, grab her rifle and haul her up. She is flustered and drenched. I ask her if she is okay, and she quickly asks if I have her rifle. With the help of Maj Messenger she is pulled out of the stream. I, too, climb out and Lt Fyjis-Walker comes over to me and whispers, 'Well done, that's very gallant. I don't think I would have got my feet wet for Charlie. She's a big girl, you know, she can look after herself.' Sgt Maj Taylor appears on the scene and adds: 'Women – they'll do anything for a bit of attention.' Everyone laughs and we head off through the village.

For a brief moment it seems that the soldiers have all forgotten that we are in the throws of a violent battle until one of the senior non-commissioned officers says to everyone: 'Okay the fun's over. Everybody switch on – don't you know there is a war on?' We all chuckle quietly but understand the point.

Gradually, the temperature starts to cool but the heat of the day has already done its damage. A member of the ANA is suspected of suffering from heat exhaustion and has been extracted back to the hospital at Camp Bastion by helicopter. A British soldier, who has a suspected broken back, joins him. It is feared that the weight of his pack may have cracked several vertebrae after he slipped and fell into an irrigation ditch.

Another soldier struggling with the heat is Private Luke Harris, 20. He had badly sprained his ankle on an operation in Kajaki. Such has been the intensity of operations since then that it has barely had time to heal. The weight of his pack, the heat and the distance walked overnight have all taken their toll. Pte Harris is dehydrated and vomiting. As we rest, I approach him and ask what is the problem? He looks utterly shattered. His blue eyes are half closed and he looks much older than his 20 years. 'I was struggling, it was my ankle,' he says.

> It's happened before. I need to get some physio on it but there just hasn't been any time. Every time I go out the same thing happens, it gives way. It makes walking so difficult. The lads have taken some of my load. I don't want to go back to Inkerman, I want to stay here with the lads. I want to do my share.

His courage and determination are admirable but he's not going to make it to the end of the operation. He is extracted back to Inkerman in one of the armoured Vikings which have come to resupply the troops with water, food and radio batteries.

The company spends the night in another deserted compound. We have covered around 10km but it feels like much more. Sentries are posted and the soldiers start to cook their boil-in-the-bag meals. A few hold an incongruous conversation about the merits of eating a chicken curry in a hot climate, but mostly the soldiers are quiet, seeking comfort in a cigarette or a few moments of quiet reflection. Everyone is exhausted. Within an hour, darkness has fallen and most of the soldiers are asleep.

The operation recommences at first light but the Taliban have fled back to their farms or into the hills. A few suspects are seized close to one of the crossing-points on the Helmand river, which leads up to Musa Qala. They are plasti-cuffed, have blackout goggles placed over their eyes and are taken back to Inkerman for questioning.

Back at Inkerman, Lt Col Carver is pleased that the operation has gone well but disappointed with the body count.

> We wanted to kill about 300 Taliban, that would have been great. That would have really given them something to think about but it looks like we only got 30. But no operation ever goes to plan and it looks as though they knew we were coming. But we did get a few of their leaders and we think we killed a 'high value target'.

His mood changes as he explains that there is a possibility that they may have caught or killed the Taliban commander of the Russian-made anti-tank weapon which was used to kill Capt Dave Hicks two weeks earlier. 'If that's the case, then the whole thing would have been worth it,' he adds enthusiastically.

I ask whether the Taliban are likely to return to this part of the Sangin Valley. 'Oh yes,' he says stroking his three-day-old beard. 'They'll be back, they always come back but they will be weaker. These operations embolden us and it sends a valuable message to the local people that the Taliban can be beaten, so their position is emboldened as well.'

Late that day A Company take part in a heliborne operation to seize a town across the Helmand river. It is a high-risk strategy because nobody knows whether there will be any Taliban in the area. From the safety of a sangar in Inkerman, I watch as the helicopter lands close to the village without incident. There are sighs of relief all around. Lt Col Carver tells me that his troops are hoping to make contact with the local elders and tell them that the troops are here to bring peace and to help in the reconstruction of Sangin and the valley. 'There will be people in that village who have never seen a British soldier before. The Taliban will have told them that the British are infidels who will kill their children and rape their wives, so hopefully they will be pleasantly surprised.'

I later discover that a dog called 'Jihad', which had been adopted by the soldiers, accompanied them on the entire operation. It seems that the dog made history by being the first animal to take part in a British heliborne operation in Helmand.

After the first phase of Operation Palk Ghar had been successfully completed, the battalion headquarters, together with Justin Sutcliffe and myself, moved by road on Route 611 to Sangin. The dirt track served to underline how much reconstruction work need to be carried out in Afghanistan to bring the country into the twenty-first century.

Months of tactical failures had forced the Taliban to reconsider its approach. While it was still happy to send poorly trained but brave and hopelessly naive young fighters to their deaths across Helmand, the organization's leadership was aware that they would have to fight the British and NATO in a different way if they were to force the 'infidel' to leave Afghanistan. It was no surprise, therefore, that the Taliban began turning towards a greater use of improvised explosive devices. Twelve months earlier, the IEDs which were used against British troops were relatively unsophisticated devices which were composed of old bits of ordnance, such as mines or artillery shells, triggered by a command wire. Advances had since been made: so-called 'Spider' IED trigger devices had been perfected in Pakistan and were being produced for the Taliban on a virtually industrial scale. The Spider IEDs could be linked to several different explosives and triggered by a remote control device. Route 611 was becoming the Taliban's favoured point of attack. The increase in troop numbers compared with the number of helicopters available to the British effectively meant that soldiers in Helmand were now at more risk from IEDs than ever before because of the need to travel by road.

Thus, as we left Inkerman for Sangin on 2 September, we did so with a certain amount of trepidation, even though we were housed inside one of the newly arrived Mastiffs, the virtually impregnable troop carriers. During the three weeks I spent in Helmand, at least three Mastiffs were attacked with IEDs but none was seriously damaged and all managed to make it back to base. The only obvious draw back of the Mastiff is that it has wheels rather than tracks. Its manoeuvrability is therefore limited.

The convoy arrived in Sangin at about 0130hrs without incident. As we walked into the District Centre, I was struck by the quiet of the evening. How different it all must have been just 12 months earlier when the base was home to the 3 Para battle group. The whole of the area would have been illuminated by automatic fire as tracer rounds flew back and forth across no man's land. It was a major mission, using artillery, air strikes and Apache attack helicopters, just to carry out a routine relief-in-place operation and casualties would be expected to be taken. By contrast, on this evening in early September 2007 the area could not have been more peaceful.

While Sangin was once regarded as a tough posting for troops, it had now become a favourite location for the men of the Royal Anglians because of the presence of the fast-flowing canal – a tributary of the Helmand river – which ran through its centre. This was where the troops would wash their clothes and bathe their bodies after a tough patrol through the town's hot and dusty streets – little wonder the soldiers dubbed the canal 'morale'. During the mornings or just before sunset, soldiers of all ranks would stroll down to the canal for a swim or a wash and, for a few minutes a least, forget that they were in one of the most dangerous and violent places on Earth.

While the canal made life infinitely more bearable, day-to-day living was still something of a trial for most soldiers. The cramped and frankly squalid living conditions meant that outbreaks of D and V were common and would often lay waste to large numbers of soldiers at any one time. Unlike in the comfortable, air-conditioned tents at Camp Bastion, Gereshk and Lashkar Gar, there was no escape from the baking summer heat in Sangin. Despite having a military presence there for more than a year, soldiers were still being forced to defecate into open pits, the stench of which was so bad during the heat of the day that they were rarely used.

The food, too, was poor. A single hard-pressed cook had to prepare two hot meals for over 150 men every day, using 10-man ration packs for weeks on end. Such a feat would certainly test the skills and mental well-being of even the most robust of celebrity chefs. Little wonder that breakfast was always the same: beans and something which was called a 'bacon burger' which had the taste and consistency of spam. Six days out of seven, the evening meal was a bland stew served with rice, mashed potatoes or noodles, and often all three.

After one particularly testing supper, I asked a couple of soldiers why they were still eating army rations rather than fresh food. 'We have been asking ourselves the same question,' said one South African junior non-commissioned officer, who was eating congealed mince and gravy from a plastic tray.

Food is fuel, man, we need to eat but this stuff is grim. It's not the cook's fault, although we have had better. We had this Fijian cook once, he was awesome. We caught fish from the canal and he prepared a BBQ. Look around you. There are no fat soldiers here. We have all lost weight because of the food. It's bloody awful.

Despite these complaints, the morale at Sangin, at least during the time I spent there, seemed to be remarkably high. Of course, this may well have been because the soldiers knew the tour was coming to an end.

As has already been shown in Chapter 9, Operation Silver drove the Taliban out of Sangin in April 2007, and there was a question as to whether the security of the town should be left in the hands of the ANA and ANP. However, it was agreed to follow the views of Lt Col Carver of the Royal Anglians and others that the best thing that the British could do was to stay and help restore the town while continuing to protect it. As Sangin re-emerged as a bustling market town, Lt Col Carver managed to get the Ministry of Defence to fund a number of irrigation projects in the area. The cash was used to pay the locals, who did the work themselves rather than simply relying on the British to solve their problems. A weekly medical clinic was also established so that sick locals could get professional medical advice, and one of the local schools reopened. Slowly, thanks to the foresight of Lt Col Carver, the British were winning the hearts and minds of the local people.

Despite these successes the malevolent presence of the Taliban was never far away. There was a covert Taliban presence in the weekly *Jirgas* attended by the locals and a British Army officer, and the Taliban continued to attack the District Centre and the various ANA patrol bases in the area, although much less frequently. It was also rumoured that the latest governor in Sangin, a former mujahideen fighter, was on speaking terms with the Taliban.

Lt Col Caver explained:

> You have to remember that these people grew up with one another. They might not like each other but they are pragmatic people. They know that the British will not stay forever but the Taliban might. They are not going to put all their eggs in one basket. They need lines of communication between both sides. It's not a case of Taliban bad, everyone else good. The tribal politics are immensely complex. The Russians never understood that and that is why, ultimately, they lost.

Despite the complexities, Sangin is tangible proof of what can be achieved in Helmand, and Afghanistan, if the will of the politicians matches the effort of the military.

By the beginning of September 2007, the situation in Sangin was stable enough for the British to make its boldest move yet in the battle for hearts and minds by compensating the Afghans for their losses in the fighting of the past year. During a secret meeting attended by Lt Col Carver and Haji Isatullah, the Chief of Police, compensation was agreed for everything from the loss of a sheep, to the death or injury of a relative, to the destruction of an entire farm. Brig Lorimer's staff had managed to secure $100,000 from the ISAF which he was going to give to anyone who could prove that they had sustained a loss directly because of coalition activity.

It was a risky strategy. There was absolutely no guarantee that the cash handed over in goodwill to the locals would not end up in the hands of the Taliban, hence the meeting was held in secret. There was also the very real risk that Lt Col Carver would be ripped off by fraudulent claims and over-inflated prices. The rates agreed included $300 for a 2km² field of wheat; $5,000 to rebuild a farm complex; $4,000 for an accidental death and $1,200 for someone who was wounded. The going rate for a dead sheep was agreed at $80 – a figure which was probably similar to UK prices.

It was during one of the *Jirgas* in which Lt Col Carver was agreeing compensation with the main Sangin negotiator that a British Army officer who was also present lent over to me and whispered, 'The FCO would have a fit if they knew this was going on. They would be trying to impose rules and procedures and telling us that we were doing it all wrong. But they won't come down here and see the size of the task we are facing.' It was just one of several comments which reflected the simmering contempt many officers had for the FCO staff.

Perhaps the best indication that life was returning to some sort of normality was the fact that many locals were now prepared to publicly voice their complaints at how the authorities were running the town. During one routine foot patrol into the bazaar, I asked many shopkeepers what they thought of the British and whether they had any complaints. The majority of those I spoke to refused to comment one way or another, except to say that they wanted security and the presence of soldiers brought trouble. However, when I asked whether they wanted the soldiers to leave, they all agreed that they did not. The local traders' greatest grievance was with the Afghan National Police. Many seemed to regard them as little better than thugs who were quite happy

13

FIX BAYONETS

Every Regiment contains men whose mere existence seems to epitomize the character of the unit. Sergeant Simon Panter of the 1st Battalion The Royal Anglian Regiment is one of those.

Sgt Panter has two battlefield rules – 'when the fighting gets close, always fix your bayonet' and 'kill him before he kills you'. When I met Simon Panter, he had been in the Army for 16 years and was already a legend within 1 Royal Anglians. He is as strong as an ox, fearless and bright.

Like many amongst the ranks of the Royal Anglians, after six months in Helmand he was a veteran of a multitude of ferocious and bloody battles with the Taliban. He has fought with bullet and bayonet throughout the broiling heat of the Afghan summer and has witnessed his own men fall and die in battle. He has seen it all and done it all. However, even he was not prepared for the events which unfolded on 7 August 2007 in the Green Zone just north of Patrol Base Inkerman.

At the time, Simon Panter was the Platoon Sergeant of 3 (Coruna) Platoon in A Company, which was then based in Sangin. On that Tuesday, he formed part of a security convoy tasked with taking Maj Charlie Calder, Acting Commanding Officer of 1 Royal Anglians, to Inkerman for a routine visit to C Company who were located at the base. The plan was for Maj Calder to accompany members of C Company on a routine patrol into the Green Zone. When they arrived, it soon emerged that C Company were short of men, so Sgt Panter 'offered his services' and volunteered to lead a section as part of the patrol. The whole patrol was under the command of Capt Dave Hicks, who just five days later would be tragically killed in action.

It was a typically hot August day as the soldiers prepared for the patrol. The number of attacks against Inkerman Patrol Base and the

Taliban activity in the Green Zone were both increasing. Everyone knew that the chances of being attacked were very high, if not certain. The men checked their equipment, ensured their radios were working and packed enough food, water and ammunition to sustain themselves for 24 hours. The patrol was going to be hard work: it always was in the Green Zone.

One by one, the soldiers left the base and headed north into enemy territory. The possibility of death lurked everywhere. This was Taliban territory and the British were unwelcome. The Taliban had a point to prove and, just 30 minutes after leaving the relative safety of the base, the much-anticipated attack came.

The troops dived and sprinted for cover as burst after burst of machine-gun fire was ranged on to the Royal Anglians. As the bullets cracked and whizzed over their heads, RPGs thumped into the ground amongst them. Sgt Panter was the reserve section commander of 3 platoon. At this stage, his soldiers were not directly in contact with the enemy but he could hear the sound of AK47s firing a few hundreds metres to his north. He waited and listened as his men took cover behind the bank of one of the numerous irrigation ditches in the area.

Sgt Panter told me of the events which unfolded that day during a rare quiet morning in Sangin in early September 2007. Despite his formidable reputation, I found him charming, friendly and thoughtful. I thought that 20 years earlier, when I was a young platoon commander in the Parachute Regiment, I would have been proud and honoured to have him as my platoon sergeant. I instinctively knew that the soldiers would have followed every word of his command without question as he began to tell me of the extraordinary events of Tuesday 7 August 2007.

Like most firefights, the battle was quite confused. I was assessing the situation when we started taking some fire from our left flank. My men were in cover so we were quite safe at that stage. The bullets were above us and close to our position so I was convinced that whoever was firing in our direction actually knew we were there. I suspected that it was the Taliban but it could have quite easily been the ANA so I didn't just want to return fire and end up having a blue-on-blue. I was aware that if we moved over to our left and it was the ANA, they might end up shooting at us, so for a few minutes we remained in position.

The firing continued so Sgt Panter decided to investigate. Pointing at Private Patrick Carey, a young soldier who was lying down a few feet away, Sgt Panter smiled and said, with his calm East Anglian twang, 'Come on, let's earn our pay.' With that, the two soldiers jumped into a ditch and began slowly moving towards the sound of the shooting. 'It was the only way I was going to find out whether it was ANA or the Taliban so I took one of the lads with me and we started moving along one of the irrigation ditches. The water was stinking but it gave us the cover we needed.'

However, wading through the knee-deep, muddy water was slowing their progress. After a few hundred metres, Sgt Panter peered above the embankment. The firing was now very close, although no enemy were visible, so the two soldiers climbed out of the irrigation ditch and began moving quickly along the bank.

As they approached a crossroads of irrigation ditches, Sgt Panter spotted the unmistakable sight of four Taliban fighters. 'By that stage I thought we were going to run into a group of ANA, then there they were, four Taliban, and I shouted out loud, "Fuck me, they're Taliban".'

As the fighting echoed around them, the two soldiers inched their way forward.

We managed to creep up on the Taliban and got quite close before they spotted us and started shooting. We attacked them and cleared the position using close-quarter battle skills. This is where all of the hard hours spent in training pay off. We moved forward giving each other covering fire. I shot dead the first Taliban fighter. He was hiding further up the irrigation ditch. I saw him crawling away and thought 'the fucker's trying to outflank us'. But he wasn't quick enough. I broke cover and fired two shots into his chest. He slumped down and I could see that I had killed him. I felt nothing. I looked back, checked that Pte Carey was okay and then prepared to go after the others.

It was at this point that I thought to myself: 'Right this could now get close and personal.' My heart was thumping; the adrenaline was flowing. I was excited and pumped but at the back of your mind you're thinking 'am I gonna make it out of here?' but I don't think its fear. It's a kind of resignation. If it happens then it happens – just don't fuck up.

So I put a fresh magazine on my weapon, fixed my bayonet and threw a grenade into the enemy position. I moved forward with the other lad a few metres behind me. We were now in the thick of it. There was no going back, only forward.

As Sgt Panter moved forward through the thick, dense vegetation, he saw a black-robed figure kneeling on the ground, armed with an AK47.

We almost bumped into each other and that wouldn't have been the first time that has happened in the Green Zone. I fired off two shots – a double tap – in quick succession. I hit him twice, he staggered and went down but I could see that he wasn't dead. He was still a threat. I was moving forward so I charged at him. I was screaming, my blood was up and I rammed my bayonet into his chest – that finished him off. I stared into his face and I saw that I had killed him. It was either him or me but I got there first. He would have killed me if I had given him the chance or if he had been quicker, of that I have no doubt. It sounds callous, I know, but you don't go out on to the battlefield to make friends. So we moved on and I got another one of them in my sights and I shot and killed him – and I have to say I was knackered at that stage, really knackered. The sweat was pouring off me and my heart was thumping but I was like a man possessed. I stopped and called Pte Carey over to me. We checked our ammunition and made sure we were both okay. It was at that stage I sat down and thought 'fucking hell', but in that situation you just have to keep going forward. That's what you are trained to do.

As Sgt Panter and Pte Cary caught their breath, the rest of the section joined them. Sgt Panter knew that there had been at least one last member of the Taliban team hiding in the fields immediately to his front, but he assumed that he had fled after watching his three colleagues die. As they were scanning the ground in front of them for signs of life, they were fired on. The fire was accurate and sustained.

We started getting some incoming again. The guy had obviously returned. He must have been very brave or stupid. I had the whole section with me at that stage so we returned fire with our SA–80,

GPMG, the grenade launcher and our anti-tank weapon. It was an enormous weight of fire. After that we stopped receiving fire from his position so we assumed that we had killed or injured him. He wouldn't have lasted long with that lot coming at him. I've often wondered why he came back. He had just seen three of his mates die and he legged it and then came back. Maybe he thought he was going to die anyway so he would take some of us with him. I think that's what I would have done.

With the four Taliban dead, Sgt Panter received a message to withdraw. An air strike was about to be launched against the main Taliban stronghold. As he withdrew, he grabbed one of the dead Taliban's AK47s and claimed it as a Sergeants' Mess trophy.

Reflecting on the incident, Sgt Panter recalled that he had been in many firefights over the last six months and in some of those he had managed to kill the enemy. But that attack on 7 August was different:

I've killed men before, but not that close. Not so that you can see the man's face when you take his life – that makes it very personal. I never thought it would get that close, when you are in touching distance. When it's that close, it can go either way. I was lucky that day, we all were. We were in the right place at the right time. For the Taliban – bad luck. They didn't expect us to come left flanking and that is how we got them.

Two of the men Sgt Panter killed were foreign fighters who had probably been recruited in Pakistan and indoctrinated in a madrassa close to the border before being dispatched to go and fight with the Taliban.

'They were armed with AKs and RPGs and at least two of the three dead were foreign fighters, dressed in black wearing chest webbing. The third one looked like an Afghan. He was dressed like an Afghan.'

I asked Sgt Panter how he felt about taking human life. He thought before he answered and said:

Actually, I've killed six, at least six. I can't say I really spend a lot of time thinking about it. For some people, including some soldiers, that might be difficult to live with but not for me. This wasn't cold-blooded, I killed them all in the heat of battle. It's what I have been trained to do. On the battlefield it's kill or be killed.

My way of thinking is I've got six of them but they could have got me and that's six less who might kill other soldiers – that's the way I look at it. I sleep very well. I don't toss and turn wondering if killing the Taliban was the right thing to do. To me it comes down to killing the enemy or losing one of your lads – there's no choice. I saw a young lad die at the beginning of the tour and I don't want that to ever happen to me again.

Sgt Panter turned to the importance of training and trusting in the weapons issued to soldiers. He spoke passionately about bayonet training and how vital a weapon it has been in Afghanistan. He recalled the minutes just before going into battle when the order is passed to fix bayonets.

There is silence followed by a clicking sound all around. Click, click, click – the sound of bayonets being fixed. It's a sound that stirs the soldiers, you can see it in their eyes.

My number one rule on the battlefield is always fix bayonets. In the Green Zone the fighting can be very close and you can quite literally bump into the enemy. If you get a stoppage with your rifle or you run out of bullets, you still have a weapon to hand if you have fixed bayonets. And a British soldier in a bayonet charge is a pretty frightening thing to see.

The role of the platoon sergeant is of paramount importance within the infantry. A good platoon sergeant, like Simon Panter, should be able to advise and steer a young and inexperienced officer while allowing him to take command. The platoon sergeant is in many ways a father to the rest of the soldiers. He is responsible for their discipline and morale. When they get injured he is the man who, with the help of the medics, will keep them alive.

Another young soldier from the Royal Anglians who, by sheer force of circumstance, was catapulted from obscurity into the limelight was Lance Corporal Oliver 'Teddy' Ruecker.

LCpl Ruecker was part of a convoy which left Sangin on 17 May 2007. Although the threat of enemy attack and ambush was always high everywhere in the Sangin Valley, there was no intelligence to suggest that the convoy might be attacked.

The Vikings fired up their engines and the soldiers in the turrets checked their machine-guns before the order to move was given. As the long column of around 30 vehicles snaked through the alleyways beyond the camp gates, all seemed quiet.

The peace lasted for just two minutes. As the convoy moved into an area less than 10m wide and overlooked by high, thick-walled compounds, it was attacked.

From above, dozens of Taliban fighters fired on the 100 men of B Company with AK47s, RPGs and a 12.7mm Dshk Russian-made heavy machine-gun. Those inside the vehicles could hear the bullets pinging off the armour and the thunderous boom of RPGs exploding nearby.

As the soldiers sought out the enemy's firing positions, an RPG struck the rear cabin of LCpl Ruecker's Viking and immediately ignited the cans of diesel stored on the roof. Cpl Dean Bailey, who was standing in the turret, was engulfed in flames which also poured into the cramped interior, threatening the half-dozen soldiers inside. With 30lbs of plastic explosive on board, there was no choice but to abandon the vehicle.

LCpl Ruecker, a trained sniper, was the first man out and sprinted down an alley to find cover. He ran straight into a Taliban fighter who was apparently delighting in the successful attack. As he recalled in a *Daily Telegraph* interview, 'Luckily for me he wasn't concentrating on the battle. He was carrying an AK47 so I drew my pistol and killed him, emptying my magazine of 13 rounds from 10 yards away.'

LCpl Ruecker attempted to get into another Viking but it was full. He then he realized that Cpl Bailey was missing.

As bullets and rockets flew around him, LCpl Ruecker had to make a choice: to keep his head down or risk his life to save one of his comrades. Looking back at the blazing Viking, he realized that his comrade was still inside and that at any moment the flames could ignite the plastic explosive. As he watched, another three RPG rounds hit the vehicle.

It took just a second for the soldier to decide to return to the burning wreck. 'I didn't really think at the time. I just did it,' he said. 'I was scared shitless. When I got to the Viking I could not see much because of the thick black smoke. I found Deano lying on the floor, very badly injured and barely conscious.'

The corporal had taken the brunt of an RPG round that had torn off most of his left arm. He also took a bullet in the chest and head after throwing off his burning body armour and was suffering with a collapsed lung.

'I made a quick assessment and realized I had to get him the hell out of there. I grabbed hold of Deano by his one good arm and began dragging him along the ground shouting everything was going to be fine.'

The soldier then braved a furious barrage of bullets and rockets as he dragged his friend to a nearby Viking. A medic helped him get Cpl Bailey inside the vehicle but LCpl Ruecker's ordeal was not yet over. There was no room for him so he had to run another 100m to a different Viking. After he made it, his colleagues began checking him for a wound because he was covered in his friend's blood.

'I then went into a little bit of shock and smoked about 20 cigarettes in five minutes,' he said.

Considering the firepower employed by their attackers it was remarkable that none of the Royal Anglians was killed, although three were seriously injured. During the encounter, eleven Taliban were killed by the patrol and another nine died under air attacks.

Cpl Bailey was taken to Camp Bastion, where surgeons operated for more than seven hours to save his life. He was unconsciousness for several days. At the time of writing, Cpl Bailey is still recovering from his injuries.

Like many of his colleagues in the Royal Anglians, LCpl Ruecker was involved in dozens of firefights with the Taliban. By the end of the tour, he was estimated to have killed more than 20 men, the majority of which were picked off through the cross hairs of his sniper rifle.

'I don't feel anything about it, to be honest,' he said with a soldier's typical understatement. 'That's what you do, that's your job. It's like fixing a car for a mechanic.'

He admitted that the Sangin incident had 'changed me a bit'. He had become quieter and more introspective. 'The blokes always ask if I am OK and tell me that they are proud of me and I am a brave lad,' he added.

Although the soldier, from Norfolk, had explained to his father what had happened he told his mother only that 'it had got a bit hairy'.

Major Mick Aston, the commander of B Company, said:

The battle was one of the most intense experiences of my life. We had small arms fire, RPGs and armour-piercing rounds going off. It was like something out of the movies.

It's difficult to describe how intense that whole action was but the guys who were there will never forget it and Teddy Ruecker's outstanding bravery was witnessed by the whole company.

This soldier was completely selfless in his actions which were made all the more poignant because he was going to the aid of one of his best mates.

In March 2008, LCpl Ruecker was awarded the Military Cross for his actions in Afghanistan.

Another of those who often found himself in the thick of the action was Major Andrew Tredget, the Regimental Medical Officer of 1 Royal Anglians.

The 34-year-old Major was known to almost everybody in Sangin, where he was largely based, as 'Doc'. He had been an Army doctor for almost 13 years, but his 6 months in Afghanistan were by far the most busy and dangerous.

'I've seen a lot of trauma before,' he said as we chatted inside his 'surgery' in the Sangin District Centre. The room is basic. There is just one window, which is filled with sandbags to prevent injury from sniper fire. Injured soldiers are treated on a stretcher on a table, beneath which a bucket has been strategically placed to prevent blood spilling on to the floor. The doctor went on:

In Iraq I saw gunshot wounds and injuries from mines and IEDs. But the amount of injuries you see in Afghanistan is of a different order. I've probably seen more battle trauma in the last six months than most consultants would see in a lifetime.

Over a period of just a few weeks, I had to deal with five members of the ANA who had shot themselves. Some of them had been smoking opium and didn't know what they were doing while others had shot themselves after their relief-in-place was delayed. They shot themselves in the foot so they could be taken out of Sangin.

Maj Tredget also recalled an incident in which one ANA soldier had a bet with another that he wouldn't be prepared to shoot himself in the chest. 'I know it seems crazy but after they had this bet, I don't know if they were high on drugs, one of them picked up his rifle and shot himself. It's not the first time I've seen that sort of thing.'

Even when the bullets are not flying, keeping soldiers fit and healthy is a challenge in the unsanitary conditions of Sangin. In a 6-week period from the middle of July to the end of August 2007, the doctor had to attend to 47 cases of diarrhoea and vomiting, 5 cases of sand fly fever, 2 cases of tonsillitis and a damaged knee ligament. On top of this there were 6 soldiers who had sustained gunshot wounds, 4 of whom were members of the ANA.

Despite being a medical professional, the doctor talked of the stress of having to deal with injured colleagues.

> We are like an extended family. So, of course, when someone who you might know and like comes in with a terrible wound, it gets to you but you have to be professional and you always are. The job is to save life and that's all you are concerned with. Afterwards, when he has been flown back to Bastion, that's when you can take account of what has happened.

During the tour, Maj Tredget encouraged a relaxed relationship with the soldiers even though he was a senior officer.

> This is a very hard environment and anyone who witnesses the death or injury of a colleague will suffer some sort of traumatic experience. If the soldiers are having problems with that, then I want them to come to me and talk about it. I then have to make a risk assessment. I have to ask the question: 'Could this man compromise an operation because he is not mentally fit?' If that is the case then I will approach his Commanding Officer and tell him there is a problem. It is always a tricky position because the soldier would have come to me in confidence. But, if I think there is a problem, I will tell the soldier that he isn't fit for ops and that I will have to tell his Commanding Officer. Fortunately, it's quite rare that this happens. So far we have had two soldiers who have been taken out of theatre due to Post-Traumatic Stress Disorder. One was a Marine and the other was a Royal Anglian. There is no shame attached to it. Everyone is much better educated on such matters these days and we all know that everyone has a breaking point.

The doctor then talked of his own fears and concerns. He often accompanies soldiers into battle and is the veteran of several ambushes and firefights. He is one of the few medics who have actually fired a weapon in anger.

When I go on patrol or on an operation, I feel like everyone else. I get a bit scared. On Operation Palk Ghar, we had a long first day. It was emotionally and physically exhausting. There were a string of contacts and it got quite hairy. On the second day, we conducted an air assault into one of the small villages on the opposite side of the river. As we were waiting to go in one of the ANA told Dom Biddick, the OC, that no soldiers had been there for months. The last to enter were US Special Forces, who had been forced out by the Taliban.

That got a lot of people thinking. We were all wondering, 'What's it going to be like when we charge out of the aircraft?' I kept thinking of the opening scenes of *Saving Private Ryan*. Everyone was very apprehensive. We had a lot of time to wait and think about what was going to happen. But then someone cracks a joke and the tension is broken. On so many occasions, it's the soldiers' humour that gets you through the darkest moments.

Maj Tredget then turned to the death of LCpl George Davey who died inside the Sangin base on Sunday, 20 May 2007. LCpl Davey was one of the most popular junior non-commissioned officers in the company and his death came as a hammer blow to the entire force.

The company was coming to the end of a busy period of operations and patrol. In the 48 hours before LCpl Davey's death, 13 soldiers had to be evacuated from the Upper Sangin Valley after sustaining wounds in combat with the Taliban. LCpl Davey had just completed an arduous but uneventful patrol. The troops had arrived safely back inside the base in Sangin, relieved that no one else was injured, and set about cleaning their weapons as part of their post-patrol administration. Several of the soldiers were sitting beneath the shade of one of the few trees inside the base's perimeter, smoking cigarettes and shooting the breeze.

What happened next can only be put down to the fact that LCpl Davey, who like everyone else was exhausted, was momentarily distracted. As is the drill when soldiers clean weapons, the rifle is cleared of ammunition and made safe. It appears that at some stage LCpl Davey replaced a full magazine of 30 rounds on his weapon and somehow inadvertently recocked his rifle and thereby placed a bullet in the chamber. As he was leaning over his rifle so that the butt was on the floor and the barrel was pointing up towards his chest, he pulled the trigger. A shot rang out and LCpl Davey slumped to the floor. Elsewhere in the camp, other soldiers froze and waited for either more gunfire or to be given the all clear. Instead, cries of 'medic, medic' rang out.

Major Tredget, who was close by, ran in the direction of the commotion and saw that a soldier was lying prostrate on the ground, being given first-aid by his ashen-faced colleagues. LCpl Davey, who was still conscious, was rushed to the medical centre where Maj Tredget began assessing his injury.

> I knew it was bad as soon as I saw the wound. A gunshot wound to the chest is always going to be bad, we all knew that and so did LCpl Davey. Sgt Maj Newton came into the medical centre and held on to LCpl Davey's hand and began giving him words of encouragement.
>
> Then LCpl Davey said, 'I'm going to die, aren't I?' It was awful. Sgt Maj Newton was brilliant. He held his hand and said 'No, don't think like that, be positive, think of your family. You're going to make it George, you're going to be okay.'
>
> The helicopter came and LCpl Davey was taken to the field hospital at Bastion but he died on the operating table. His wounds were virtually non-survivable. There was nothing anyone could do. The surgeons fought for hours to keep him alive but in the end the damage done was just too much.

LCpl Davey's death had a devastating impact on the Company.

> We had just been through a tough patch with a lot of guys getting injured and then that happened to LCpl Davey. People were thinking, 'When is all of this going to end?' I knew LCpl Davey quite well so I found it particularly hard. But you just have to plough on and that's what we did, that's what we always do. A few tears are shed and then people get on with their jobs because out here there is no alternative.

LCpl Davey was just 23 years old when he was killed. He was married to Joanna with whom he had two young daughters, Millie and Morgan, whom friends said were the centre of his life.

After his death, Lt Col Carver paid this tribute to him:

> As a section second-in-command in 5 Platoon B (Suffolk) Company he had been serving in Helmand Province, Afghanistan, on Operation Herrick 6 since early April 2007. George was a kind-hearted, loyal and selfless commander who worked tirelessly for the benefit of others. His quiet and unassuming demeanour helped him achieve impressive results. He sought little praise or recognition for his actions, preferring to get on with the job in hand with the minimum of fuss. The welfare of his men was always uppermost in his mind.
>
> In the face of the enemy, he displayed all the attributes of a first-class soldier. On a recent mission in the Sangin Valley, under intense fire from the enemy, he was fearless in the support he provided to his Platoon Sergeant, as he attempted to suppress the enemy at close quarters. LCpl Davey was a pillar of strength to all those around him and he was a proven combat soldier whose influence will be missed in the Company.

The doctors, nurses and combat medical technicians were some of the hardest working soldiers in Helmand. On operations they would often be at the forefront of the battle, ready to treat the injured as and when they fell. Several medics were also injured themselves as they moved into the open to treat a fallen soldier or were just simply unlucky enough to be struck by a stray bullet during an ambush.

As well as carrying all of the equipment of an infantry soldier, they were also laden down with bandages, stretchers, saline for drips and drugs. A shortage of doctors, a problem which exists right across the defence medical services, would often mean that relatively inexperienced combat medics would be responsible for several hundred soldiers at any one time. At any hour of the day or night, a 20-year-old medical orderly with just a couple of years' experience could be called upon to deal with anything from a traumatic amputation, to a bullet wound in the head, to treating an outbreak of D and V.

All wars are fought by young men, and the war in Afghanistan is no different. The average age of the men in the Royal Anglians was 19, the same age as the US conscripts who fought in Vietnam in the 1960s. At the age of just 18, Private Kane Hornigold was the youngest British soldier serving in Afghanistan. He said:

> It's exactly what I joined to do. I wanted to do something which would test me and push me to my limits and that is what has happened here. It's been hard and dangerous but it's a real adventure. Most of my mates at home spend their evenings getting drunk and taking drugs. I don't have anything in common with them any more – this has changed me.

Private Hornigold was just a 12-year-old schoolboy when British troops entered Afghanistan in November 2001. When I met him in Sangin he was rapidly becoming a hardened veteran of the war in Afghanistan. The soldier from Norfolk was sent out to Afghanistan four days after his 18th birthday in August 2007. A week later he was patrolling the dangerous streets of Sangin with other members of 1 (Almanza) Platoon, A Company. On that very first patrol, he was one of a group of soldiers who discovered an IED which had been primed for detonation. Two days later he was deployed on Operation Palk Ghar and had his first taste of battle.

He told me his thoughts as he became involved in a series of contacts which would last for the next seven hours as his company moved through the dangerous Green Zone in the Sangin Valley:

> I was a bit scared, to tell the truth, but it was very exciting. The bullets were coming in just above my head, trees were exploding around me and all I could think was, 'Fucking hell, this is it, this is the real thing.' An RPG exploded 50m away. It was really terrifying, I was shitting myself and then you relax into it a bit. I was quite close to Sgt 'Larry' Holmes and he looked after me. At one point we couldn't move forward so we sat there and shared a cigarette.
>
> The battle lasted all day and my job was to help distribute the ammo. It was knackering. I was running all day long, up and down rivers, carrying link ammunition to the forward sections. I also had to carry all my own equipment as well and I just wasn't used to carrying that much weight.

Squinting against the bright Afghan sun, Pte Hornigold went on:

> I actually found the hardest thing about coming out here was saying goodbye to my family because in the back of your mind you know you might not see them again. We all know what the risks are and you have to learn to live with them. If you come here to Helmand thinking that you might not get injured you are being stupid. In the end it's just the luck of the draw. Wrong time, wrong place and that could be you – dead. That's what it comes down to in the end: luck.

Pte Hornigold's take on life was no different to that of hundreds of other 18-year-old soldiers serving in Helmand. They all knew that at any moment they could be killed or injured.

Just two days after chatting with Kane Hornigold over a cup of tea inside the Sangin DC, the first 18-year-old soldier was to die in the conflict. Private Ben Ford of the newly created Mercian Regiment was killed on Wednesday 5 September 2007. The vehicle in which he was travelling with three other soldiers and an interpreter was blown up 17km north of the town of Lashkar Gar. The soldier from Chesterfield had been in the Army for little over two years when he died alongside Private Damien Wright, who was five years' his senior. The interpreter who was travelling with them was also killed and the two other soldiers were seriously injured. At the time of writing an investigation was still attempting to discover whether their deaths were caused by a mine or an IED.

While much of the media was focused on the north of Helmand, little was written about the 1st Battalion of the Worcestershire and Sherwood Foresters Regiment which, during the course of their tour in Helmand, had been amalgamated into the Mercian Regiment and became its 2nd Battalion.

While I was in the north of Helmand with the Royal Anglians, the men of 2 Mercian were preparing for one last crack at the Taliban before handing over their area of operations to the incoming British unit. The aim was to move into what had effectively become no man's land and push the Taliban back from their forward positions. In theory, and albeit temporarily, this would disrupt their ability to strike against British forces in Garmsir and thus give the new incumbents a few weeks breathing space before the fighting started again.

It was Friday 7 September 2007 and the men of A (Grenadier) Company were about to take part in Operation Palk Pechtaw. As last light fell, the soldiers slowly and carefully moved out of their base at Camp Delhi and began to move forward towards the Taliban lines. The operation began at 2200hrs and by midnight the troops had reached what was generally regarded as Taliban territory. The enemy were now believed to be just 1km away and the Mercians knew that if the Taliban were aware that the British were in the area, they might well be walking into an ambush. Progress was slow. Irrigation ditches and the threat of landmines meant that the soldiers would move a few hundred metres at time, then stop, listen and scan the horizon using night-vision goggles to see if they could detect any movement. The plan was to head for a series of farms, compounds and areas of tactical importance to clear them of the enemy. They might be unoccupied or full of Taliban – no one knew. As in most operations in this part of Helmand, intelligence was at best sketchy. The Mercians had broken down the area into three stages, characterized by three objectives known as 'Three Walls', 'Strip Wood' and 'Snowdon', the last being a hill that had been used by the Taliban to attack British troops on numerous occasions. The Mercians were understandably anxious. In about seven weeks' time they were due to fly home to their families and friends. Getting killed or severely injured after having survived months of combat was a thought which played on everyone's mind.

The responsibility for guarding the southern flank of the advance lay with 1 Platoon which was commanded by Lt Simon Cupples, a 25-year-old officer from Chesterfield in Derbyshire.

Just before 0100hrs, the young officer ordered his platoon to halt – 'go firm' – so that he could move forward to his point section and conduct a 'nav check' to confirm his platoon's position. Lt Cupples was about 10m short of the front section when the Taliban opened up from two positions. He and his front section had been caught in the killing zone. Machine-gun fire tore into his men, hitting Privates Luke Cole, a member of the Territorial Army who, in civvy street was a forklift truck engineer, Sam Cooper, who, having just turned 18, was one of the youngest soldiers serving in Afghanistan, and Johan Botha, a South African who had joined the British Army four years earlier. Their section commander, Cpl Lee Weston, had also been hit. In an instant Operation Palk Pechtaw had transformed from a 'company fighting patrol' mission to a casualty evacuation operation.

Panic descended upon the Mercians. The front section had been taken out and the screams of the injured could be heard between the breaks in automatic gunfire. Lt Cupples dived to the sandy desert floor as bullets splattered into the ground around him.

Just a few yards in front of Lt Cupples, Pte Luke Cole was lying on the ground in terrible agony. The 22-year-old territorial, who had also served in Iraq, had been injured in the first volley of fire when a bullet smashed into his femur. Although Pte Cole had lost a lot of blood, he was still able to fire his weapon. As reported by the *Guardian* on 12 January 2008, he said:

> I looked down and I could see that I had been hit. There was a big hole in my leg and a lot of blood. I knew it was bad but I also knew that I couldn't take morphine – if I did I might not be able to fire my weapon properly.
>
> The Taliban were close. I could see them and hear them, so I knew they could see me. They were close to where I thought Botha had gone down so I opened fire at them. The problem was that every time I opened fire I gave my position away and they started shooting at me.

Lt Cupples crawled forward to assess the situation and to locate the injured. As the bullets zipped above his head, Lt Cupples explained to Pte Cole that he was leaving him in order to organize a rescue party. He later admitted that leaving a seriously wounded colleague lying injured in no man's land was one of the hardest decisions of his life.

As Lt Cupples crawled away, Pte Cole was shot again, this time in the stomach, which had left his bowel exposed. 'I just tucked it back in. There was nothing else I could do.'

The weight of fire falling on the platoon had left the soldiers disorientated. A very real risk began to emerge that those in the rear could end up firing on those at the front. Sergeant Mike Lockett, who had almost been killed by enemy fire himself in the opening burst, told his men to check fire and wait for further instructions.

Lt Cupples crawled back to where his Platoon Sergeant was organizing the casualty evacuation and told him that there were at least three injured soldiers trapped in the Taliban's killing zone. Botha, Cooper and Cole were alive but injured, he explained, and he wasn't sure how long they could survive.

Sgt Lockett quickly assembled a rescue party composed of just five men – the only ones who could be spared. The party consisted of Lt Cupples, Sgt Lockett, Lance Corporals Jonathan McEwan and David Chandler and 20-year-old 2nd Lt Rupert Bowers, who was shadowing Lt Cupples. He had just completed his platoon commanders' course and had only been in Helmand for a week. The two teams set off for the injured; Lt Cupples and LCpls McEwan and Chandler were in one team and Sgt Lockett and 2nd Lt Bowers were in the other. The rescue party dashed forward in a bid to cover as much ground as possible before the Taliban spotted them.

As the teams moved forward, Sgt Lockett saw Pte Cole lying in the sand, firing his weapon. In the *Guardian* article of January 12, he recalled:

> I was shouting to Cole, 'Get the fuck over here, you need to get the fuck over here.' I was absolutely fucking gobbing at him, egging him on: 'As soon as you get to me, you're out of the line of fire.' He was making his way towards me with a morphine auto jet, shouting, 'Put this in me', but he wasn't a massive casualty at this point and I was saying, 'No, I haven't got fucking time, I've got fire coming in and I've got to get Cooper.' I said, 'As soon as we get 10m away, I will smash you with that morphine.' If we moved, we were going to get hit.

Lockett and Bowers went back into the killing zone and found Pte Cooper lying motionless on the ground. A bullet wound to his head had left his brain exposed. His body was cold and limp and it was clear that he was very close to death. 2nd Lt Bowers, a tall, thin man, hoisted him on to his shoulders and began running back to the first aid post. Bullets whizzed past the junior officer as he ran, then walked and eventually crawled to safety with Pte Cooper on his back. Bowers assumed that he too would become a casualty and was amazed that he survived the route back to the ditch, where Pte Cooper was checked for signs of life. 2nd Lt Bowers recalled: 'I said, "Cooper, have you got a girlfriend?" Someone said, "Has she got big tits?" And he lashed out – that was the only response he gave that night.'

By now the company doctor, Captain Henry Nwume, and Company Sergeant Major Peter Lewis arrived with a series of armoured fighting vehicles to assist in the casualty evacuation and to resupply the troops with more ammunition.

As Lt Cupples' team began searching for Pte Botha, they realized that the Taliban were trying to outflank them. Initially, the fire was coming from their front but the weight of it began to drop off as the Taliban started to move around to their left. 'We could actually see and hear them moving. We could hear them talking to one another.' Lt Cupples realized that he had just a couple of minutes before he would be caught in a deadly crossfire. There was no other option but to pull back, but LCpl McEwan did not want to leave without Pte Botha. 'McEwan was saying, "I can hear him screaming, boss," but I had to explain that wasn't Botha, it was the Taliban. They were taking casualties too.'

The situation was now critical. Major Jamie Nowell, the Company Commander, who was trying to control the battle from the rear, ordered 3 Platoon to move forward to provide covering fire for 1 Platoon so that they could locate and extract Pte Botha. Just before 3 Platoon moved forward, Sgt Lockett said to Sgt Craig Brelsford, the Platoon Sergeant, who was also his best friend: 'Botha is up there, can you make sure you bring the big man back to me?' 'Don't worry, we'll get him,' replied Sgt Brelsford.

Sgt Brelsford told his men that one of their own was left behind and that there was no way that they were going to leave him to become a Taliban trophy. Every British soldier serving in Helmand had heard the stories of how the Taliban would often mutilate the bodies of dead soldiers. No one needed to be told twice that this was a vital mission.

However, as Sgt Brelsford moved into the killing zone he was struck in the neck by a Taliban bullet and died a few minutes later. The situation was going from bad to worse. A few minutes later, another British casualty would be sustained when a US jet dropped a 500lb bomb on the Taliban position. At 'Three Walls', once a farmstead but now a ruin serving as the company first aid post, the soldiers waited anxiously for the aircraft to attack. The Forward Air Controller gave a running commentary over the radio of the jet's progress, enabling everyone to prepare for the impact. Pte Lee Stacey, who was acting as the company medic, noticed that one of the injured soldiers looked particularly scared. Just before the bomb struck, Pte Stacey covered the soldier with his own body to protect him from the blast. The shockwave smashed into the ruin where the soldiers were taking cover and part of it collapsed on top of Pte Stacey, seriously damaging his neck.

After that the platoon was ordered to return to Camp Delhi. It was now 0630hrs and the Mercians had been in continuous contact with the enemy for over five hours. The men were exhausted and morale was low but, worst of all, they had been forced to leave Pte Botha behind.

When they arrived back at camp, Lt Cupples went straight to Maj Nowell and the two men began to prepare a rescue plan to retrieve Pte Botha. Although neither said so, they both assumed that in all likelihood Pte Botha was either dead or seriously wounded.

The plan was relatively simple. It needed to be: time was running out. Scimitar armoured vehicles would advance towards the position where Pte Botha was last seen alive. The light tanks would blast the Taliban positions with their 30mm Rarden cannons. The search party would dismount from Vikings and retrieve Pte Botha.

While the two officers hatched their plan, Sgt Lockett began to rally his troops, who were quiet and exhausted. For the most part, they were sitting in silence. Of the 25 who had left the base on the previous evening, only 16 had returned unscathed, 8 had been injured and a soldier was missing in action. Some of those close to Botha were crying. Others were staring into space. They all knew that volunteers would be called upon to go back out again.

Lt Cupples said:

There were people who did not want to go back out, and you couldn't blame them. There was only space for nine of us and you could see on the faces of the guys that it was a big ask. But combat makes you closer than brothers and pretty soon there were volunteers coming in from all over the camp.

At 0730hrs, the rescue party left the safety of Camp Delhi for the second time in less than 12 hours. The plan went like clockwork and Pte Botha was found 20m from the Taliban's position. Although Capt Nwume checked for signs of life, it was clear that Botha had been dead for some time. His pupils were covered with dust – a sure sign of death. He was sitting upright and the ground around him was smoking. He had been shot in both the shoulder and the arm and he probably died from internal bleeding.

Pte Botha's body was wrapped in a poncho and he was placed on the floor of the Viking. For 15 long minutes, the soldiers were jammed in the back of the vehicle with Pte Botha lying by their feet. No one spoke.

At Camp Delhi there was a sense of despair and exhaustion. Many of the men were crying openly for several hours. Even the more experienced soldiers such as Sgt Maj Lewis and Sgt Lockett struggled with their emotions. 'It would have made a massive amount of difference if we had lost Botha's body. How everybody felt, getting him back was a massive, massive bonus. I would have been a lot more haunted than I am,' Sgt Maj Lewis told the *Guardian* when he returned to the UK.

The bodies of Sgt Brelsford and Pte Botha were later placed in body bags and were sent back to Camp Bastion. Twenty-four hours later, the rest of the company joined them.

At the time of writing, those who were injured in battle are still recovering from their wounds. Pte Sam Cooper, who was shot in the head, suffered brain damage and is still undergoing treatment. Pte Luke Cole, who was awarded the Military Cross, has had several operations but is expected to make a full recovery. It is unlikely that Pte Lee Stacey will serve on operations again.

For his actions on that night, Lt Cupples was awarded the Conspicuous Gallantry Cross (CGC) and Sgt Lockett won the Military Cross (MC). Sgt Brelsford was awarded a posthumous MC. In all, 2nd Battalion The Mercian Regiment won 28 awards during the tour, including two CGCs and five MCs. A further five soldiers were given a Mention in Dispatches.

Out of respect for the two men who died during the battle, the Union Jack was flown at half-mast in British military bases across Afghanistan. This dignity appeared to be absent from a number of civilians from the Foreign and Commonwealth Office based at Lashkar Gar, who decided to have a party. Unlike soldiers, the FCO civil servants are allowed to bring 'small amounts' of alcohol into the base for their own personal consumption. Brig Lorimer was furious when he found out about the party, as were many officers and soldiers serving at Lashkar Gar. The Brigadier spoke to David Slinn, the FCO's senior man at the base, and told him that the behaviour of some of his personnel was a disgrace.

Civil servants from the Ministry of Defence, the Foreign and Commonwealth Office and the Department for International

Development routinely send volunteers to both Iraq and Afghanistan to advise on foreign policy, coordinate reconstruction efforts and to work as press officers. For their pains they receive very generous allowances. MoD civil servants can boost their salaries by up to £29,000 a year on top of their salaries, included in a host of allowances. They are also entitled to two weeks of leave every nine weeks. FCO staff are believed to receive similar entitlement. By comparison, soldiers get an allowance of just £2,400 for six months and two weeks R and R at some stage during the operations.

A few weeks earlier, General Sir Richard Dannatt, the Chief of the General Staff, had spoken of the disconnection between the military and civilian life – there can be no more nauseating demonstration of this than the FCO staff deciding to hold a drunken party just hours after two soldiers had been killed. Many of the soldiers already found the FCO staff quite irritating, not least because they rarely ventured beyond the walls of relatively safe bases like Lashkar Gar, and avoided the more dangerous and uncomfortable outstations such as Sangin.

By the end of October 2007, the Royal Anglians and the rest of 12 Mechanized Brigade were safely back in the UK with their families and friends. It had been a long, difficult and bloody six months which had changed the lives of many who took part forever.

In March 2008, Brig Lorimer and Lt Col Carver were both awarded the Distinguished Service Order for their actions in Afghanistan. The Vikings won 78 awards in total, including 6 Military Crosses and 1 Queen's Gallantry Medal, and 6 soldiers received a Mention in Dispatches. The fact that the battalion had won just 4 Military Crosses in the previous 44 years is a measure of the intensity of the fighting in which it was involved in Helmand

It was now the turn of 52 Infantry Brigade to secure Helmand for the next six months. The brigade was composed of troops from 40 Commando, the 2nd Battalion The Royal Gurkha Rifles, the 2nd Battalion The Yorkshire Regiment (The Green Howards) and the 2nd Battalion The Royal Highland Fusiliers, the Royal Regiment of Scotland.

The brigade was operational by mid-October 2007. They would experience a different conflict as the nature of the battle changed. By late 2007, the Taliban knew that there was little point in conducting mass attacks against the British bases. Their growing casualty statistics meant that they simply could not win. Even with the Taliban's impressive spin operation, they were beginning to have trouble attracting volunteers for what was effectively certain death. Gradually, and perhaps inevitably, the use of improvised explosive devices by the Taliban began to increase even more. The IEDs remained relatively unsophisticated, but they were deadly and accounted for all of the nine combat deaths sustained by the brigade from October 2007 to April 2008.

14

THE FALL OF MUSA QALA

By early December 2007, the main focus of NATO troops in southern Afghanistan was Musa Qala. High in the Sangin Valley, the dusty town, which is about the size of Cambridge in the UK, had become a refuge and stronghold for the Taliban. It was here that they now trained, recruited and equipped themselves for the fight against the British. While the Taliban remained in the town, the Sangin Valley and the Kajaki Dam complex were always vulnerable to attack.

Musa Qala had been in Taliban hands since February 2007. After the Taliban were pushed out of Sangin, the town also became the new narco-centre for northern Helmand. As described earlier, the British troops pulled out of the town in October 2006 following a peace deal brokered between the town elders and the Taliban. The US were against the deal at the time and there was a cry in the NATO headquarters of 'I told you so' when the Taliban reoccupied the town.

After the truce collapsed, soldiers from the Special Forces Support Group (SFSG), as 1 Para were now known, became involved in a secret project called Operation Rego. The plan was to create an Afghan militia which would force the Taliban out and take control of the town. The SFSG has been involved in Afghanistan, providing extra firepower such as additional mortar or machine-gun support, almost from the day it was created in 2005. Raising a militia was a completely different task which would not be met with such success. The basic tactic seemed to be to pay hundreds of thousands of US dollars to the local elders in the hope that they would encourage their young men to join up. The plan was taking too long and was fraught with too many problems. By August 2007, Operation Rego had been post-poned indefinitely and NATO commanders were looking at more traditional means to retake Musa Qala.

The battle for Musa Qala began in mid-November 2007, when US Special Forces began to probe the town's defences and look for ways in which they could be penetrated.

Fighting patrols were also conducted by elements of the British Brigade Reconnaissance Force, which would push up to the Taliban positions in Wmik Land Rovers and armoured vehicles, cause mayhem and then return to the safety of the surrounding desert.

By the middle of December, the main Taliban positions both inside and outside the town were being attacked on an hourly basis. US Spectre gunships would lead the charge, firing their powerful machine-guns and Howitzers at Taliban defensive positions whilst flying a continuous figure of 8 over the target. US A–10 Warthog tankbusters and Apache helicopter gunships also joined the fray. While many of the Taliban positions on the outskirts of the town were reduced to rubble, the centre of Musa Qala was left relatively untouched. NATO commanders were aware that there was little point in 'liberating' the Afghans if they had nowhere to live once they were free.

As the bombings intensified, the highly effective Taliban PR-machine swung into life. The commanders claimed that there were '2,000 mujahideen' armed and ready to fight to the death in Musa Qala. Despite these confident boasts, the British knew that the number of fighters was closer to 200 and the reality was that few if any of these men would actually hang around to take part in a pitched battle against regular, well-equipped troops.

Despite this, the NATO force, which was composed of US Special Forces and airborne troops, the Afghan National Army, troops from the Royal Marines, the Scots Guards in their Warriors and troops from the 2nd Battalion of the Yorkshire Regiment, were not going to take any chances.

The battle proper for the town began on the weekend of 9 December 2007. Amid an artillery barrage, 14 Chinook helicopters, each laden with members of the US Airborne, raced towards a heavily defended landing zone in a *wadi* north of the town. In a few short minutes, more than 300 troops were on the ground and pushing south to head off the Taliban. As the troops moved forward, Apache gunships picked-off Taliban bunker positions with their 30mm cannons and Hellfire rockets. More heavily defended positions, hidden inside the ubiquitous compounds situated in the villages surrounding the town, were dispatched with deadly efficiency from 500lb bombs dropped by NATO jets flying high above.

Resupplies for the troops involved in the battle were largely driven in from Camp Bastion, around 70km further south. Although relatively short in distance, the terrain made for slow progress and drivers had to be constantly aware of the threat of both mines and IEDs.

'We've had to fight our way through with every convoy so far,' said 2nd Lt Ali Dray, the commander of one 20-vehicle convoy.

> The main frustration we have is with the aging fleet of vehicles we've got. They are always breaking down and usually at the time you don't want them to. A few weeks ago the wheel came off my wagon en route. We fixed it only for it to break down minutes later. Then we started getting mortared and you think 'I could do without this.'

Although the British forces remained under the command of Brigadier Andrew Mackay, a tough, white-haired officer with a formidable reputation, the assault on Musa Qala was a truly multinational operation and senior officers were keen for the Afghan National Army to play a central role.

High on a ridge overlooking the town, British soldiers from the BRF brought their guns to bear on the Taliban position. 'I fired eight rounds into the Taliban position,' said Lance Bombardier Alex Smith, a member of the BRF who was manning the .50 calibre heavy machine-gun on his Wmik. 'After it burst into flames, I saw three Taliban fighters running away so I continued to fire at them. I'm not sure if I hit any of them or not but it was a huge adrenaline buzz.'

As with many battles against the Taliban, the outcome is generally never in doubt but that does not mean that such operations are not without their dangers. Shortly after 1000hrs on Saturday 8 December, Sgt Lee 'Jonno' Johnson, 33, a member of B Company, was killed when his Vector vehicle struck a mine. Sgt Johnson, who had a partner and two children, was one of the most popular sergeants in the battalion. His death was all the more tragic because he volunteered to delay his leave so that he could take part in the battle.

The vehicle detonated a mine, probably left over from the Soviet era, as it passed by a broken-down Afghan truck. The six-wheeled Vector was thrown down a slope by the force of the blast and Sgt Johnson was killed instantly. He was later pronounced dead by a US Special Forces medic.

The demands of the on-going operation meant that his body could not be extracted until the following day so his comrades kept a silent vigil on a hillside overlooking the Sangin Valley. Although Sgt Johnson had been killed, the others inside the same vehicle escaped unscathed. Pte Lee Bellingham said, 'I knew in my subconscious that he was dead already. But I just felt I ought to do something. I didn't want to let go. I never normally pray but I said something that day and I feel someone looked after me.'

By the time the soldiers from the Yorkshire Regiment had arrived in Musa Qala, the Taliban – who had earlier claimed they would fight to the death – had fled. The reception from the locals was muted. Many shouted at the soldiers to 'go away' while others were outwardly happy that the Taliban had been forced to leave.

Some of the locals quickly pointed out to the British troops the places where the Taliban hanged 'criminals' and beheaded 'informers'. In one case, a market trader had been dragged from his home at 3.00am and beheaded. His head was then stuck on a pole in the centre of the market. Despite these horrendous acts of savagery, however, many of the locals felt secure amongst the Taliban. Crime was virtually non-existent and many people benefited from the cash which came with harvesting the poppy. Much was also made of the fact that the ANA won the battle for Musa Qala. This crass and heavy-handed propaganda did the British and NATO little credit. The ANA may have been the first into the town, but they were shown the way by the US and British forces who effectively ensured that there was little or no resistance.

The success of Musa Qala instantly presented a problem for the British forces. Once taken, the town had to be secured. This put a considerable strain on the limited resources in Helmand. While the town would be largely garrisoned by the ANA, it was immediately clear that extra British troops would have to be shipped into Musa Qala if it was not to fall back into Taliban hands. The British would also have to start rebuilding the town and its infrastructure – much of which had been destroyed when the Paras and the Royal Irish occupied the town in 2006 – if the hearts and minds of the locals were to be won and retained.

52 Infantry Brigade had played an important role in the retaking of Musa
Qala. Overall, like the previous Operation Herrick tours in Helmand, 52
Infantry Brigade's tour was full of incidents, some heroic and others less
so. Many may never be made public and will exist only in the memories of
those who took part. However, there was one event which, in terms of
individual bravery, stands head and shoulders above all others.

Isolated and vulnerable, Patrol Base Inkerman remained a key
Taliban target. Between October 2007, when 52 Infantry Brigade took
over, and February 2008 it was attacked on 57 separate occasions. The
troops were also constantly vulnerable to attack and ambush when they
were on patrol in the Green Zone. It was against this backdrop that a
series of reconnaissance missions was launched to try and find the
headquarters of a local Taliban unit which, according to intelligence
gleaned from locals, had established a bomb factory in one of the
hamlets close to the British base.

On 11 February 2008, a reconnaissance patrol composed of 32
members of 40 Commando left Inkerman and headed into the Green
Zone. The plan was for the soldiers to get in and out of the Green Zone
under the cover of darkness.

About an hour before dawn, the patrol approached the suspected
bomb factory. The troops stopped short of the target and four members
of the patrol were ordered to carry out a 'close target recce' (CTR) of a
compound. Using night-vision scopes, the Marines scanned the area
looking for bodies inside the buildings.

One of those who took part in the operation was LCpl Matt
Croucher, 24, from Birmingham, a Royal Marines reservist with a liking
for war zones. He had already completed three tours of duty in Iraq –
but this was his first in Helmand.

Within five minutes of searching a compound over 200kg of fertil-
izers had been discovered. The troops had found their bomb factory. As
they moved deeper into the compound, LCpl Croucher's foot brushed
against a wire.

> I felt it on my shins and saw the 4m wire. The grenade was stuck to
> a stick with tape behind a tree two feet from me. It was a pineapple
> type like the ones you see in the old World War Two films. The
> force of the pin coming out knocked the grenade off its stick and I
> saw it fall right by my feet.

I was pretty threaders [seriously upset]. I shouted 'grenade take cover'. Two of the guys were 2m behind me and the other a little further.

I knew a grenade like this has a killing circumference of about 5m. I'd been through this scenario in my mind and realized there was nowhere to take cover – there's no point running off because you're going to catch shrapnel.

The lads behind me would have caught a lot too. I'm very tight with the other three guys. There have been a few times when they've saved my bacon. So I went down next to the grenade. I thought that if I could keep my torso and head intact I'd probably survive any other injuries – although I fully expected to lose a limb. I thought, 'I've set this bloody thing off and I'm going to do whatever it takes to protect the others.' So I got down with my back to the grenade and used my body as a shield. It was a case of either having four of us as fatalities or badly wounded – or one. I brought my legs up to my chest in the brace position and waited for the explosion. When it went off the bang was the loudest I've ever heard. There was a flash of light and a big plume of smoke and orange sparks jetted into the air. I was flung through the air. My head was ringing. Blood was streaming from my nose. It took 30 seconds before I realized I was definitely not dead.

His patrol commander, Corporal Adam Lesley, witnessed the whole event and was dumbstruck by such an outstanding act of individual bravery. 'My reaction was, my God, this can't be real,' said Corporal Adam Lesley. 'Croucher had simply lain back and used his day-sack to blunt the force of the explosion. You would expect nine out of 10 people to die in that situation.'

Then they waited for the blast to come. 'It felt like a lifetime,' said Lesley. When the grenade went off it blew Croucher's rucksack more than 30ft and sent a burning radio battery fizzing into the air. As the noise died down, one of the patrol, Marine Scott Easter, was standing 'just completely frozen' and untouched. Croucher was in deep shock but, apart from a bloody nose, had few injuries.

'He had shrapnel in his helmet, in the plate of his body armour, but he was basically okay,' said Lesley. 'His day sack had taken the blast.'

His backpack, which had been filled with a medical pack, shoulder-launched 66mm rockets and radio equipment, had been shredded.

It was blown straight off my back. The blast shunted me a full metre. The lithium battery for my communication equipment took the brunt of the shrapnel – it landed 10m away with sparks and flames flying from it.

I was completely disorientated. The shockwave had exploded the blood vessels in my nose. All I could hear was a loud ringing and the faint sound of people shouting 'Are you ok? Are you ok?' Then I felt one of the lads giving me a top to toe check. A minute later someone said 'you were fucking lucky'. They were like 'what are you doing, you nutter?' But you could feel their relief.

Fearful that the Taliban would have heard the blast, the four-man team headed back to the rest of the patrol. LCpl Croucher said:

We patrolled back to where our Captain was. He was told what happened and just looked at me with a little smile in his eyes and said, 'That was a bit crazy, Croucher.'

I was checked over by a medic who wanted to evacuate me – but I wanted to stay. We knew the Taliban would want to come and see what had happened.

The Marines, now convinced that the Taliban would not be able to resist coming to investigate, settled into a nearby ditch and waited.

Within an hour or so our team spotted a guy with an AK47 approaching our position. He was in his early 30s and wearing traditional Afghan dress. I don't know for sure if he spotted us but when he lifted his weapon as if to shoot in our direction we opened up. I'm more or less certain I shot him. For all I knew this guy had set the booby trap. He was my 10th or 11th kill in five months in Afghanistan.

LCpl Croucher's actions prompted his colleagues to pass a written citation to their Commanding Officer, Lieutenant Colonel Stuart Birrell, recommending him for the Victoria Cross.

It's a pretty unusual thing but the lads put me forward for the VC themselves. It's entirely out of my hands. But if it was to happen it would be a massive honour not just for me but for the regiment and all my comrades.

It was LCpl Croucher's second close shave in just four months. In November, his patrol was ambushed by 30 Taliban near Putay in the Sangin Valley. One of his team had been shot through the chest and was close to death. As the team medic it was Matt's job to keep the Marine alive. He said, 'I patched him up under fire for 45 minutes. I put chest seals over the bullet wounds so his lungs wouldn't collapse and ran a drip into his arm. Bullets were landing everywhere and at one stage a rocket-propelled grenade landed 3m from us. It injured four other guys.' The Marines were saved when three Apache gunships arrived and laid down covering fire so they could get away.

At the time of writing this closing chapter, in June 2008, it is two years since the British Army arrived in Helmand and the battle with the Taliban continues. The cost in blood has been high: 97 soldiers have been killed while hundreds more have been wounded and many of those have sustained life-changing injuries. Men, some as young as 18, have been maimed, paralysed, blinded and burnt beyond recognition. Others have been forced to leave the frontline, unable to continue on operations after witnessing friends and colleagues killed and injured in battle. The war in Afghanistan has exacted a terrible price for many soldiers and Marines and all the signs suggest that the war will last for many years yet.

The Afghans have also paid a high price. There are no accurate statistics for the number of civilians killed and wounded across Afghanistan in the same period, but the figure is likely to be in the thousands.

Just under two years ago, Dr John Reid, the then Defence Secretary, made his now infamous statement in which he said he would be happy to see British troops leave Helmand in three years time without having fired a shot. He also said at the same time that British troops would not be 'running around the hills of Afghanistan chasing down the Taliban'. In the intervening period, several million bullets have been fired in anger and thousands of missiles and bombs have been dropped. Villages and homes which have been caught in the crossfire have been flattened. In some parts of Helmand, where the fighting was heaviest, the landscape has been completely transformed by bombing.

Was Mr Reid, one of the most media-savvy cabinet ministers of his era, ill-informed, out-of-touch or simply spinning a line to the British public, the majority of whom were very much against getting involved in another foreign war? We will have to wait for his memoirs, I suppose.

Whatever the truth, the British military looks set to become bogged down in another costly war in which success is not guaranteed. It is true that great strides have been made in Helmand. The Taliban are no longer the most powerful force in the area. The Afghan National Army, and to a lesser extent the Afghan National Police, are becoming more professional and capable by the day but there is still much to do. Reconstruction continues apace in Sangin, which just a few months ago was a Taliban stronghold. Schools which were closed down by the Taliban are reopening and farmers, who left their homes and land as they fled the fighting, are beginning to return to their land. The hydro-electric station at the Kajaki Dam will eventually bring electricity to thousands of homes in the Sangin area, transforming the lives of tens of thousands of rural people who still live an impoverished existence and who are often cynically exploited by the Taliban.

By the end of each of the so-called fighting seasons, the Taliban have been 'tactically defeated' yet again, or so our military commanders tell us. But what does this mean and does it actually matter to the Taliban? They know that they can never win, in military terms at least, a war against NATO. But do they need to? While they have a seemingly inexhaustible supply of volunteers who are prepared to fight and die for an apparently hopeless cause, they are keeping thousands of troops pinned down in Helmand and the wider Afghanistan. They know that a time will come when many western governments will decide that the cost in blood and hard cash is too high. Even now, the NATO alliance appears fragile. Canada, which is largely responsible for securing the neighbouring province of Kandahar, only agreed to maintain its commitment to the ISAF plan when the US said they would send an additional 1,000 troops into the province to assist the Canadian military. There are also questions over the usefulness of allies who have to operate under impossible restrictions – such as the Dutch not being able to fly helicopters at night or the German government not allowing its forces to be deployed to dangerous areas of the country – that they become a tactical liability.

As with other post-war insurgent groups, the Taliban know that they do not need to defeat NATO to win the war: they just have to survive as a viable force until NATO leave.

The Afghans are a pragmatic people. They are used to being invaded and then dealing with the consequences when the invaders leave. Much of the population outside of the main cities will happily support NATO forces while they believe NATO are the dominant force, but if and when that changes they will just as happily switch sides – this is the Afghan way and it has been like this for centuries.

In many towns and villages, where British and NATO troops may visit just once a week, the Taliban remain a dominant force. Here, they convince young men that NATO troops want to destroy Islam and are intent on raping their wives and daughters and stealing their land. And NATO's counter-narcotics policy of eradicating the poppy seems to be playing into the Taliban's hand. For many farmers, the poppy is their main cash crop and it is sold either to drug lords or to the Taliban, who use it to fund the insurgency. Those farmers who refuse to grow poppy on behalf of the Taliban run the risk of being murdered. There have been numerous examples of village elders who have been publicly beheaded after ordering the Taliban to leave their tribal area.

As well as controlling large parts of Helmand, another worrying factor for NATO is the fact that al-Qaeda is now a resurgent force in the tribal areas of northern Pakistan which border Afghanistan. Although not welcome in some tribal areas – in some cases al-Qaeda fighters have been attacked and killed in large numbers – the organization is starting to grow and attract new volunteers which are used to fill the ranks of the Taliban.

There was a time when the Taliban was almost exclusively composed of Afghans. This is no longer the case. The organization now attracts Saudi Arabs, Chechens, Punjabis and Pakistanis, and there have even been reports of British Muslims joining the jihad against NATO, although no British fighters have ever been found either dead or alive.

As I write, 16 Air Assault Brigade are back in Helmand, two years after they first arrived, conducting operations against the Taliban. They returned to Helmand on Operation Herrick 8 with more men, around 7,000. The force was composed of 2 and 3 Para; the 1st Battalion The Royal Irish Regiment; the brigade recce platoon known as the Pathfinders; the 5th Battalion The Royal Regiment of Scotland, the Argyll and Sutherland Highlanders; and units from the engineers, the artillery, the signals and the medical support groups who are vital in the killing fields of Helmand.

While I was in Helmand in September 2007, Brig Lorimer told me that he believes that the UK will have a military presence in Afghanistan until at least the middle of the next decade. Whether the war against the Taliban will continue for that long is, he said, 'anybody's guess'. Like many senior officers and diplomats, he believes that the counter-narcotics problem will take another 25 years to solve if, in fact, it is actually solvable. It could be well into the middle of this century before NATO eventually leaves Afghanistan. By that stage the country will be of an economic standing equivalent to that of Bangladesh – in short it will still be one of the poorest countries in the world.

Brigadier Mark Carleton-Smith, who at the time of writing is the Commander of 16 Air Assault Brigade in Helmand, believes that the conflict in Afghanistan has reached a 'tipping point'. The Taliban have sustained more than 7,000 casualties in the past two years. He argues that they are short on weapons and ammunition, and that their command and control ability have been seriously disrupted by surgical strikes conducted by British Special Forces.

The 44-year-old brigadier, who many in the military believe is destined for command at the highest level, described the Special Boat Service's killing of Mullah Dadullah, one of the Taliban's senior leaders, as a 'seminal moment'. Unlike the mujahideen who fought the infidels two decades earlier, the Taliban have a limited support base within the country. Thus Brig Carleton-Smith argues that 'the Taliban insurgency is failing', although he stresses that it has not yet failed.

Afghanistan's strategic position has always made it a valuable prize for foreign powers and that is equally true today. Its eastern borders hug China while the north of the country provides a gateway to the 'Stans' that occupy what was once the southern border of the Soviet Union. Its southern borders sit alongside Pakistan, where the al-Qaeda leadership has been hiding since the fall of the Taliban regime in 2001, and to the west lies Iran. Afghanistan undoubtedly sits in the middle of the most volatile area of the world.

Then there is the oil, not in Afghanistan itself but in the area of the Caspian Sea which has an estimated 21 billion barrels of crude – a reserve equivalent in size to that of the US – which the oil-thirsty West will need in the near future. The Caspian Sea area is landlocked so a pipeline is being built which will transport it through Afghanistan to Pakistan, where it will be pumped onboard super tankers and transported to western Europe and the US. It adds to the strategic importance of Afghanistan, for the pipeline can only be built and secured if Afghanistan is stable and free from the Taliban.

ACKNOWLEDGEMENTS

This book would not have been possible without the help of a vast number of serving members of the Army and Royal Marines who must remain nameless. I would especially like to thank those members of the Royal Marines and the 1st Battalion The Royal Anglian Regiment who kept me safe during my visits to Helmand in 2006 and 2007. I would also like to thank the team at Constable for their encouragement and efforts. Most importantly, I would like to thank my beautiful wife, Clodagh, and my two wonderful children, Luca and Rafe, for their love and support.

PICTURE CREDITS

All photographs reproduced in this book are provided courtesy of Sean Rayment, with the exception of the following:

Sean Rayment on Operation Palk Ghar
An exhausted British soldier at Operation Palk Ghar
Soldiers washing in the Helmand River
The Killing Zone, Helmand Valley

which are © Justin Sutcliffe.

INDEX